Turbo C++

A Self-Teaching Guide

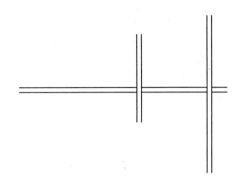

Turbo C++
A Self-Teaching Guide

Bryan Flamig

John Wiley & Sons, Inc.

New York • Chichester • Brisbane • Toronto • Singapore

Publisher: Therese A. Zak
Editor: Katherine Schowalter
Managing Editor: Ruth Greif
Copy Editor: Sheck Cho
Design and Production: Lenity Himburg and Rob Mauhar, The Coriolis Group

Recognizing the importance of preserving what has been written, it is a policy of John Wiley & Sons, Inc. to have books of enduring value published in the United States printed on acid-free paper, and we exert our best efforts to that end.

Turbo C++® is a registered trademark of Borland, Inc.

This publication is designed to provide accurate and authoritative information in regard to the subject matter covered. It is sold with the understanding that the publisher is not engaged in rendering legal, accounting or other professional service. If legal advice or other expert assistance is required, the services of a competent professional person should be sought. FROM A DECLARATION OF PRINCIPLES JOINTLY ADOPTED BY A COMMITTEE OF THE AMERICAN BAR ASSOCIATION AND A COMMITTEE OF PUBLISHERS.

Library of Congress Cataloging-in-Publication Data

Flamig, Bryan.
    Turbo C++: a self-teaching guide / Bryan Flamig.
        p.   cm.
        Includes index.
        ISBN 0-471-52903-6 (paper)
        1. C++ (Computer program language)   2. Turbo C++ (Computer program)
    I. Title.
    QA76.73.C15353   1991
    005.26'2—dc20   90-13036
                                                                        CIP

Printed in the United States of America
91   92   10 9 8 7 6 5 4 3 2

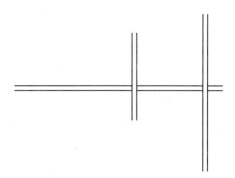

Contents

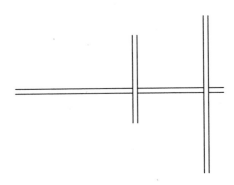

Preface

To some, C++ has earned the undeserved reputation for being a hard language to program with. The problem in the past was that the available C++ programming environments weren't easy to use. Borland has now removed the barriers by creating Turbo C++—the complete C++ programming environment that provides an interactive debugger, a mouse-controlled windowed environment, and sophisticated help system. To help you learn how to use Turbo C++ and write useful C++ programs, *Turbo C++: A Self-Teaching Guide* provides a practical "hands-on" approach to programming.

Here are some major highlights of this book:

- Emphasizes the learn-by-doing approach to writing Turbo C++ programs
- Incorporates self-checks throughout the book to help you learn at your own pace
- Includes a set of programming exercises at the end of each chapter to test your knowledge of the subject matter
- Helps you learn how to program in the object-oriented programming style

Who Should Read This Book

If you're familiar with the C language and have always wanted to learn C++, but have been put off because you thought C++ was a difficult and mysterious language, then you've come to the right place. Throughout the book short, easy-to-follow programs are used to demistify C++ programming. You'll learn how to progress from the C style of programming to the C++ style. If you're the kind of person who likes to learn at your own pace, you'll especially benefit from the self-checks provided in each chapter.

How This Book Is Different

This book is more than just a reference guide to the C++ language. You not only learn what the features of C++ are, but how they are used, and what problems you might have using them.

Instead of long examples that lose the point of what's being discussed, or incomplete code fragments that don't show the whole story, this book provides numerous small but complete examples that concentrate on one concept at a time. Each topic is covered thoroughly, but is kept at a level understandable to someone new to C++.

What You'll Need

To use this book, you'll need the Turbo C++ compiler, as well as an IBM PC, XT, AT, PS/2, or compatible computer. All of the examples run in text mode, so you won't need any particular graphics adapter. While some of the programs utilize color, the output screens are viewable in monochrome as well.

A Quick Look Inside

This book progresses from the basics to more advanced topics in a way that lets you put previously learned skills to use quickly. In each chapter, you'll find a set of self-checks to help you review the material that has been presented. We've also included special notes and tips throughout the book to point out important programming issues.

Chapter 1: *Turbo C++: An Introduction* gets you up and running with Turbo C++. You'll get an overview of the C++ language, and how it relates to C. You'll learn how C++ supports object-oriented programming, and get your first looks at the most important feature of C++—classes. A small sample Turbo C++ program is included.

Chapter 2: *Working with the Turbo C++ Compilers* shows you how to compile

C++ programs, both with the command-line compiler and from the Integrated Development Environment. You'll learn how to organize C++ programs, and what compiler options are important.

Chapter 3: *C++ Fundamentals: Part 1* is the first half of two chapters on the fundamental building blocks of C++. Covered are identifiers, constants, and data types. This chapter is both a review of how C implements these building blocks, and how they differ in C++.

Chapter 4: *C++ Fundamentals: Part 2* picks up where Chapter 3 left off and discusses the attributes that data components can have, such as their storage class, duration, linkage, and scope. Also covered is how C++ extends the way variables can be declared.

Chapter 5: *Functions in Turbo C++* discusses what's new for functions in C++. You'll learn new ways to pass arguments to functions using reference arguments and default arguments. You'll also learn about two new types of functions—inline functions and overloaded functions.

Chapter 6: *Learning About Classes* provides a step-by-step discussion showing you how to transition from the structures of C to the classes of C++. You'll learn how classes implement encapsulation, an important object-oriented programming concept.

Chapter 7: *Creating and Initializing Objects* explains how to create objects from classes, and how to initialize and destroy objects using constructors and destructors. Also covered is how to create dynamic objects.

Chapter 8: *More Class Features* discusses some additional class features that allow you to solve a wider range of problems. Covered are static members, constant members, and friend functions. You learn how to create classes that work in tandem.

Chapter 9: *Inheritance and Derived Classes* shows you how to reuse and extend existing classes for new applications. It's here that you'll learn how C++ programming can differ radically from C programming. The topics covered are inheritance, derived classes, virtual functions, and polymorphism.

Chapter 10: *Using Operator Functions* shows how the operators of C++ can be overloaded using special operator functions. You'll also learn how to create your own type conversion functions.

Chapter 11: *The C++ Stream I/O Library* is the concluding chapter to the book. It discusses a new object-oriented way to input and output data from a program using the new C++ I/O library. By using this library, you'll see what a working system of classes can do for you.

Contacting the Author

After working through this book, you may wish to correspond with me about the subject matter. I invite you to do so either by electronic mail or by U.S. mail. The quickest way is to reach me through CompuServe. My ID is 73057,3172. My address is P.O. Box 13433, Denver, CO 80201.

Acknowledgments

I would like to thank the following individuals for their contribution to this book:

- To Katherine Schowalter, for providing the means to get this book published.

- To Rob Mauhar and Lenity Himburg for their excellent design and production work.

- To Loren Heiny, for his thorough review of the manuscript and helpful insights to the problems of a C programmer trying to learn C++.

- To Keith Weiskamp, for suggesting this book to me and providing the right contacts to have it published.

- To Holly Mathews, for convincing me to move to Colorado, where I could work in the beauty and solitude of the mountains.

- Finally, to Dogzilla, for thoughtfully chewing on my socks instead of the manuscript.

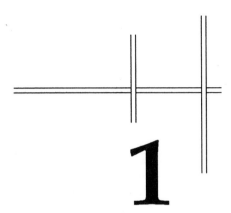

Turbo C++: An Introduction

With the release of Turbo C++, programming in C++ became much easier. This book will show you how to use this new language. In this chapter, you'll be introduced to what Turbo C++ is, and how it relates to the C language. In addition, an overview of the features available to you when writing Turbo C++ programs is provided.

A sneak preview of the most important Turbo C++ construct—*classes*— which allows you to bundle up data and functions into user-defined types can also be found in this chapter. Classes are central to a new style of programming, *object-oriented programming* (OOP), to which you will also be introduced.

The chapter ends with a sample Turbo C++ program. This sets the stage for Chapter 2, where you'll learn all about compiling and running programs using the Turbo C++ programming environment.

After completing this chapter, you'll know:

- How C++ relates to the C language
- What classes are and how they relate to OOP
- Three basic ways that C++ extends the C language
- What a sample Turbo C++ program looks like

What Is C++?

C++ is an extension to the C language that was created by Bjarne Stroustrup of AT&T. The most notable extension that Stroustrup added was the class construct, which was borrowed from the language Simula, a relatively obscure language developed in the 1960s. As Figure 1.1 suggests, C++ can be thought of as "C with class."

Classes are basically extensions to the structures of C. With classes, you can create user-defined types that not only represent data, but the operations to be performed on that data. Variables created from classes are called *objects*, and programming with objects is called *object-oriented programming*. OOP is very popular today, which accounts for the increasing interest in languages such as Turbo C++.

Note ‖ C++ has gone through several incarnations before reaching its present state. The current definition of the language is called C++ 2.0, and it is the version which Turbo C++ implements.

If you thought that C was diverse, then C++ is even more so. C++ has all the features of C, even down to low-level pointers and null-terminated strings. However, with the classes of C++, you can develop programs at a very high level. The types you define using classes can be integrated into your programs almost as naturally as the built-in types.

Even though C++ has all of C's low-level features, they have been toned down slightly. For example, C++ is much stricter about type checking, especially on function calls. In addition, C++ provides ways to define routines that can be automatically called to initialize your variables and objects. These initialization routines can reduce many of the errors caused by using uninitialized data. With features such as these, it's possible to write safer programs in C++ than in C.

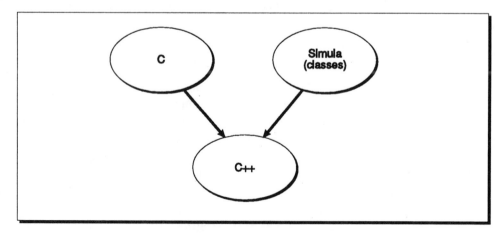

Figure 1.1. C++: C with Class

The new features that C++ adds still have the spirit of C. That spirit is one of efficiency, spartan syntax, and above all, complete programmer control over the use of the variables and functions in a C++ program. C++ tries to follow the syntax of C as much as possible. Thus if you're a C programmer now, you've already cleared one major hurdle on your way to the C++ finish line—the C language. You're now ready to sprint toward the more powerful extensions in C++.

The C++ Extensions

Recall that in C, the ++ operator is used to increment the value of a variable by one. That's where the name C++ comes from, for C++ goes one step beyond C. All of the familiar C constructs are available, such as assignment statements, **for** loops, **while** loops, **if** statements, functions, variables, and structures. The C language has recently been standardized into ANSI C. C++ incorporates most of the changes to C language that ANSI C brought about—most notably, function prototypes.

C++ incorporates many new features not found in ANSI C. As shown in Figure 1.2, the extensions provided can be grouped into three categories:

1. Miscellaneous extensions that make C++ a "better C"
2. Extensions to the data typing system that allow for more robust user-defined types
3. Extensions directly supporting OOP

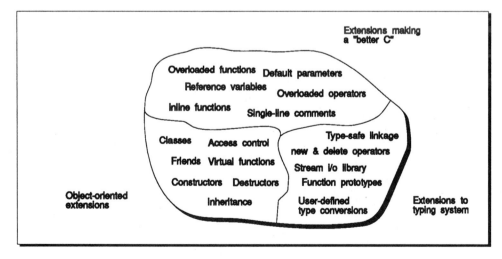

Figure 1.2. The Features of C++

Tables 1.1, 1.2, and 1.3 summarize the extensions in each category. It's interesting to note that while the extensions listed in Tables 1.1 and 1.2 aren't specific to the object-oriented style, they came about primarily to support that style.

Table 1.1. Miscellaneous Extensions

Extension	Purpose
New style of comments	Provides better code readability.
Inline functions	Allows functions to be expanded inline, similar to the way macros are. Increases code efficiency.
Reference types	Simplifies the syntax for passing parameters by reference.
Function overloading	Allows a group of functions performing similar operations to be given the same name.
Operator overloading	Allows the standard C operators to work with user-defined types, such as using the + operator to add strings together.
Default parameters	Allows you to specify default values for parameters to functions.

Table 1.2. Extensions to the Typing System

Extension	Purpose
Struct, union, and enum tags are type names	Simplifies the syntax of user-defined types.
Function prototypes	Provides better type checking for function calling.
Memory allocation operators	Supports dynamic allocation of user-defined types. Makes for safer dynamic memory management.
Type-safe linkage	Catches more parameter passing errors by performing type checks at link time.
New stream library	Allows greater flexibility in inputting and outputting user-defined types. Supports object-oriented input/output (I/O).
User-defined type conversions	Allows you to specify routines to convert from one type to another.

Table 1.3. Object-Oriented Extensions

Extension	Purpose
Classes	Allows functions and data to be grouped together. Used to create objects.
Access control	Allows you to restrict access to data and functions inside a class.
Derived classes	Let's you to inherit, or reuse, existing classes and extend them for new applications.
Virtual functions	A more powerful mechanism for function calling, where the function to call is determined at run time, not at compile time.
Friends	Allows selective access to otherwise restricted members of a class.
Constructors	Used to create user-defined routines for the initialization of objects.
Destructors	Used to create user-defined routines for performing cleanup tasks for objects.

Your First Turbo C++ Program

Let's see what a Turbo C++ program looks like. Listing 1.1 gives a small C++ program, **welcome.cpp**. (In Turbo C++, your source files will normally have a **.cpp** extension, rather than the **.c** extension used in C.)

Listing 1.1. The welcome.cpp Program

```
// welcome.cpp: Program to welcome you to Turbo C++
#include <iostream.h> // New stream I/O library header

main()
{
  char name[80];                   // Variable declarations as in C
  cout << "Enter your name: "; // New way to output data
  cin >> name;                     // New way to input data
  cout << "Welcome, " << name << ", to Turbo C++\n";
}
```

While the program is similar in structure to a C program, the first line shows a new style of comments. In this style, each comment starts with a pair of slash characters, and continues to the end of the line.

The program also shows a new method for doing I/O using the **iostream** library, which is discussed in Chapter 11. The **iostream** library uses the >> and << operators to indicate input and output, respectively. The program inputs a name, and then outputs a message using that name.

Assuming you've installed your Turbo C++ compiler correctly, here's how to compile **welcome.cpp** from the DOS command line:

```
tcc welcome.cpp
```

The following is a sample run of the **welcome.cpp** program:

```
Enter your name: Sam
Welcome, Sam, to Turbo C++
```

Note ‖ You'll probably be compiling from the Turbo C++ integrated development environment most of the time. We'll show you how to do that in Chapter 2.

Sneak Preview of Classes

Since classes are the most important part of C++, you're probably anxious to see what they look like. The following code shows an example of a class that represents employees.

```
// Class declaration

class employee {
private:            // Start of private members
  int id;           // Employee's data
  char name[80];
  float wage;
public:             // Start of public members
  employee(int i, char *n, float w); // Constructor
  void print_payinfo(float hrs);     // Member function
};

// Class implementation

employee::employee(int i, char *n, float w)
// Implements the constructor, which is used to
// initialize an employee object
{
    id = i;  strcpy(name, n);  wage = w;
}

void employee::print_payinfo(float hrs)
// Member function to print out pay information
// for an employee. Note that printf() is still
// available in C++
```

```
{
  printf("Employee #%d: %s\n", id, name);
  printf("Hours worked:  %6.2f\n", hrs);
  printf("Amount paid: $%7.2f\n\n", hrs * wage);
}
```

Since we won't be explaining every detail about class definitions here, don't worry if you can't understand every line of code. You'll have plenty of opportunity to learn the details of classes in Chapters 6 through 9.

Classes are organized into two parts: (1) A *class declaration* and (2) A *class implementation*. A class declaration is similar to a structure declaration; it lists the members that belong to the class. Classes can have data members, called *instance variables*, and functions, called *member functions*. The instance variables of **employee** are **id, name,** and **wage.** The member functions are **employee()** and **print_payinfo().**

Only forward declarations are given in the class declarations for the member functions. These declarations are called *function prototypes.* If you're familiar with the newer C compilers, you'll have seen function prototypes before. The bodies to the functions are usually defined after the class declaration, and the collection of member function definitions is known as the *class implementation.*

One of the member functions, **employee(),** is a special type of function called a *constructor,* which is called whenever an **employee** object is created. The following is an example of creating an **employee** object and calling its constructor:

```
employee john(1, "John Jackson", 15.00);
```

This statement declares **john** as an **employee** object and then initializes **john** to have an **id** of 1, a **name** of "John Jackson", and a **wage** of $15.00 per hour. The parameters given are passed to the constructor which does the initialization.

Once you've created an object, you can use it in much the same way you can use a structure variable. For instance, you can access the object's members using the dot notation. The difference is that we can not only access instance variables, but member functions too. In this manner, we can call a function that belongs to an object. For example, let's call the **print_payinfo()** function for **john:**

```
john.print_payinfo(40.0);
```

In this function call, we pass the number of hours worked, and then the payroll information is printed out. In this case, we get the following output:

```
Employee #1: John Jackson
Hours worked:  40.00
Amount paid:  $600.00
```

By calling the **print_payinfo()** function through the object **john**, we're letting **john** decide what is to be printed. We've shifted the orientation of the program to the object. That is, we've made the program *object oriented*.

In the employee class declaration, you'll notice two new keywords, **private** and **public**. These keywords allow you to control the access to the members of the class, and they are an essential part of programming with classes. Basically, only the public members can be accessed outside the class. The private members are internal to the class, and they can only be accessed by other members of the class.

All of the instance variables are private in the **employee** class. This means we can't change **john**'s hourly wage, since **wage** is private. Thus the following statement is illegal:

```
john.wage = 100.0; // Can't do since wage is private
```

However, we can access the two functions **employee()** and **print_payinfo()**, since they are public. By restricting access to the instance variables, we can better hide how the **employee** class is implemented.

To review, the two most prominent features of classes are that they can have data and functions as members, and that you can control access to the members. Taken together, these two features comprise what is known as *encapsulation*, an important concept in OOP. In Chapter 6, you'll learn more about encapsulation.

Your Second C++ Program

Let's take the **employee** class and build a complete program around it. Listing 1.2 gives the program **employ.cpp**, which is a small employee payroll program. It defines the **employee** class, creates some **employee** objects, and it then prints out payroll information for the employees.

To compile the program, use the following command line:

```
tcc employ.cpp
```

The output of the program is:

```
Employee #1: John Jackson
Hours worked:    40.00
Amount paid:  $600.00

Employee #2: Karen Butler
Hours worked:    52.00
Amount paid: $1144.00
```

Listing 1.2. The employ.cpp Program

```c
// employ.cpp: A simple payroll program
#include <stdio.h>
#include <string.h>
// Class declaration

class employee {
private:                // Start of private members
  int id;               // Employee's data
  char name[80];
  float wage;
public:                 // Start of public members
  employee(int i, char *n, float w); // Constructor
  void print_payinfo(float hrs);     // Member function
};

// Class implementation

employee::employee(int i, char *n, float w)
// Implements the constructor, which is used to
// initialize an employee object
{
    id = i;  strcpy(name, n);  wage = w;
}

void employee::print_payinfo(float hrs)
// Member function to print pay information
// for an employee
{
  printf("Employee #%d: %s\n", id, name);
  printf("Hours worked:  %6.2f\n", hrs);
  printf("Amount paid: $%7.2f\n\n", hrs * wage);
}

main()
{
  // Create some employee objects
  employee john(1, "John Jackson", 15.00);
  employee karen(2, "Karen Butler", 22.00);
  // Print out payroll information
  john.print_payinfo(40.0);  // John worked 40 hours
  karen.print_payinfo(52.0); // Karen workd 52 hours
  return 0;
}
```

Summary

In this chapter, you were introduced to the features that C++ adds to the C
language. Some of the features were added to make improvements to C, such

as better type checking and automatic initialization of variables. However, many of the features were added for one purpose: to support OOP.

Central to OOP is the class construct, which is used to create user-defined types. These types can have functions as well as data associated with them, and variables created from such types are called objects.

Exercises

1. C++ is one of the languages available for the IBM PC that supports OOP. Make a list of some of the other languages.

2. Name the two most prominent features of classes. What concept do they represent?

Answers

1. *Some of the other OOP languages currently available for the IBM PC are: Smalltalk, Objective-C, Quick Pascal, Turbo Pascal 5.5, and Actor.*

2. *Classes can have both data and functions as members, and you can control access to class members through the **public** and **private** keywords. These two features— bundling functions and data together, and hiding members—represent encapsulation.*

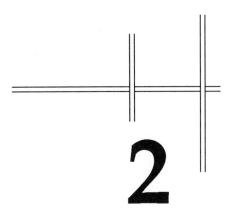

2

Working with the Turbo C++ Compilers

Before getting into the details of Turbo C++ programming, it's a good idea to look at the overall process of compiling and running C++ programs. While the process is similar to compiling and running C programs, there are some differences that we'll be highlighting in this chapter.

First, we'll discuss how Turbo C++ programs are organized. Then, we'll discuss how to compile programs from the command line, and we'll discover which compiler options are important. After this, we'll explore the new Turbo C++ integrated development environment (IDE).

Many of the details about compiler options and the IDE are best left to the Turbo C++ manuals. The purpose of this chapter is to point out those features that are specific to compiling and running C++ programs. There are some pitfalls in using the Turbo C++ compilers that we will be showing you how to avoid.

After studying this chapter, you'll know:

- How to organize multiple-file C++ programs
- What to include in header files
- How to avoid confusion when using both C and C++ files
- How to use the command line compiler
- What the major compiler options are
- How to use the IDE
- How to work with project files

Organizing Your C++ Programs

In general, Turbo C++ programs are organized as a set of header files and source files, just as C programs are. As an example, let's take the payroll program from Chapter 1 and reorganize it. Figure 2.1 shows the new organization, which is typical of a C++ program. We have a file containing the main program, **payroll.cpp** (Listing 2.1), a header file declaring the **employee** class, **employee.h** (Listing 2.2), and another file implementing that class, **employee.cpp** (Listing 2.3).

Header files in Turbo C++ usually have a **.h** extension, and source files usually have a **.cpp** extension. Other implementations of C++ use different extensions. For instance, Zortech C++ uses **.hpp** and **.cpp**, whereas many Unix implementations use **.h** and **.C** (with an uppercase C). Keep this in mind if you're porting from other C++ platforms.

Tip | | You can use any extensions you like for header and source files, but the Turbo C++ conventions of **.h** and **.cpp** are recommended.

Listing 2.1. The payroll.cpp Program

```
// payroll.cpp: The main source file for the payroll program

#include "employee.h"
```

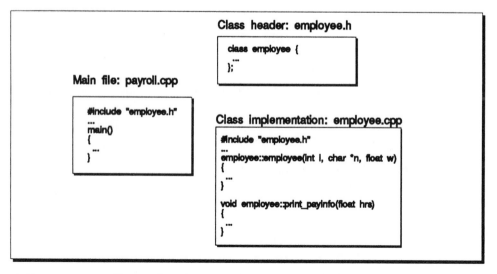

Figure 2.1. Organization of a C++ Program

```
main()
{
  // Create some employees
  employee john(1, "John Jackson", 15.00);
  employee karen(2, "Karen Butler", 22.00);
  // Print out payroll information for specified hours
  john.print_payinfo(40.0); // John worked 40 hours
  karen.print_payinfo(52.0); // Karen worked 52 hours
  return 0;
}
```

Listing 2.2. The employee.h Header File

```
// employee.h: Class declaration for the employee class

#ifndef H_EMPLOYEE
#define H_EMPLOYEE

class employee {
private:
  int id;
  char name[80];
  float wage;
public:
  employee(int i, char *n, float w);
  void print_payinfo(float hrs);
};

#endif
```

Listing 2.3. The employee.cpp Source File

```
// employee.cpp: Class implementation for the employee class

#include <stdio.h>
#include <string.h>
#include "employee.h"

employee::employee(int i, char *n, float w)
{
   id = i;  strcpy(name, n);  wage = w;
}

void employee::print_payinfo(float hrs)
{
  printf("Employee #%d: %s\n", id, name);
  printf("Hours worked:  %6.2f\n", hrs);
  printf("Amount paid: $%7.2f\n\n", hrs * wage);
}
```

Declaring main()

Each C++ program must have one file that contains the function **main()**, just as in C. One source of confusion is what return type to use for this function. In the past, the function **main()** has taken many forms. Some C++ implementations don't require a return value for **main()**, others, however, do. Thus in order to make it easy to port programs from different platforms, Turbo C++ allows three forms for **main()**:

```
main()            // Form 1: No return type specified
{
   ...
}

int main()        // Form 2: An int return type
{
   ...
   return 0;
}

void main()       // Form 3: A void return type
{
   ...
}
```

Form 1, where no return type is specified, is the most common way of specifying **main()**. You don't have to return a value in this form, but you may want to anyway. (Recall that in C, if a function has no return type specified, then **int** is assumed. The same is true in C++.)

The integer value returned from **main()** is passed as an exit code to DOS. This code can be used to control the flow of operations in a batch file. If you don't specify a return value, then the exit code to DOS will be undefined, and your program may not work properly with batch files.

One way to use the exit code is to return an error flag back to DOS if your program fails, as in the following scenario:

myprog.c:

```
main()
{
   ...
   if (failure) return -1; else return 0;
}
```

runme.bat:

```
myprog
if errorlevel -1 echo Program failed
```

If you use form 2 of **main()**, with an **int** return type, you *must* return a value, therefore this is the safest form for **main()**. In form 3, with a **void** return type, no return value can be used. The exit code passed back to DOS will be undefined in this case, therefore you may want to avoid using this form.

In addition to the return type, Turbo C++ allows **main()** to have up to three parameters:

```
main(int argc, char *argv[], char *env[])
{
   ...
}
```

The first parameter passes the number of arguments on the command line, the second is an array of those command arguments, and the third passes back the current DOS environment strings. All of these parameters are optional.

What's in a Header File?

In C, you normally restrict what goes in header files. These files should only contain definitions, such as the types and names of external variables, structure definitions, constants, macros, and function prototypes. The variable declarations (where memory is actually allocated) should be placed in code files, along with the function implementations. Figure 2.2 shows some sample legal and illegal header file components.

The same rules about header files apply for C++, except there are some additional constructs to worry about. In particular, you might have class declarations and *inline functions*.

Classes are handled like structures. A class declaration typically goes in a header file where it can be accessed by other source files. Typically, the class implementation (the functions associated with the class) are placed in a separate source file. Our sample files Listing 2.2, **employee.h**, and Listing 2.3, **employee.cpp**, illustrate this arrangment.

Inline functions are a special type of function similar to macros (See Chapter 5). Like macros, inline functions can be placed either in header files or in source files. If you want an inline function to be global in a multifile program, you must place it in a header file and include this header in the other files, just as you would for global macros.

Note || C++ treats constants differently than C does when it comes to including them in header files. (See Chapter 4 for details.) In addition, C++ treats the inclusion of inline functions differently from normal functions (see Chapter 5).

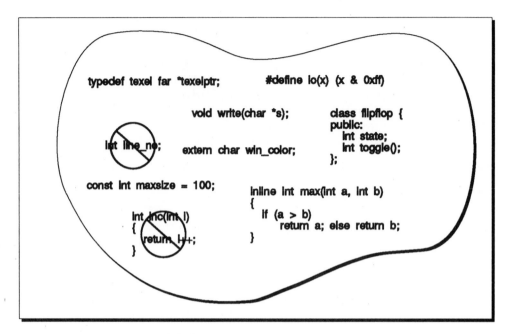

typedef texel far *texelptr;   #define lo(x) (x & 0xff)

                     void write(char *s);   class flipflop {
                                                 public:
                                                     int state;
int line_no;   int toggle();
                     extern char win_color;   };

const int maxsize = 100;
                                                 inline int max(int a, int b)
                                                 {
        int inc(int i)   if (a > b)
        {   return a; else return b;
            return i++;   }
        }

Figure 2.2. Some Legal and Illegal Header File Components

Avoiding Multiple Definitions

One problem with header files is that they are sometimes hard to organize properly. The organization problem becomes more apparent when using the object-oriented style of programming, since you'll have numerous header files for all your class definitions. Managing these header files can be tricky.

You want to avoid putting all your definitions into one giant header file, because it will cause each source file to compile more slowly. Yet you don't want too many header files to manage either. Then there is the problem of having the same header file included more than once in a source file compilation. The problem with including a header file more than once is that the definitions it contains will be multiply defined. In many cases, this will result in compilation errors.

You can avoid the problem of having multiple definitions easily. In each header file, you can use the compiler directives **#ifndef**, **#define**, and **#endif** to put a wrapper around your definitions. An example of this was used in the Listing 2.2 **employee.h** header. The method is summarized as follows:

```
#ifndef H_EMPLOYEE      // Guards against recompiling
#define H_EMPLOYEE      // Sets "guard"
```

```
class employee {          // Here's the class definition
  ...
};

#endif                    // End of the guard
```

The basic idea is to define macro constants for each header file. These constants, which we'll call *guard macros*, are used to guard against multiple compilations of the header file.

For example, the first time the compiler visits the header file **employee.h**, the value for the guard macro H_EMPLOYEE is undefined. Therefore, the whole header file will be compiled, including the statement that defines a value for H_EMPLOYEE. Should the header file be included more than once in the same source file, either directly or indirectly, the compiler will see that the H_EMPLOYEE is defined and skip over the contents of the header file after the first inclusion.

Tip You'll want the guard macros you use to have unique names. One way to do this is to use the names of the header files prefixed with **H_**, as we did in the **employee.h** file.

Finding Include Files

As with C, you can control where Turbo C++ looks for header files, by using either angle brackets or double quotes around the file names. For example, the following statements

```
#include <stdio.h>
#include <string.h>
#include "employee.h"
```

tell the compiler to look for **stdio.h** and **string.h** in the default directories, and to look for **employee.h** either in the current directory or in one of the default directories. The default directories can be controlled both from the command line and from options in the IDE, as you'll learn later in this chapter.

You can specify relative path names as well in **#include** statements. For example,

```
#include <sys\stat.h>
```

tells the compiler to look for **stat.h** in the directory **sys** which is a subdirectory of one of the default directories.

Tip || You can use either forward "/" or backward slashes "\\" in path names for include files.

Compiling C++ Programs

It's now time to see how to compile a Turbo C++ program. We'll first discuss some of the differences between C and C++, and how this affects the compilation process. Then, we'll explain how to use the command-line compiler, including the options that pertain to C++ programming. Later in this chapter, we'll see how to compile from the IDE.

Two Compilation Modes

The Turbo C++ compiler has two compilation modes. One of the modes is for C programs, using either the ANSI, UNIX, TURBO C, or Kernighan and Ritchie dialects. The other mode is for C++ programs. But why two modes? Isn't C++ a superset of C? Why couldn't the C++ mode be used to compile straight C programs?

The answer is that, even though C++ is in many ways a superset of C, there are some features common to both C and C++ that are implemented differently by the two languages. For example, structure tags are type names in C++, but not in C. Also, C++ requires function prototypes, C does not. There are some other differences that will be discussed in Chapters 3, 4, and 5. For now, remember that C++ isn't quite a superset of C. Because of this, it's important to realize which mode you are compiling in.

Using the Command Line Compiler

The command line compiler is the program **tcc.exe**. When invoking **tcc**, you can specify source files to compile as well as object modules and libraries in which to link. To run **tcc**, you give a list of compiler options and a list of files to compile and link. Here's how to compile our sample payroll program:

```
tcc payroll.cpp employee.cpp
```

The two files will be compiled, using the C++ mode, and then linked to form the executable **payroll.exe**. If you run this program, you should get the following output:

```
Employee #1: John Jackson
Hours worked:    40.00
Amount paid:  $600.00

Employee #2: Karen Butler
Hours worked:    52.00
Amount paid: $1144.00
```

Here are some other examples of using **tcc**:

```
tcc -ms myprog.c func1.obj
tcc -c database.c
tcc mainprog.cpp func1.c mylib.lib
```

The first example compiles the program **myprog.c** using the C mode, and using the small memory model (indicated by the **-ms** option). The generated **myprog.obj** file is then linked with **func1.obj** and with the standard libraries, creating the file **myprog.exe**.

The second example compiles the file **database.c** using the C mode, but does not create an executable, due to the compile-only option, **-c**.

The third example is a little more complicated. It first compiles **mainprog.cpp** using the C++ mode. It then compiles **func1.c** using the C mode, and links both together with the library **mylib.lib**, as well as with the standard libraries. The resulting program is named **mainprog.exe**.

You probably did a double take when you read the last paragraph. Note that both C and C++ files were compiled and linked together. What's going on here? It's time to find out.

Keeping C and C++ Straight

With **tcc** (and the compiler in the IDE as well), you can compile both C and C++ source files and link them together. The **tcc** program invokes the appropriate compiler mode by looking at the extensions of the files. By default, files ending with **.c** are compiled using the C mode, and files ending with **.cpp** are compiled using the C++ mode. You can change this by using the -P (uppercase P) option. For instance, the following command compiles both **mainprog** and **func1** as C++ files, even though they have different extensions:

```
tcc -P mainprog.cpp func1.c
```

Tip ‖ It's best to compile either for C or for C++, and not mix the two (unless you're trying to use existing C code in your C++ program). If necessary, Chapter 5 shows you how to mix the two languages.

In the examples we've shown so far, we've always included file extensions. By default, if an extension is not given in a file name, then **tcc** looks for a file with extension **.c**, and compiles that file as a C file. If, however, you use the -P option, then **tcc** looks for a file with extension **.cpp**, and compiles it as a C++ file.

Tip ‖ To avoid confusion, always include the file extension for files compiled with **tcc**.

Other extensions can be used. For instance, a file ending with **.obj** is assumed to be an object file ready for linking. A file ending with **.asm** is assembled with the Turbo Assembler (TASM). A file ending with **.lib** is assumed to be a library file ready to be linked. A file with any other extension is assumed to be a C file, unless the -P option is used to make the default a C++ file. These rules are summarized in Table 2.1.

Note ‖ The -P option forces all files to be treated as C++ files, unless those files end ‖ with **.asm**, **.obj**, or **.lib**.

Recall that header files are usually given a **.h** extension. This is true for both C header files and C++ header files. The question remains, then, which compilation mode is used for header files? The answer is: For header files, **tcc** uses the mode that's in effect for the source file that the header is included in. Thus, if you include a header in a C file, the C mode is used for the header. Include that same header in a C++ file, and the C++ mode is used.

Table 2.1. Determining which Compiler to Use

file.c	Uses the C compiler, or if the -P option is specified, the C++ compiler.
file.cpp	Uses the C++ compiler
file.h	Uses the C compiler, or if the -P option is specified, the C++ compiler
file	Looks for file.c, and uses the C compiler. If the -P option is specified, then it looks for file.cpp, and uses the C++ compiler.
file.asm	Assembles with TASM
file.obj	Links in the file as an object file
file.lib	Links in the file as a library file
file.xyz*	Uses the C compiler, or if the -P option is given, the C++ compiler.

* xyz is assumed to be any extension not already listed in the table.

Tip || To compile a C++ header file by itself, use the -P option to avoid having the C compilation mode used, and possibly causing compilation errors.

1. Suppose the current directory contains the following files:

   ```
   test.c
   test.cpp
   ```

   Which file is compiled with the following command?

   ```
   tcc test
   ```

   What if the command is the following?

   ```
   tcc -P test
   ```

2. Which compilation mode is used in the following program (assuming default behavior)? Assume that the **employee** class has been declared correctly, and that it is implemented in another file to be linked in. Will the program compile? Why or why not? (Hint: Look at the file names.)

   employee.h:

   ```
   class employee {
   private:
     int id;
     char name[80];
     float wage;
   public:
     employee(int i, char *n, float w);
     void print_payinfo(float hrs);
   };
   ```

   myprog.c:

   ```
   #include "employee.h"

   main()
   {
     employee e(101, "John Doe", 4.25);
     e.print_payinfo(10.0);
   }
   ```

3. Suppose you were to compile **employee.h** by itself with

   ```
   tcc -c employee.h
   ```

   What happens? How can you fix it?

1. *In the first case, the default is to compile a C file, thus the compiler looks for **test.c** and compiles it. In the second case, the default is to compile a C++ file, thus the file compiled is **test.cpp**.*
2. *No, because **employee.h**, which contains a class declaration, and is therefore in C++, was included in the C file **myprog.c**. You must change the file name to **myprog.cpp**, or use the -P command line option.*
3. *The C compilation mode is used, and the compilation fails since C doesn't know about classes. Try using*

```
tcc -c -P employee.h
```

Other Command Line Options

There are some other command line options relevant to C++ programming. These options have to do with *inline functions*, debugging, *virtual functions*, and warning messages.

One command line option has to do with *inline functions* (see Chapter 5). When you declare a function inline, it serves as a hint to the compiler that the function is small and should be expanded inline wherever called, much the way that macros are expanded. However, expanded inline functions are hard to debug with the debugger, thus there is an option, -vi, to turn off inline expansion. The -vi option works in conjunction with the -v option, which controls the inclusion of debugging information in the object file. The following are five ways you can use these two options:

-v	Turn on debugging, turn off inline expansion
-v-	Turn off debugging, turn on inline expansion
-vi	Turn inline expansion on
-vi-	Turn inline expansion off
-v -vi	Turn on debugging, turn on inline expansion

Another option has to do with *virtual functions* (see Chapter 9). Virtual functions are implemented using a table of function pointers. The -Vx switches (uppercase V) control the placement of these tables in the executable. Use of these switches requires advanced knowledge of C++. Normally, you'll want to use the default switch, -Vs, which stands for "Smart virtual function tables."

There are over 50 options for controlling the generation of warning messages. We recommend that you enable all warnings. While you may not like getting picky messages (such as the one which complains about mixing signed versus unsigned characters), it's better to be informed of potential problems rather than having them blindly accepted. This is especially true if you're just starting out in Turbo C++ programming.

The trouble is, it's a lot of work to turn all the warning messages on from the command line. However, there is a way around that. You can create a special file that **tcc** can read to determine the options it is supposed to use. Such files are discussed next.

Using .CFG files

In addition to the options you give on the command line, you can also specify options in special configuration files that have **.cfg** extensions. When **tcc** begins compiling, it looks for the default configuration file **turboc.cfg** in the current directory. If it can't find it there, then **tcc** uses the file **turboc.cfg** in Turbo C++'s home directory.

After you've installed Turbo C++, the **turboc.cfg** file, as given in Turbo C++'s home directory, contains two options that tell **tcc** where to look for library and include files. The configuration file looks something like this:

```
-Ic:\tc\include
-Lc:\tc\lib
```

The -I option tells **tcc** where to look for include files. The -L option tells **tcc** where to find library files. You can add other options to this file. For instance, you might add the -P option to cause **tcc** to always compile for C++:

```
-Ic:\tc\include
-Lc:\tc\lib
-P
```

You may want to make changes to the configuration file that affect only compilations in the current directory. You can do this by including a version of **turboc.cfg** in your working directory. This file overrides the one in Turbo C++'s home directory. You can also create other **.cfg** files with different names. To access these, you use the + option on the command line. For instance, the command

```
tcc +myopt.cfg -c myfile.cpp
```

tells **tcc** to use the configuration file **myopt.cfg** when compiling **myfile.cpp**. Note how we've also used an additonal -c option on the command line. Options given on the command line are used in addition to the ones in the **.cfg** file. You can even override the ones in the **.cfg** file. The rules for this are a little tricky, though. Consult the Turbo C++ manuals for more details about this.

There is still the problem of turning on all the warning options. One way is to use TCINST program to set the warnings on in a global fashion. Another way is to use the IDE, since you can easily set all the compiler options from within the IDE. (However, these options are valid only while using the IDE, and not when compiling from the command line.)

The Turbo C++ IDE

If you've used Turbo C in the past, you'll notice a dramatic change in the integrated development environment for Turbo C++. The IDE now uses multiple windows and supports the mouse. You start up the IDE by using the **tc.exe** program (not to be confused with **tcc.exe**). An IDE session can be started by simply typing

```
tc
```

at the DOS command line. Figure 2.3 shows a typical IDE screen.

Note | We'll refer to IDE menu entries using the syntax **entry/sub_entry/ sub_sub_entry...**, which tells you to first select **entry** from the main menu, and then **sub_entry** from the submenu, and so forth.

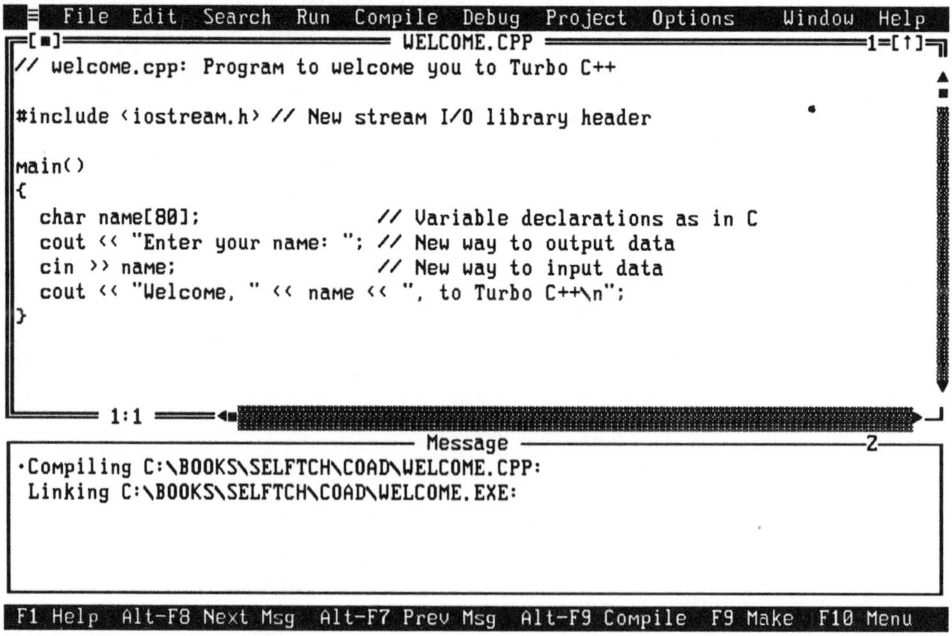

```
  File  Edit  Search  Run  Compile  Debug  Project  Options    Window  Help
[■]═══════════════════ WELCOME.CPP ═══════════════════1=[↑]
// welcome.cpp: Program to welcome you to Turbo C++                        ▲

#include <iostream.h> // New stream I/O library header          •

main()
{
  char name[80];              // Variable declarations as in C
  cout << "Enter your name: "; // New way to output data
  cin >> name;                 // New way to input data
  cout << "Welcome, " << name << ", to Turbo C++\n";
}



  1:1                                                                      ▼
──── Message ────────────────────────────────────────────2─
•Compiling C:\BOOKS\SELFTCH\COAD\WELCOME.CPP:
 Linking C:\BOOKS\SELFTCH\COAD\WELCOME.EXE:


 F1 Help  Alt-F8 Next Msg  Alt-F7 Prev Msg  Alt-F9 Compile  F9 Make  F10 Menu
```

Figure 2.3. A Typical IDE Screen

Let's type in and run a small program. First, open up a new file by selecting **File/New**, and then type in the following program (which came from Chapter 1) into the editor window:

```
// welcome.cpp: Program to welcome you to Turbo C++
#include <iostream.h>

main()
{
  char name[80];
  cout << "Enter your name: ";
  cin >> name;
  cout << "Welcome, " << name << ", to Turbo C++\n";
}
```

Save the program file as **welcome.cpp** by selecting the **File/Save As...** entry. Then, compile and link the program by selecting **Compile/Make**.

Tip

Before compiling a file from within the IDE, make sure to select the window containing the file as the active window. You can tell when a window is selected by looking for a highlighted border with scroll bars.

Assuming you've entered the program correctly, it should compile with no errors. You can now run the program by choosing **Run/Run**. The display flips to the output screen while the program runs. After you've typed in your name, the program responds with

```
Welcome, <your name>, to Turbo C++
```

and the display flips back to the IDE.

You may have had some problem compiling and running the sample program. You might have typed it in wrong, or you may have installed Turbo C++ improperly and have configured the IDE wrong. We're now going to show you how to set up the IDE specifically for compiling C++ programs. Keep in mind that the settings we're going to use are suggestions only, and these settings are the most helpful when you're first learning Turbo C++.

Other than setting up the options, we won't be going into much detail on how to use the IDE. It's fairly intuitive, especially if you have a mouse, or have used the previous Turbo C IDE. Consult the appropriate Turbo C++ manuals for further information.

Suppose you're trying to compile a file you have open in an editor window in the IDE, but the **Compile/Compile** menu entry option is grayed out, meaning the option can't be selected. What's most likely the problem?

The file you're trying to compile is not in the active window.

Setting Options from the IDE

In this section, we'll show which options are pertinent to C++ programming and recommend settings for them. Most of the options are found in the **Options** entry of the main menu. Turbo C++ allows you to have two settings for the menus: short and full.

Note ‖ For the following discussion, you'll need to use the full menu setting.

Compiler Options
The first set of options we'll work with are in the **Compiler Options** menu, as shown in Figure 2.4. The entries we're concerned about are **Code Generation**, **C++ options**, **Optimizations**, **Source**, and **Messages**. We'll discuss each in turn. The **Names...** entry is for advanced use only and doesn't concern us here. If you've installed Turbo C++ properly, then leave this last set of options alone.

Code Generation Options
Recommended settings for the **Compiler Options/Code Generation** dialog box are given in Figure 2.5. You want to be using the small memory model with a standard stack frame, and want to test for stack overflow.

More important, you'll want the **Unsigned characters** option set off. This option tells the compiler to treat all characters as **unsigned**. This is a convenient

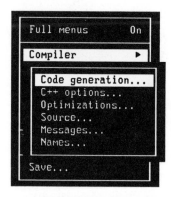

Figure 2.4. The Compiler Options Menu

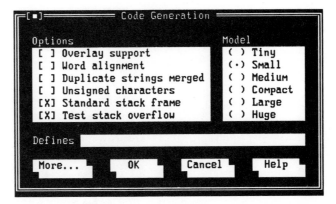

Figure 2.5. The Code Generation Dialog Box

option in C, but unfortunately, it's not so convenient in C++. The reason is that C++ is stricter on type-checking function calls. In particular, C++ has "type-safe" linkage (discussed in Chapter 5), in which argument typing information is embedded in the object file for each function. If you have the **Unsigned characters** option on, and try to pass a character to a function requiring a signed character, you may get a linker error.

You'll notice that there are more code generation options you can set. Select the **More...** button to see another options dialog box. The most important option to set here is the function calling convention. You want to use the C calling convention, rather than the Pascal calling convention.

Try compiling and linking **welcome.cpp** with the **Unsigned characters** option set. What happens?

You get a linker error due to C++'s type-safe linkage. By turning on the **Unsigned characters** *option, you've forced all the character strings used in the program to be unsigned. But the linker couldn't find an appropriate I/O function that takes unsigned character strings. (The only candidate takes signed character strings.)*

C++ Options

The next set of options have to do explicitly with C++. Select **Compiler Options/ C++ Options ...** and the dialog box in Figure 2.6 appears. Three options can be set from this dialog box. The first is related to the -Vx option used for virtual functions, as we explained earlier. You'll probably want to select the **Smart** option.

Figure 2.6. C++ Options

The second option corresponds to the -P command line option. Selecting **C++ always** is equivalent to using -P. The **CPP extension only** option is the default. However, it's recommended that you use the **C++ always** option. The reason is that if you try to compile a C++ header file by itself in the environment, you'll most likely get numerous error messages. This is because the default compiler for **.h** files is the C compiler, and if your header file contains C++ code, such as class declarations, you're in for trouble. Setting the **C++ always** option alleviates this problem.

The last option in the **C++ Options** dialog box has to do with whether or not inline functions are expanded. As pointed out earlier, having expanded inline functions makes debugging difficult. Therefore we're recommending you turn off the expansion. Later, when you get ready to make "production-quality" code and want maximum efficiency, you might want to turn the expansion back on.

Optimization Options
The **Optimization Options** dialog box is shown in Figure 2.7, with the recommended settings. As with expanded inline functions, having the optimizations turned on makes it hard to debug programs, thus we're recommending you turn off the optimization until you want production-quality code.

Source Options
Another dialog box you need to visit is **Source Options**, as shown in Figure 2.8. This box allows you to specify nested comments. It also controls what type of C or C++ dialect you wish to use, and controls to what length identifiers are unique. We recommend you turn off nested comments (it will eventually get

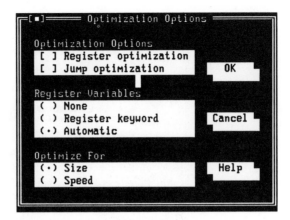

Figure 2.7. The Optimization Options

you into trouble). Since we'll be working in C++, set the keyword option to **Turbo C++**. You should set the identifier length to 32, so that you can create the longest names possible. In Turbo C++, the maximum unique identifier length is 32 characters.

The Message Options
Selecting **Compiler Options/Message...** pops up a dialog box to control the display of warning and error messages, as shown in Figure 2.9. You'll first want to specify how many errors or warnings you'll accept before the compilation is canceled. Using 25 and 100, respectively, is a good start, although you might prefer lower numbers. Be sure that the **Display Warnings** option is checked, otherwise, you won't get any warning messages at all.

You'll want to go through and set each message option individually. The four buttons in the main dialog box pop up further dialog boxes for this purpose.

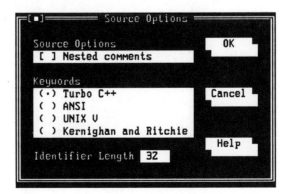

Figure 2.8. Source Options

Figure 2.9. Compiler Message Dialog Box

Tip | You should turn on *all* warnings. This is especially helpful when you're first learning C++. Let the compiler notify you of as many problems as it can.

Editor Options

To make it easy to work with C++ files in the IDE, you should change the default file extension for editor windows. You can do this by selecting the **Option/Preferences/Editor...** dialog box, as shown in Figure 2.10. The option we're concerned with is **Default Extension**. Set this to **.cpp**, and then every time you open a file the IDE will look for **.cpp** files rather the **.c** files, which is its default behavior.

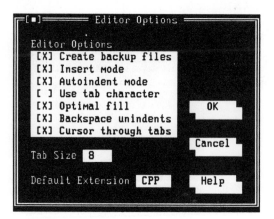

Figure 2.10. Editor Options

Make Options

The Turbo C++ IDE has a built-in Make facility. Figure 2.11 shows the **Options/ Make...** dialog box that's used for setting various options for Make.

You can set Make to abort on varying conditions. Figure 2.11 shows setting Make break on **Fatal Errors**. The choice is somewhat arbitrary. What isn't so arbitrary is checking the **Check auto-dependencies** entry. This option allows Make to make better decisions about which files need recompiling. We'll leave discussion of this to the section on project files. You'll probably always want to have the **Check auto-dependencies** option on.

Setting up the Debugger

Compiling your programs so that debugging information is included is most helpful when you're learning C++. Selecting the options as shown in Figure 2.12 is a good starting point. In particular, setting the **Inspector** options **Show inherited** and **Show methods** allow you to see all of the variables and functions of a class when you're debugging it.

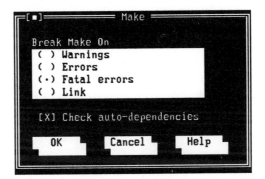

Figure 2.11. Make Options

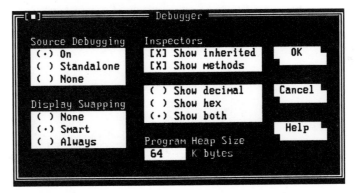

Figure 2.12. Debugger Options

One critical option sets the program heap size. When running a program from the IDE, memory is set aside for the heap in your program. If your program uses too much heap space, mysterious errors can occur while running the program from within the IDE. To avoid these errors, you should set the heap size to at least 64K. You can set it higher than 64K, but only if you're using the medium, large, and huge memory models.

Saving Your Options

Now that you've set up the desired options for compiling from the IDE, you'll want to save them by using the **Options/Save...** dialog box, as shown in Figure 2.13. You can save three different kinds of configuration data: environment, desktop, and project data.

Turbo C++ uses three types of files to store the configuration of the IDE. The compiler options are stored in the file **tcconfig.tc** in the Turbo C++ home directory. The current desktop configuration (such as which windows are open and where they are located) is stored in **tcdef.dsk**, also in the home directory. Finally, if you're using project files, they are stored in files ending with **.prj**. However, if you're not using a project, but rather just compiling a single-file program, that information gets stored in the file **tcdef.dpr** in the home directory.

Since all we're concerned with right now is the compiler options, make sure that at least **Environment** is selected, and then save it. You can save the other settings too if you like. In fact, you can have the IDE automatically save any or all of the settings each time you leave the IDE by going into the **Options/ Environment/Preferences** dialog box and selecting the appropriate auto-save behavior.

After loading a header file into an editor window and attempting to compile it, you're confronted with a number of errors, even though you know that the header file is good. What's most likely the problem?

Figure 2.13. Saving the Options

The default compiler for .h files is the C compiler. To compile a header file by itself within the IDE, be sure to set the C++ always option in the C++ Options dialog box.

Project Files

If your program is made up of multiple files, you'll have to set up a project file in order to compile the project from the environment. All you need to do is select **Project/Open Project**, and type in the desired project name into the dialog box shown in Figure 2.14. As given in the figure, type in the name of the first example in this chapter, **payroll**. A project file called **payroll.prj** will be created and a project window will appear at the bottom of the screen.

Tip ‖ The name of the project file becomes the name of the executable that will be created by the project.

You need to add files to the project. You can add C, C++, and TASM files and have them all compiled or assembled. For our project, we want to add the files **payroll.cpp** and **employee.cpp**. (However, we don't need to include the header file **employee.h**.)

Tip ‖ With the project window selected, you can press **Ins** to pop up a dialog box to add files to the project.

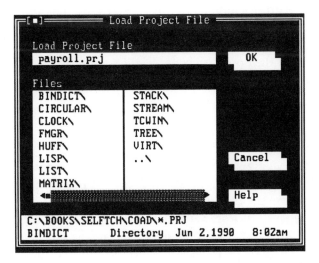

Figure 2.14. The Load Project Dialog Box

Once you've included all the source files you need for your project, you can load any of them into an editor window by selecting the file in the project window and then double-clicking with the mouse or pressing **Enter**. Try doing this for **payroll.cpp**. The screen should look something like that in Figure 2.15.

If you select a file in the project window, you can change certain options for the file, and you can view any header files included in the source. By typing **Ctrl-O**, a dialog box appears that allows you to set what you'd like the name of the object file to be, and more importantly, to set which compiler or assembler to use for that file. You can use the integrated compiler, the command line compiler, the Turbo Assembler, and in fact any other third-party compiler or translator as well. (Consult the manuals on how to do this.)

You can get a list of all header files included in a source file by pressing **SpaceBar** while that file is selected in the project window. A list of include files will appear in a dialog box. You can select any of the files and load them into an editor window for viewing.

Building the Project

You can Make a project by choosing either **Compiler/Make** or **Compiler/Build All**. The first compiles only those files that have been changed, the latter compiles everything regardless if it's needed or not.

Unlike many other compilers, Turbo C++ keeps a list of what header files are used in a source file, and stores this information in the corresponding **.obj** file. The **Make** facility can use this information to determine when a source file needs recompiling. It does this by checking the date of the **.obj** file against the date of the source file, and against the date of the header files mentioned in the **.obj** file. If any of these files is newer than the **obj** file, then **Make** knows to recompile the source. This auto-dependency check is optional, so make sure you've set it on in the **Make...** dialog box as shown in Figure 2.11.

Saving the Project File

You can save your project configuration by either closing the project file with **Project/Close Project** or by choosing **Options/Environment/Save** and checking the payroll file for saving. You might also want to go into the **Options/Preferences/Environment** dialog box and select the project file for automatic saving when you exit the IDE.

The IDE keeps track of your project in two files, a project file ending with **.prj**, and a desktop file with the same name as the project, but ending with

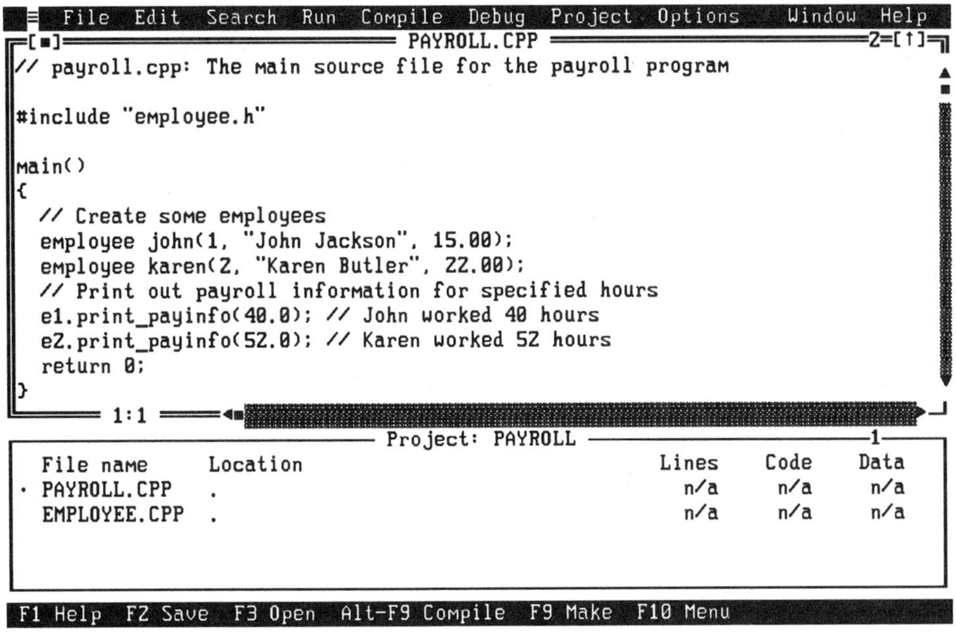

```
 File  Edit  Search  Run  Compile  Debug  Project  Options      Window  Help
[■]========================= PAYROLL.CPP =====================2=[↑]
// payroll.cpp: The main source file for the payroll program     ▲
                                                                 ■
#include "employee.h"

main()
{
  // Create some employees
  employee john(1, "John Jackson", 15.00);
  employee karen(2, "Karen Butler", 22.00);
  // Print out payroll information for specified hours
  e1.print_payinfo(40.0); // John worked 40 hours
  e2.print_payinfo(52.0); // Karen worked 52 hours
  return 0;
}
  1:1 ═══◄■▓▓▓▓▓▓▓▓▓▓▓▓▓▓▓▓▓▓▓▓▓▓▓▓▓▓▓▓▓▓▓▓▓▓▓►┘
─────────────────── Project: PAYROLL ───────────────────1──
  File name    Location                Lines    Code    Data
· PAYROLL.CPP   .                        n/a     n/a     n/a
  EMPLOYEE.CPP  .                        n/a     n/a     n/a



F1 Help  F2 Save  F3 Open  Alt-F9 Compile  F9 Make  F10 Menu
```

Figure 2.15. A Sample Project Screen

.dsk. Unlike the project files of Turbo C 2.0, the project files in Turbo C++ not only contain file information, but they also store all the compiler options you've set for that project. You don't need a separate **.tc** file as you did in Turbo C 2.0.

Working with Project Files

If you've created a project file in a directory, then every time you start up **tc** in that directory, it automatically loads the project and restores all the windows that were open at the time you last used **tc**. (It stores these window positions in the **.dsk** file associated with the project.)

If you have more than one project file in a directory, you can specify which project to use by giving the project file name on the command line, and including the file's **.prj** extension.

Summary

In this chapter, the most important thing to remember is that there is a difference between compiling for C and compiling for C++. In the next few chapters, we'll take a look at what those differences are.

You've seen many options and dialog boxes in this chapter, but three are particularly important. When using the command line compiler, the all important option is -P. When compiling from the IDE, the **C++ Options** dialog box contains the critical **C++ extension only** and **C++ always** options. If you become suspicious of compiler errors that you don't think you should be getting (especially with header files) make sure these settings are correct.

Exercises

1. Find the mistake in the following program, and suggest three ways to fix it:

```
#include <stdio.h>
int main()
{
  int k = 42;
  printf("k = %d\n", k);
}
```

2. What problem does the following header file have?

   myheader.h:

```
int compute_answer(int a, int b)
{
  return a + b;
}
```

3. What are two ways to ensure that a file is compiled from the command line in C++ mode?

4. Given the following two files **source.cpp** and **myprog.cpp**:

   source.cpp:

```
int ascii_to_num(char c)
{
  return c - '0';
}
```

   myprog.cpp:

```
#include <stdio.h>
extern int ascii_to_num(char c);

main()
{
  char nine = '9';
  printf("Decimal value is %d\n", ascii_to_num(nine));
}
```

try compiling and linking these files using the following sequence of commands:

```
tcc -c source.cpp
tcc -c -K myprog.cpp
tcc myprog.obj source.obj
```

What happens? Can you explain why?

5. What's a convenient way to manage a set of compiler options for use by the command line compiler?

6. Suppose you are using the Turbo C++ IDE and when you specify a file without an extension, the IDE puts on a **.c** extension. However, you wish to use files with a **.cpp** extension only. What can you do?

Answers

1. *The **main()** function was declared to take an **int** return type, yet no return statement was given. You can fix the problem by either supplying a return statement that returns a value, or by using a void return type, or by leaving the return type off altogether.*

2. *The header file has a function definition inside it. Normally, only the prototype for a function should be included in a header file, not the body of the function.*

3. *Either use the -P option, or give the file a **.cpp** extension.*

4. *The **myprog.cpp** file was compiled with the -K switch, forcing all **char** types to be treated as **unsigned**. Thus, the compiler sets up a call to the function **ascii_to_num()** with an **unsigned char** for a parameter. However, the **source.cpp** file was compiled without the -K switch, so the function **ascii_to_num()** was compiled to have a **signed char** as a parameter.*

   *When you try to link the two files together, you'll get a linker error stating that the function **ascii_to_num(unsigned char)** is missing. The reason is that C++ is stricter than C is about parameter types when linking functions together. (See the discussion on type-safe linkage in Chapter 5.) Note that had we compiled and linked these files in the C mode, they would have linked fine.*

5. *You can use a **.cfg** file and list the compiler options in it.*

6. *Ensure that you always use the **.cpp** extension when specifying a file, or more conveniently, set the default extension to **.cpp** in the **Editor Options** dialog box.*

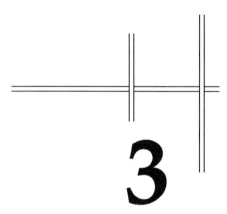

C++ Fundamentals: Part One

In this chapter, the fundamental building blocks of C++ programs, such as identifiers, constants, and data types are covered. Much of the material that's covered here is a review of the C language. However, some of the new features of C++ will also be introduced. This will help you see some of the ways that C and C++ differ.

One of the goals of C++ is to provide support for user-defined types in a more direct and natural way than is possible in C. Another important goal is to provide a safer programming environment. This chapter will explain some of the ways that these two goals are accomplished.

After studying this chapter, you'll learn:

- How constant literals differ between C and C++
- How pointers differ between C and C++
- What references are and how to work with them
- How enumerated types differ between C and C++
- About the new class types
- How constants differ between C and C++

Starting from the Ground Up

The purpose of a program is to take some data and manipulate it. The data that's manipulated comes in two forms: either as constant literals, or as memory locations that are identified by using names. We'll first look at constant literals, and then we'll look at identifiers.

Constant Literals

A literal constant can take on four different forms:

- Integers
- Floating point numbers
- Characters
- Strings

Integer constants are represented in Turbo C++ as signed integers, and they usually take up two bytes. The actual size depends on the constant. For instance, the constant 70000 won't fit in 2 bytes, so 4 bytes are used. A constant can be an unsigned type using the **u** or **U** suffixes, and a constant can be made **long** (taking up 4 bytes) by using the **l** or **L** suffixes. The following are some integer constants:

```
12       // A decimal constant having the value 12
012      // An octal constant having the value 10
0x12     // A hex constant having the value 18
0X12     // The same constant, using uppercase X
12L      // A signed, long integer constant
17l      // Another signed, long integer constant
42UL     // An unsigned, long integer constant
```

Floating point constants are by default typed as **double**, and take up 8 bytes. You can type them as **float** (taking 4 bytes) using an **f** or **F** suffix. You can also type them as **long double** (taking 10 bytes) by using an **l** or **L** suffix. Some examples are:

```
3.1419F   // A famous constant as a float
6.02e23   // Another famous constant as a double
6.02E23L  // Same constant as a long double
```

With integer and floating point constants, there's no difference between C and C++. However, there is a difference with character constants, as you'll now see.

Character Constants

A character constant is a character enclosed in quotes. For instance:

```
'A'  // A character constant
```

In Turbo C, a character constant is typed as a signed integer and requires 2 bytes of storage, even though only 1 byte is used. The sign of the low order byte is extended to the upper byte.

In Turbo C++, however, a character constant is typed as a character, and takes up only 1 byte. Most of the time, you won't notice this difference. However, it will show up when you take the size of a character constant in the two languages:

```
sizeof('A') = 2 // In C
sizeof('A') = 1 // In C++
```

This change was made in C++ to help the new stream I/O operators work better with character constants. See Chapter 11 for more about this.

Some characters aren't printable. To represent these, you can use escape sequences such as '\n'. Table 3.1 lists the escape sequences available.

Both Turbo C and Turbo C++ support another type of constant which can hold two characters. These are called wide character constants, and you represent them using quotes, prefixed by the letter L. An example is:

```
L'ab' // A wide character constant
```

Table 3.1. Character Escape Sequences

Sequence	Character	Description
\a	Alarm (bell)	Sounds the bell
\b	BS	Backspace
\f	FF	Formfeed
\n	LF	Line feed
\r	CR	Carriage return
\t	TAB	Horizontal tab
\v	VT	Vertical tab
\\	\	Backslash
\'	'	Apostrophe
\"	"	Double quote
\?	?	Question mark
\O	Any character	String of octal digits
\xH	Any character	String of hex digits

These constants were included to help support character sets where there are more than 256 characters, and thus more than 1 byte is needed to represent a character.

String Literals

A string literal is a sequence of characters surrounded by quotes. For instance:

```
"Turbo C++"
```

String literals are stored as an array of characters terminated by a byte containing 0. Thus, the sample string takes up 10 bytes.

You can concatenate string literals together in one of two ways: either by using a backslash to continue the literal to the next line, or by simply placing two string literals next to each other. For example, the following two expressions both create the literal "Turbo C++".

```
"Turbo \
C++"

"Turbo "  "C++"
```

When using the backslash form, be sure that the backslash is the last character on the line, and that the next line starts immediately with the continued string. It's easy to make a mistake using this method, so the second method, where you simply place two strings next to each other, is preferred.

You can use character escape sequences in literal strings. A common use is in ending a string with a newline:

```
printf("Turbo C++: The next generation\n");
```

It gets a little tricky if you use escape sequences involving hexadecimal or octal constants. For instance, what does the following do?

```
printf("\x0072 errors found\n");
```

Previous versions of Turbo C allowed only up to three digits in a hexadecimal constant. Thus, the **printf()** statement prints the character '\x007' (the bell) followed by the string "2 errors found\n". However, the three-digit rule has changed in Turbo C++. Now character escapes using hexadecimal constants can contain any number of digits, so in Turbo C++, the **printf()** statement prints the character '\x0072', followed by the string " errors found\n".

A way to avoid problems such as this is to simply concatenate two strings together. For instance:

```
printf("\x007" "2 errors found\n");
```

1. What potential problem exists in the following code?

```
void write(unsigned char *s);

main()
{
  write("Hello Turbo C++ Fan\n");
}
```

2. Find the mistake in the following code:

```
int i, nums[10];
// Initialize each element in the array
for (i = 0; i<010; i++) nums[i] = 0;
```

1. *If you don't have the -K option set (which defaults all characters to unsigned), then you'll get a type mismatch warning. String literals have a type of **signed char*** and we're passing this one to an argument expecting an **unsigned char*** type.*
2. *A zero was inadvertently placed in front of the constant 10, making it an octal constant instead of a decimal constant. The **for** loop would only execute 8 times instead of 10.*

Identifiers

Identifiers in C++ are composed of alphanumeric characters and underscores, just as they are in C. Identifiers can't start with a digit, and they must begin with either a letter or an underscore. The following are some valid and invalid identifiers:

```
thirtysomething  // Valid
_zorba           // Valid
len_             // Valid
12dozen          // Invalid
@sign            // Invalid
_                // Valid, but not recommended
```

The difference between C and C++ identifiers is that C identifiers are unique only up to the first 32 characters. In C++, identifiers are unique up to any length. (You can change this via command line options or from the IDE, as explained in Chapter 2.)

Some identifiers are reserved as keywords. Table 3.2 lists the reserved keywords in Turbo C++. Those marked with an asterisk are keywords added specifically for the C++ language.

You'll notice that some of these keywords start with underscores. Actually, you should treat all identifiers that start with underscores as reserved. The Turbo C++ libraries use many such identifiers for built-in variables and flags. You should avoid using names starting with underscores in your code. (Don't confuse the underscores *you* put on as opposed to the ones the compiler tacks on internally.)

Declaring Types in C++

Each variable and constant in a Turbo C++ program has a type. This type determines the storage requirements and bit patterns for that variable or constant.

The types come in two categories: fundamental types and derived types, as shown in Figure 3.1. The fundamental types are the building blocks of the typing system. They include types such as integers and characters. The derived types, such as arrays and structures, are built from the fundamental types. Let's look first at the fundamental types.

Table 3.2. Reserved Keywords in Turbo C++

asm*	_cs	extern	interrupt	register	struct
auto	default	far	_loadds	_regparam	switch
break	delete*	float	long	return	template*
case	do	for	near	_saveregs	this*
catch*	double	friend*	new*	_seg	typedef
cdecl	_ds	goto	operator*	short	union
char	else	huge	pascal	signed	unsigned
class*	enum	if	private*	sizeof	virtual*
const	_es	inline*	protected*	_ss	void
continue	_export	int	public*	static	volatile
* New C++ keywords					while

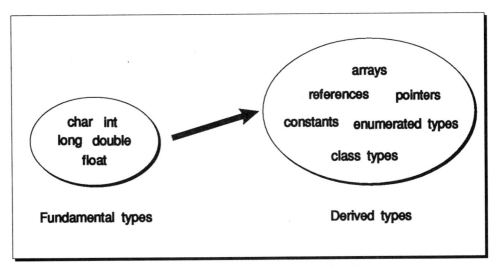

Figure 3.1. The Type Categories

Fundamental Types

Turbo C++ has the same basic types that Turbo C has, as summarized in Table 3.3. Note that some of the types have more than one name. Also, **char** can mean either **unsigned char** or **signed char**, depending on whether the -K compiler option is set.

Table 3.3. Basic Data Types in Turbo C++

Type	Bytes	Range
signed char	1	-128 to 127
unsigned char	1	0 to 255
char	1	Depends on -K option
short, short int	2	-32768 to 32767
signed short	2	-32768 to 32767
signed short int	2	-32768 to 32767
unsigned short	2	0 to 65535
unsigned short int	2	0 to 65535
int, signed int	2	-32768 to 32767

continued

Table 3.3. Basic Data Types in Turbo C++ *(continued)*

Type	Bytes	Range
unsigned int	2	0 to 65535
long, long int	4	-2147483648 to 2147483647
signed long	4	-2147483648 to 2147483647
signed long int	4	-2147483648 to 2147483647
unsigned long	4	0 to 4294967295
unsigned long int	4	0 to 4294967295
float	4	3.4E-38 to 3.4E+38
double	8	1.7E-308 to 1.7E+308
long double	10	3.4E-4932 to 3.4E+4932

The Derived Types

From the basic types, any number of derived types can be built. The derived types available in Turbo C++ are:

- Pointers
- References
- Arrays
- Enumerated types
- Class types (including structures and unions)
- Constants

Table 3.4 shows some examples of each kind of derived type.

To the derived types available in C, C++ adds reference types and class types. We'll be discussing these new additions, as well as explaining some differences in how C++ implements the types common to both languages. We'll start with pointers.

Pointers

Pointers are a prominent part of C++ programming, just as they are in C. For the most part, pointers in C++ are used the same way that they are used in C.

Table 3.4. Quick Sample of Derived Types

pointers	`char *str;` `void (*func)(char *str, int len);`
references	`int i;` `int &ref_to_i = i;`
arrays	`char msg[80];` `float surface_points[100][100];`
enumerated types	`enum seasons {winter, spring, summer, fall};`

class types	`class bin_tree {`
	`private:`
	`  bin_tree *l, *r;`
	`public:`
	`  bin_tree(void);`
	`  void set_left(bin_tree *t);`
	`  void set_right(bin_tree *t);`
	`  bin_tree *lchild(void);`
	`  bin_tree *rchild(void);`
	`};`

constants	`const int tabsize = 8;`
	`void write(const char *fmstr, ...);`
	`void stack::push(const token &tk);`
	`const char *const defmsg(void)`
	`{`
	`  return "No errors";`
	`}`

However, there are some differences. These differences include how **void** pointers may be used and how pointers to functions work.

As a review, in C, you can define a pointer **p** to any of the built-in types, or to any user-defined type as follows:

```
type *p;
```

where **type** is any built-in or user-defined type. The same is true in C++. Some examples are:

```
int *ip;  // Pointer to a integer
char **s; // Pointer to a character pointer
```

You can also declare pointers to **void** in C and C++, but there is a difference. In C++, you can't assign a **void** pointer to a non-**void** pointer without doing a typecast. (Note that both languages let you go the other way around, though.) Figure 3.2 illustrates the restriction to **void** pointers in C++.

Tip

As with most changes that C++ makes to C language, the **void** pointer restriction is meant to make programming a little safer. However, if you're courageous enough, you can always get around type restrictions like this by using typecasting.

Pointers to Functions

Both C and C++ allow you to declare pointers to functions. But again, the rules are slightly different in C++ to accommodate stricter type checking. The general form of a pointer-to-function declaration is as follows:

```
<return-type> (*fptr)(argtyp1, argtyp2, ...);
```

This declaration declares **fptr** to be a pointer to a function that has a return type of **return-type**, and takes the arguments having types **argtyp1**, **argtyp2**, and so on. For example, the following declaration declares **h** to be a pointer to a function that takes a **char*** as an argument and passes back an **int**:

```
int (*h)(char *);
```

One problem you might encounter is when porting code like the following from C to C++:

```
int strlen(char *s); /* Function prototype */

int (*g)();          /* Declare function pointer g */
```

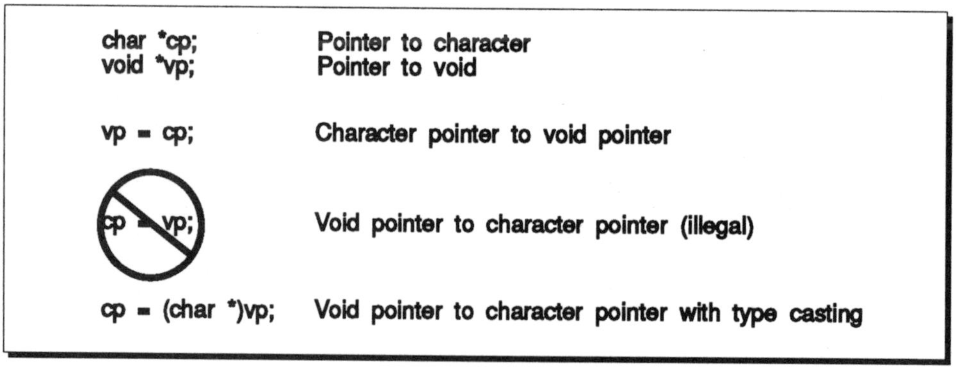

char *cp;	Pointer to character
void *vp;	Pointer to void
vp = cp;	Character pointer to void pointer
cp = vp; (illegal)	Void pointer to character pointer (illegal)
cp = (char *)vp;	Void pointer to character pointer with type casting

Figure 3.2 Using Void Pointers in C++

```
main()
{
  g = strlen;      /* Point g to strlen() */
  g("Turbo C++"); /* This indirect call compiles in C */
  g(134.17);       /* This compiles too, but what happens? */
}
```

In C, a function prototype declared with no arguments means that the function can take any number of arguments. For example:

```
int f();  /* Takes any number of arguments in C */
```

Thus, our function pointer **g** is a pointer to a function taking any number of arguments and returning an **int**. That's why the second use of **g** inside **main()** is perfectly legal in C, even though a **double** is passed instead of a **char***. The result, of course, is erroneous.

In C++, the preceding example won't even compile. In C++, a function prototype declared with no arguments means not that the function can take any number of arguments, but rather, that the function takes no arguments at all! For instance:

```
int f();  // Takes no arguments in C++
```

This interpretation is exactly the opposite of that used in C. (See Chapter 5 for more discussion of this.) Because of this difference, the C++ declaration

```
int (*g)();  // Declare function pointer g
```

declares **g** to be a pointer to a function taking no arguments and returning an **int**. Thus, calls to **g** such as

```
g(134.17);
```

are illegal. Again, the C++ rules make for safer programming.

---

1. Given the following C++ program, which of the function calls in **main()** are illegal? What if the program were compiled in C?

```
void *v;
char *c;

void f1(void *p) { ... }
void f2(char *c) { ... }

main()
{
  f1(v);  // (a)
```

```
    f1(c);   // (b)
    f2(v);   // (c)
    f2(c);   // (d)
}
```

2. Will the following program compile in C? What about C++? Why or why not?

```
#include <stdlib.h>

main()
{
  char *p;
  p = malloc(25);
  return 0;
}
```

3. Will the following code compile in C++? (Hint: Look at the assignment to **fptr.**)

```
#include <stdio.h>

int (*fptr)(...);
int strlen(char *s);

main()
{
  fptr = strlen;
  printf("Len = %d\n", fptr("Hello"));
}
```

---

1. *Call (c) is illegal, since we're trying to assign a **void** pointer to a **char** pointer in the function call. If compiled in C, this would present no problem. In both languages, the best way to make the call is:*

```
f2((char *)v);
```

2. *It compiles fine in C (you might get a warning about **p** being unused), however, in C++ you'll get a compiler error. The reason is that **malloc()** returns a **void*** type, and we're trying to assign this **void*** to a **char***. That's legal in C, but not in C++. You should use typecasting:*

```
p = (char *)malloc(25);
```

*Note that the inconvenience of using **malloc()** in C++ is mitigated by the fact that there are simpler ways of allocating memory in C++, by using the **new** operator, as you'll learn in Chapter 7.*

3. *No. Even though **fptr** is declared to be a pointer to a function taking any number of arguments (through the use of the ellipses), we can't assign **strlen()** to it, since **strlen()** takes a char* argument. When used in conjunction with function pointers, ellipses will only match other ellipses. We could set **fptr** to point to a function like the following:*

```
int somefunc(...);

fptr = somefunc;  // Okay
```

References

In C, you can use pointers to create aliases to other variables. But C++ adds another way through the use of *references*. References are like pointers in that they contain addresses to other variables. However, unlike pointers, they are implicitly dereferenced when used, and thus look more like ordinary variables.

References are declared in much the same way pointers are declared, except that you use the & operator instead of the * operator. For instance, the following makes **p** a pointer to an integer, and makes **r** a reference to the same integer:

```
int i;      // Declare an integer
int *p=&i;  // Declare a pointer to i
int &r=i;   // Declare a reference to i
```

Note ‖ You don't have to take the address of a variable when referring to it with a reference. That's done automatically.

Recall that in C the & operator has two uses: as the **AND** operator and as the **address-of** operator. We're using it as the **address-of** operator when we initialize the pointer **p**. But we're also using it a third way, which is only available in C++, when we declare the reference **r**. Figure 3.3 summarizes the different uses of the & operator.

Both **p** and **r** point to the integer **i**. However, that's where the similarity ends. The difference lies in how these variables are used. Once you've initialized a reference to alias another variable, anytime you use the reference, it's as though you're using the aliased variable. Let's contrast the use of a reference with that of a pointer:

```
i = 55;  // Updates i
*p = 42; // Updates i
r = 17;  // Updates i
```

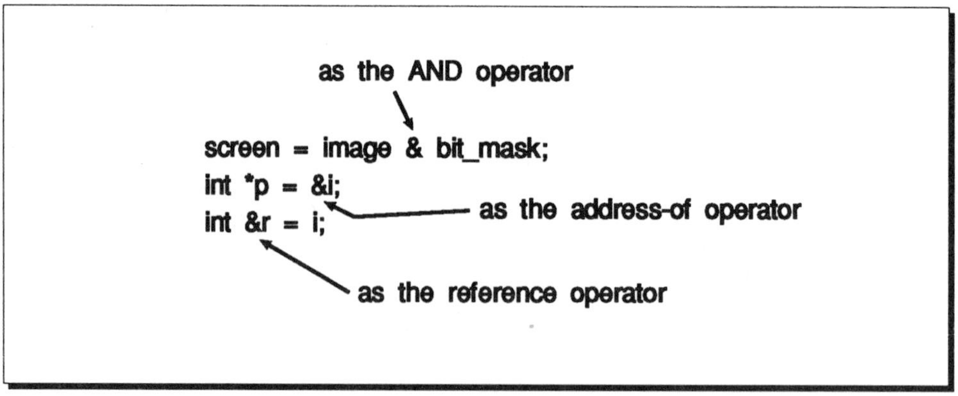

Figure 3.3. Three Uses of the & Operator

Note how all three statements update the same memory location: the location named **i**. We had to dereference the pointer **p** to get to the location of **i**, but with the reference **r**, we didn't. The reference **r** is simply another name for **i**.

Restrictions to Using References

There are three restrictions when using references:

1. References must be initialized when declared (unless when used as arguments to functions, as explained in Chapter 5).
2. Once initialized, a reference cannot be reassigned to point to another variable.
3. You can't create a reference to a reference or a pointer to a reference. (However, you can create a reference to a pointer.)

For example:

```
int i, j;
int &r = i; // Declare and initialize reference
r = &j; // Not okay, can't initialize again
r = j; // Okay, sets i = j.
int &*p = &r;  // Can't create pointer to a reference
int &&p = r; // Can't create reference to a reference
int *q;
int *&r = q; // Okay, creates a reference to a pointer
```

Aside from the restrictions mentioned, references can be used in many of the same ways that pointers can. For example, you can have constant references, references to constants, references to functions (instead of pointers to functions), and references to structures. Let's look at an example of the latter:

```
struct symbol {
  int token;
  char name[80];
};

symbol s;         // Declare symbol
symbol *p=&s;     // Declare pointer to s
symbol &r=s;      // Declare reference to s

p->token = 5;     // Member access via pointer
r.token = 5;      // Member access via reference
```

Compare the way that pointers to structures and references to structures are used. Note how with the reference **r**, we use the dot operator, not the arrow operator to access **token**.

Tip ‖ The way to remember how a reference works is to think of it as another name for the variable it references.

Although the examples we've given so far show one way to use reference variables—as direct aliases to other variables—in practice, you will seldom use them that way. Using direct aliases is somewhat dangerous. However, there are cases when aliases come in handy. One such case is when you're passing parameters to a function. It's possible to declare function arguments as references, and get the effects of pass-by-reference. This topic is discussed in Chapter 5.

1. Which of the following examples are legal:

   a. int &r;
   b. int &r = 25;
   c. int *p = 25;
   d. int i;
      int &r = i;
      r = 25;
   e. const int j = 25;
      int &r = j;

2. Having an array of references is illegal. Using the rules we've given you in the previous section, can you guess why?

1. Examples a, c, and e are illegal, but b and d are fine. In a, we're trying to declare a reference without initializing it. You must initialize a reference at the time of decla-

ration. In b, we're setting a reference to refer to a constant literal. That's legal. The compiler will allocate storage for the literal so that the reference has something to point to. Note, however, that the analogous pointer operation, shown in c, is illegal.

*Even though we can point a reference to a constant literal, we can't point it to a constant variable, as we tried to do in e. What would happen if we assigned a value to the reference? We would be updating a constant! To fix this problem, we should make **r** a reference to a constant, as follows:*

```
const int  j = 25;
const int &r = j; // Declare reference to a const
```

2. *Recall that an array name is really a pointer to the elements of the array. Thus if we tried to declare an array of references, we would in essence be declaring a pointer to one or more references, which is illegal.*

Arrays

Closely related to pointer types are arrays. Arrays are declared using the square brackets, as in

```
char msg[80];
```

which declares **msg** to be an array of 80 characters. It also declares **msg** to be pointer to a character. As you well know, the pointer and array notation can be used interchangeably. For instance, the following two statements are identical:

```
msg[5] = 'a';  // Update fifth element of msg
*(msg+5) = 'a';// Also updates fifth element
```

You can create multidimensional arrays by declaring arrays of arrays, as in

```
char msgtable[25][80];
```

which declares **msgtable** to be an array of 25 arrays of 80 characters.

Note ‖ Arrays of any type are allowed, except for arrays of references.

As in C, you can initialize arrays in C++ at the time of declaration by enclosing the initial values of the elements between curly braces, as in

```
int pair[2] = {17, 42};
```

Character arrays can be initialized both with curly braces and with string literals. For example, the following two statements are identical:

```
char msg1[6] = {'h', 'e', 'l', 'l', 'o', '\0'};
char msg2[6] = "hello";
```

Recall that string literals end with a null terminator which must be accounted for in the size of the array.

Both C and C++ allow partial initializations. That is, if you don't give enough values in the initialization, the rest of the elements are assigned the value zero. However, it's an error to give too many initializers in C++. Here's an area where C and C++ differ. In C, the following is legal. However, in C++, it's not:

```
char letters[3] = "abc"; // Legal in C, but not C++
```

The literal "abc" consists of 4 bytes (including the null), which won't fit into an array of three characters. Quite properly, C++ flags this as an error. To fix the problem in C++, you should use:

```
char letters[3] = {'a', 'b', 'c'};
```

One problem that both C and C++ have is that subscripts to arrays are never checked for out-of-bounds conditions. However, C++ provides a solution to this problem. It's possible to declare classes that simulate the look and feel of arrays, but that also have range checking on their subscripts. You'll see an example of this in Chapter 10.

Enumerated Types

C++ provides enumerated types just as C does. The general syntax is:

```
enum <tag> { member1, member2, ...} <variables, ...>;
```

For example:

```
enum seasons { winter, spring, summer, fall } s1, s2;
```

As Figure 3.4 illustrates, the identifier **seasons** is called an *enumeration tag*. The members **winter, spring, summer,** and **fall** are called *enumerators*. In our example, we declared two variable *enumerations* **s1** and **s2**. Declaring variables at the time of defining an enumeration is optional. You could also write:

```
enum seasons { winter, spring, summer, fall };
enum seasons s1, s2;
```

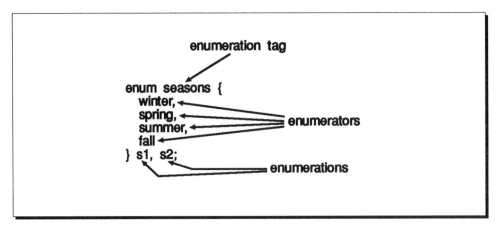

Figure 3.4. Components of an Enumerated Type

The enumerators of an enumeration are given default values, starting at zero and increasing by one. You can, however, specify the enumeration values yourself. For example, here's an equivalent way to declare **seasons**:

```
enum seasons { winter=0, spring=1, summer=2, fall=3 };
```

If you don't specify a value for an enumerator, the value used is one plus the value of the previous enumerator. If it's the first enumerator, then it is assigned the value 0. Two enumerators in the same enumeration can have the same value. For example, in

```
enum dirn { up, down, left, right, none = 0 };
```

both **up** and **none** have the value 0. The enumerators **down, left** and **right** have the values 1, 2, 3, respectively.

C++ allows you to have anonymous enumerations. These are enumerations without tags. For instance:

```
enum {good, bad, ugly};
```

Even though the enumeration has no name, you can use its members. That is, you can use **good, bad,** and **ugly.** They have the values 0, 1, and 2, respectively. Of course, you can't use an anonymous enumeration to declare variables (unless you declare them at the time you define the enumerator).

Tip || Anonymous enumerations allow you to group a set of constants without having to give the overall set a name.

While you use enumerations in C++ much like you do in C, there are three differences:

1. C++ is stricter about assigning to enumerations
2. Enumeration tags are type names in C++
3. Enumerators are hidden in C++ classes, but not in C structures.

Let's look at the first difference. In C, you can assign any integer value to an enumeration, as well as assign it the value of one of its enumerators. However, in C++, you can only use enumerators in an enumeration assignment. For instance:

```
enum seasons { winter, spring, summer, fall } s;

s = winter; // Legal in both languages
s = 0;      // Legal only in C
```

Even though 0 is the value of one of the enumerators—**winter**—C++ won't let you use the value directly. You'll get a warning if you try. This is in keeping with C++'s stricter type checking. However, you can always use a typecast, even if it makes no sense:

```
s = (enum seasons) 47;  // User beware
```

The other two differences to the way C++ treats enumerators will be discussed in Chapter 4, when we talk about *name spaces* and *scopes*.

1. What's wrong with the following header file?

   myheader.h:

   ```
   enum time_of_day { morning, noon, night } t1;
   ```

2. Suppose we changed the header file to the following. Is it okay now?

   myheader.h:

   ```
   struct navig_data {
     enum time_of_day { morning, noon, night } t1;
     float x_posn, y_posn;
   };
   ```

1. *The enumerated type* **time_of_day** *is defined. That's okay, but a variable of that type,* **t1**, *is declared as well, causing storage to be allocated. Such memory allocation shouldn't be done inside header files.*

2. *Yes, it's fine now. Even though we're still declaring the variable **t1**, that declaration is inside a structure template. No storage is allocated, since we're only defining the structure, not creating variables from it.*

Class Types

In C programs you use **structs** and **unions** to represent user-defined types. For example, here is a **struct** declaration that declares a **point** type:

```
struct point {
  float x, y;
}
```

The problem is, even though you might think of **point** as being a type, it really isn't a true type in C. You can't use the name **point** directly when declaring **point** variables, you must prefix the variable declarations with the **struct** keyword. Here's an example:

```
struct point p; /* Must use struct keyword in C */
```

C++ fixes this problem by making **structs** and **unions** bonafide types. This means that we can use the name of a **struct** or **union** just as we can any type name. Thus we can write statements such as:

```
point p; // Don't need struct keyword in C++
```

In C++, **structs** and **unions** are collectively called *class types*, or *classes* for short. In fact, C++ extends the capabilities of structures and unions by allowing them to have functions as members as well as variables. For example, we could include a **set()** function inside our definition for **point**:

```
struct point {
  float x, y;
  void set(float xi, float yi);
}
```

There's also another way to declare class types, and that is to use the **class** keyword. An example is:

```
class point {
private:
  float x, float y;
public:
  void set(float xi, float yi);
};
```

You'll notice some additional keywords, **private** and **public**, used in our class declaration. These control access to the members of the class.

Don't worry if you don't understand what this access control is about, or how the functions inside the class declaration work. We won't be discussing classes in detail until Chapter 6. For now, the important thing to know is that classes are types, and that they can be declared with either the **class**, **struct**, or **union** keywords.

Some additional examples of classes are:

```
class window {
private:
  int x, y, wd, ht;
public:
  window(int w, int h);
  void draw(void);
  void erase(void);
};
struct employee {
  int id;
  char name[80];
  void set_info(int i, char *n);
};
union token_data {
  double d;
  char name[32];
  void set_num(double n);
  void set_name(char *n);
};
```

In the new C++ terminology, variables declared from classes are called *objects*. The following are some declarations of objects using the preceding class declarations:

```
window w; // Declare window object w
employee e;  // Declare employee object e
token_data td; // Declare token data object td
```

Using Typedefs

In C, one way to get around using the **struct** and **union** keywords in variable declarations is to use the **typedef** keyword. For example, we could declare the **point** structure as

```
typedef struct {
  float x, y;
} point;
```

and then write variable declarations such as

```
point p; /* Okay now, since point was declared as a type */
```

As you learned in the last section, such use of **typedef** is no longer necessary in C++. However, **typedefs** are still useful. Recall that the **typedef** keyword can be used to make synonyms for types. For example:

```
typedef char *string;
```

Note ‖ Unless coupled with **struct** or **union** declarations, **typedefs** do not create new types, they simply define alternate names for existing types.

Another use for **typedefs** is to simplify complex type declarations, such as those used in declaring pointers to functions. For instance:

```
// Make synonym for void pointers
typedef void *vptr;
// Make synonym for pointer to function returning a void pointer
typedef vptr (*vpf)(void);
// Make synonym for an array of such function pointers
typedef vpf ten_vpf[10];
ten_vpf ftable;
```

Contrast the last statement with the following, which is an equivalent (but much more complicated) definition for **ftable**:

```
void *(*ftable[10])(void);
```

Write a C++ declaration equivalent to the following C declarations, without using **typedef**:

```
typedef struct { int wd, ht; } rect;
```

struct rect { int wd, ht; };

Type Conversions

As in C, C++ allows both implicit and explicit type conversions. An example of an implicit type conversion is when you use a character where an integer is

C Form	Alternate C++ Form
d = (double)i;	d = double(i);

Figure 3.5. Typecasting Syntax in C++

expected. The compiler will use the lower byte of the character and then either pad the high byte with zeros, or sign extend the high byte if the character is signed. Similar implicit conversions exist for going from short to long integers, from integers to doubles, and so on.

The rules for implicit type conversions can get complex. You should consult the Turbo C++ manuals for details of these rules. It's often better to use explicit type conversions. In that manner, you and whoever reads your code won't have to remember any complicated conversion rules.

In C, you specify an explicit type conversion by prefixing the identifier with the desired type to convert to, enclosed in parentheses. For instance, you can convert an **int** to a **double** as follows:

```
int i = 5;
double d;

d = (double)i;
```

The same syntax is valid in C++. However, there's an alternate form in C++, shown in Figure 3.5, that makes the conversions look more like function calls. An example is:

```
d = double(i);
```

There's a reason for this alternate syntax. C++ allows you to specify your own type conversion functions. (In Chapters 7 and 10 you'll learn ways to do this.) The new syntax lets you invoke these user-defined conversion functions with normal function calls.

Is it possible to use the new type conversion syntax when converting a long integer to a character far pointer? Here's how to do it the old way:

```
char far *p = (char far *)0xb8000000L;
```

If you try using

```
char far *p - char far *p(0xb8000000L);
```

*you'll get a syntax error. A work-around is to use a **typedef**, as in the following code:*

```
typedef char far *cfptr;

cfptr p - cfptr(0xb8000000L);
```

Constants

Both C and C++ allow you to declare identifiers of any given type to have fixed values. Such identifiers, called *constants*, can be specified using the **const** keyword. For instance,

```
const int tablesize - 100;
```

declares **tablesize** to be an integer, and to have the fixed value of 100. Declaring a constant tells the compiler that the identifier will never change values. In certain cases, this lets the compiler perform better optimizations on expressions involving that identifier.

You can not only declare constants of simple types, such as integers, but as aggregates (arrays and objects) as well. For instance:

```
const char prompt[] - "Ready"; // Constant array

enum linetype { solid, dashed };

struct linestyle {
  linetype ltype;
  int pixelwidth;
};

const linestyle x - { solid, 3 }; // Constant object
```

Constant Pointers and References
Constants can be used in conjunction with pointers and references. You can declare pointers to constants, constant pointers, and constant pointers to constants. In an analogous way, references to constants, constant references, and constant references to constants can also be declared. Table 3.5 lists examples of each.

Table 3.5. Using Constants in Pointers and References

Example	Description
const char *p;	Pointer to a constant character
char *const p;	A constant character pointer
const char *const p;	A constant pointer to a constant character
const char &p;	Reference to a constant character
char &const p;	A constant character reference
const char &const p;	A constant reference to a constant character

What's the difference between a pointer to a constant and a constant pointer? A pointer to a constant can only point to a constant. However, you can change the pointer at any time to point to another constant. In contrast, once a constant pointer is initialized, you can't make it point to anything else. Analogous rules exist for references.

There are two ways to declare a pointer to a constant. (Similar methods exist for references.) The following are two ways to declare a pointer to a constant character:

```
const char *p; // One way
char const *p; // Another way
```

The first way is preferred. The second way is too easy to confuse with

```
char *const p;
```

which means something entirely different: a constant pointer to a character.

1. Given the declarations,

```
const char x - 42; // A character constant
char y - 17;       // A character variable
const char *p;     // A pointer to a constant
```

which of the following assignments are legal:

```
p - &x;  // (a)
*p - 55; // (b)
p - &y;  // (c)
*p - 55; // (d)
```

2. Given the following two character declarations,

```
const char x = 42;  // A character constant
char y = 17;        // A character variable
```

which constant pointer declaration is legal?

```
char *const p = &x;  // (a)
char *const q = &y;  // (b)
```

3. Given the declarations from Question 2, which of the following assignments are legal?

```
*q = 55;  // (a)
q = &x;   // (b)
```

---

1. *Assignments (a) and (c) are legal. You can point a pointer to a constant character to any character, regardless of whether that character is constant or not. Thus, pointing p to x and y is perfectly fine. However, assignments (b) and (d) are not legal. Assignment (b) tries in effect to update x, but x is constant. Assignment (d) tries to update y. However, even though y is not a constant, as far as p is concerned, it is!*

2. *Declaration (b) is legal, but for (a), we need a typecast:*

```
char *const p = (char *const)&x; // Need typecast
```

The reason for the typecast is the following: First, x a constant character, so &x is a constant pointer to a constant character. However, p is a constant pointer to a character. Thus, we must typecast &x to be a constant pointer to a character.

Of course, such typecasts are not safe. For instance, with the typecast just given, we could have an assignment that updates the constant, leading to unpredictable results, such as:

```
*p = 55;  // Updates the constant x!
```

3. *Assignment (a) is perfectly fine. However, in (b) we're trying to change the pointer q to point to something else. Since q is a constant pointer, and already points to y, we can't point q to x.*

Using Constants

Constants in C++ work much more smoothly than they do in C. For example, in C, you can't use constants to build up other constants. You can in C++, as in:

```
const MaxSize = 100;
const IndexLimit = MaxSize - 1; // Legal in C++, but not in C
```

In a similar vein, you can't use a constant to declare the size of an array in C, but you can in C++:

```
const int TableSize = 100;
int HashTable[TableSize]; // Legal in C++, but not in C
```

Using Constants in Header Files

Another subtle, but important, difference between C and C++ constants is their linkage. By *linkage*, we mean whether an identifier is visible to other modules in a program (external linkage) or whether the identifier is local only to the file it's declared in (internal linkage).

In C, constants have external linkage by default. In C++, they have internal linkage. This means if you declare a constant in a header file, and include this header in multiple files, you won't get a duplicate definition error in C++ when the files are linked. You would in C.

Since a C++ constant declared in a header has internal linkage, it means each source file that includes the header has its own copy of the constant. You might think that this wastes storage. However, in many cases, it does not. If a constant you declare is simple enough (such as an integer), then Turbo C++ does not allocate storage for it. This lets you use constants the way that you used to use macros. For example, the following statements are equivalent in terms of their use and storage requirements:

```
#define TableSize 100      // The C way
const int TableSize=100;   // A better C++ way
```

If a constant you declare is an aggregate (such as a class or an array), then Turbo C++ has to allocate storage for it. Thus, using a constant aggregate in a header file can cause memory to be wasted in duplicate storage locations. To get around this problem, use the same technique you would use for variables: declare the constant as an external in the header file, but don't actually initialize it there. Then, in one (but only one) of your source files, initialize the constant to some value.

Figure 3.6 shows an example of this arrangement. We declare the **texel** constant **blank** external in the header file **screen.h**, and initialize it in the source file **screen.cpp**.

Tip | When you want to declare a constant for a simple type, rather than use a **#define** macro, use a **const** declaration instead. Using **const** is much less error prone than using **#define**, and is just as efficient.

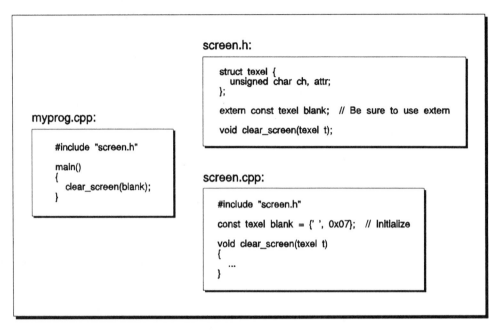

screen.h:

```
struct texel {
    unsigned char ch, attr;
};

extern const texel blank;  // Be sure to use extern

void clear_screen(texel t);
```

myprog.cpp:

```
#include "screen.h"

main()
{
    clear_screen(blank);
}
```

screen.cpp:

```
#include "screen.h"

const texel blank = {' ', 0x07};  // Initialize

void clear_screen(texel t)
{
    ...
}
```

Figure 3.6. Using an Aggregate Constant in a Header File

1. Show a better way to arrange the following C++ files:

file1.cpp:

```
const double pi = 3.14159;
...
```

file2.cpp:

```
const double pi = 3.14159;
...
```

2. The total amount of storage used by the constants in Question 1 is:

   a. 8 bytes
   b. 16 bytes
   c. None

3. What would happen if you compiled the files in Question 1 in C?

4. Suppose you had the following statement in a C++ header file. Rewrite it so that it would work equivalently in a C header file:

```
const char newline = '\n';
```

1. *Even though it's legal, it's not a good idea to declare and define the same constant in two separate files. You may accidentally give the constant two different values, causing much confusion. It would be better to arrange **file1.cpp** and **file2.cpp** as follows:*

   ***header.h**:*

   ```
   const double pi = 3.14159;    // Make up a header
   ```

   ***file1.cpp**:*

   ```
   #include "header.h"
   ...
   ```

   ***file2.cpp**:*

   ```
   #include "header.h"
   ...
   ```

2. *No storage is required, because Turbo C++ doesn't normally allocate storage for simple constants.*
3. *You'd get a duplicate identifier error in the linker in C. But in C++, you would not.*
4. *In C++, constants have internal linkage, so the equivalent C statement would be:*

   ```
   static const char newline = '\n';
   ```

Volatiles

The counterpart to constants are volatiles. Volatile variables are declared with the **volatile** keyword:

```
volatile int port66;
```

Declaring a variable volatile tells the compiler that the value of that variable may change at any moment. For instance, the variable may be associated with an interrupt that can change the variable at any time. For volatiles, the compiler makes no assumptions about the value of the variable staying the same between assignments to that variable.

Would it ever make sense to declare a variable to be both constant and volatile?

Yes. If you wanted a variable that's manipulated by a interrupt routine or is aliased to a hardware port, you should declare that variable as being volatile. And, by declaring it to be a constant as well, you also prevent anyone other than the interrupt routine or the hardware itself from updating that variable. Other routines could only read the value of the variable. Thus, you can get read-only volatile variables by declaring them constant.

A Practice C++ Program

Listing 3.1 gives a program that you can type in and try out. It fills the screen with a fill pattern, and then draws a shadowed blue box with the message "Turbo C++" in the middle. This program uses many of the constructs we've discussed in this chapter; mainly types, **typedef**s, constants, and type conversions. The output from the program in shown in Figure 3.7.

Figure 3.7. Output from ch3ex1.cpp

Listing 3.1. A Sample Program Using Types and Constants

```cpp
// ch3ex1.cpp: An example of using constants and types.
// This program fills the screen with a pattern, and then
// draws a shadowed box.
// Note: This program works best on color monitors

#include <conio.h> // Required for getch()

// Define a type representing a text video element
struct texel {
  unsigned char ch;     // The character byte
  unsigned char attr;   // The attribute byte
};

typedef texel scrnarray[25][80]; // A screen array type
typedef scrnarray far *scrnptr;  // A pointer to a screen array type

scrnptr color_screen; // Declare a screen array pointer

// This macro makes screen accesses more convenient
#define screen (*color_screen)

// Define constant indicating where video ram resides
// Use 0xb0000000L for monochrome adapters
const long vram_addr = 0xb8000000L;

texel fill_pattern   = {0xb2, 0x07}; // Makes a white fill pattern
texel shadow_pattern = {0xb2, 0x08}; // Makes a gray fill pattern
texel solid_pattern  = {' ', 0x10};  // Makes a solid blue pattern

texel msg[] = { // Define a white on blue message
  {'T', 0x1f}, {'u', 0x1f}, {'r', 0x1f}, {'b', 0x1f},
  {'o', 0x1f}, {' ', 0x1f}, {'C', 0x1f}, {'+', 0x1f}, {'+', 0x1f}
};

main()
{
  int i, j;
  // Initialize screen pointer. Note the type conversion syntax.
  color_screen = scrnptr(vram_addr);

  // Fill the screen with a patterned background
  for (i = 0; i<25; i++)
      for (j = 0; j<80; j++) screen[i][j] = fill_pattern;

  // Now put a solid blue box in the middle
  for (i = 5; i<15; i++)
      for (j = 30; j<50; j++) screen[i][j] = solid_pattern;

  // Put in the vertical and horizontal shadows
  for (i = 6; i<16; i++)
```

```
      for (j - 50; j<52; j++) screen[i][j] - shadow_pattern;

   for (j - 31; j<51; j++) screen[15][j] - shadow_pattern;

   // Write message
   for (j - 0; j<9; j++) screen[9][j+36] - msg[j];

   getch();  // Wait for a key press
   return 0; // Value returned is optional here
}
```

Summary

In this chapter, the fundamental building blocks for representing data in Turbo C++ programs were discussed. Many of these building blocks are very similar to their C counterparts. There are differences, however. In almost all cases, the differences came about because the designers of C++ wanted to improve on the C language in some way, either to make it a safer language, or to make it easier to express certain constructs.

All the improvements and changes discussed in this chapter lead eventually to the ability to support object-oriented programs in a clean fashion. However, before we get to such intriguing applications, you need to learn a few more fundamentals. In Chapter 4, we continue where we left off and talk about statements, declarations, names spaces, and scopes.

Exercises

1. List four things wrong with the following program:

```
main()
{
   int _i - 019;
   char *12months;
   char *this - 12months;
}
```

2. Given the following structure and function declarations,

```
struct point { float x, y; }

double origin_dist(point &p)
{
   return sqrt(p.x*p.x + p.y*p.y);
}
```

correct the following call to **origin_dist()**:

```
point *mugu;
double od - origin_dist(mugu);
```

3. Given the array below, what is the array name's type?

```
int first_nums[3] - {1, 2, 3};
```

4. How do we change the declaration of **first_nums** in Question 3 to be an array of constant integers?
5. Since neither C nor C++ has a boolean type, it's common to use macros like the following to represent false and true:

```
#define FALSE 0
#define TRUE 1
```

Try defining an anonymous enumerated type to represent these two values. What are the advantages of doing so? Is using an enumerated type less efficient than using macros?
6. Which of the following declarations declare classes?

```
a. class two_nums {
      int a, b;
   }
b. struct circle {
      int x, y, radius;
   }

c. union number_parts {
      float num;
      struct parts{
       char exp;
       char mantissa[3];
      };
   };
```

7. Would the following header file work correctly in C++? In C? Suggest fixes for any possible problems.

myheader.h:

```
const char bell - '\a';
```

Answers

1. *(a) You shouldn't use underscore in variable **i**, since such usage is reserved, (b) the octal constant 019 is illegal since 9 is not an octal digit, (c) you can't start identifier **12months** with a digit, and (d) **this** is a reserved keyword in C++.*
2. *To pass a pointer to a structure where a reference to a structure is expected, you must dereference the pointer, as in*

   ```
   point *mugu;
   double od = origin_dist(*mugu);
   ```

   Even though you've dereferenced the pointer, the structure is still passed by reference. (The Turbo C++ compiler will internally pass a pointer to the structure.)
3. *The array name **first_nums** is a constant pointer to an integer. It's a constant pointer because you can't change what **first_nums** points to. For instance, the following is illegal:*

   ```
   first_nums = &some_other_array; // Illegal
   ```

4. *Here's how:*

   ```
   const int first_nums[3] = { 1, 2, 3 };
   ```

5. *You could define an anonymous enumerated type like the following:*

   ```
   enum { FALSE=0, TRUE=1 };
   ```

   This is better than using macros, because the two constants are kept grouped together. Note that we don't need to declare variables of the enumerated type, we're only using it to group the two related values together. Thus, we can make the enumerated type anonymous, and avoid having to give the group a name. Since we've only declared a type, and haven't declared any variables, using the enumerated type doesn't require any storage. Thus, it's just as efficient as using macros.
6. *All three declarations declare classes.*
7. *The header file would work fine in C++. Since constants have static linkage in C++, initializing the constant **bell** in the header won't ever cause problems. In C, though, the constant has external linkage, so you'll get duplicate definition errors in the linker should you include the header in more the one file in the program. For C, you should write:*

   ```
   static const char bell = '\a';
   ```

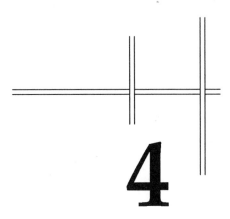

4

C++ Fundamentals: Part Two

T his chapter is the second half of the discussion on the fundamentals of C++. We pick up where we left off and discuss other attributes that data items have besides their types, such as *storage class, duration, linkage,* and *scope.* These attributes determine where data items are stored, when they come into existence, how long they stay in existence, and who can access the data.

After discussing the various data attributes, we'll cover how data is manipulated using operators, expressions, and statements. One particular type of statement—compound statements—affects the scoping and visibility of identifiers. There will be an in-depth look at compound statements, followed by discussions on scopes. Related to the scope of identifiers are *name spaces,* which are categories that determine how identifier names interact. In addition, name spaces are covered in this chapter.

As in Chapter 3, many of the topics discussed here are a review of features available in C, but we'll be pointing out how these features differ in C++. For example, C and C++ differ in how they handle variable declarations, as you'll see in the last part of the chapter.

After reviewing this chapter, you will learn:

- What storage class, duration, and linkage are
- What operators are available in Turbo C++
- How to declare expressions and statements
- What scope and visibility of identifiers are
- How name spaces relate to scope and visibility

- What the special rules for nesting enumerators inside classes are
- What the special rules for nesting classes inside other classes are
- That C++ has more flexible ways to declare variables than C does

The Five Data Attributes

Each data item in a C++ program has five attributes associated with it, as given in Table 4.1.

You've already learned about types in Chapter 3. In this chapter, we'll be discussing the other attributes, starting first with storage class and duration. Keep in mind as we go through the discussion that all of the attributes are intertwined. Changing one of the attributes for an identifier will most likely change some of the others.

Storage Classes

The *storage class* of a variable determines what type of storage is used for the variable. There are four kinds of storage, each with an associated keyword, as listed in Table 4.2. Figure 4.1 presents some examples of these different storage types.

By default, the local variables of a function have **auto** storage. They reside on the stack, and are thus automatically allocated and de-allocated during a call to the function. A **register** variable is also local to a function, but is allocated in one of the hardware registers.

Tip || Use of the **auto** keyword is rare, since it's only for local variables to functions, which have **auto** storage by default anyway.

Table 4.1. The Five Data Attributes

Attribute	Description
Data type	Determines how the data is encoded and operated on
Storage class	Determines where the data is stored
Duration	Determines how long the data exists
Linkage	Determines the accessibility of data in multiple-file programs
Scope	Determines the visibility of data

Table 4.2. The Four Storage Classes

Keyword	Type of Storage Used
auto	The data resides on the stack
register	The data resides in a hardware register
static	The data resides in this module
extern	The data resides in another module

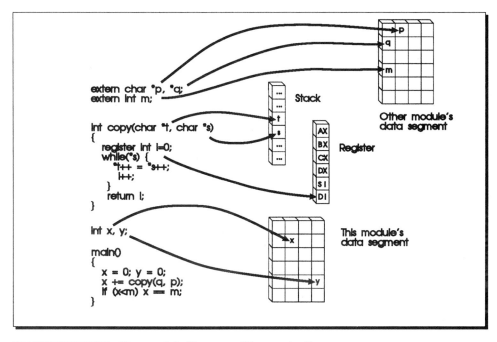

Figure 4.1. Storage Classes in C++

The other two storage classes, **static** and **extern**, are for data residing outside of any function. Variables with **static** storage class are allocated in the module they are defined in. Variables declared external with the **extern** keyword are allocated in some other module.

The **static** keyword can also be used for variables inside functions. Such variables have static storage and don't reside on the stack. Because of this, they last the duration of the program, such as with global variables. However, variables declared static inside functions can't be accessed outside the functions in which they are declared.

Note In the following discussion, you'll see that the **static** keyword has many different meanings, which can cause confusion. C++ inherits this unfortunate legacy from C.

Closely related to the storage class of a variable is its duration, as will be discussed next.

Duration

The duration of a variable determines how long that variable has real, physical memory attached to it. The memory can come from three places, which results in the three duration types given in Table 4.3.

Linkage

When you have more than one source file (also called a module) in your program, the linkage attributes of the variables come into play. There are two types of linkage: *static linkage* (also known as *internal linkage*) and *external linkage*. The linkage for an identifier is specified using the **static** and **extern** keywords.

Note Unlike the storage class and duration attributes, the linkage attribute applies to functions as well as variables.

The linkage of an identifier helps determine in which modules it is accessible. Those identifiers with static linkage are local to the modules in which they are declared. Statically linked variables and functions do not appear in the object files created by the compiler, thus the linker cannot see them. Variables and functions declared with external linkage are in the object files, and are visible to the linker. Thus, many modules can share an externally linked identifier.

Table 4.3. The Three Duration Types

Duration Type	Storage Used	Length of Existence
Static	Data segment	During the entire program
Automatic	Stack or register	During a function call
Dynamic	Heap	User controlled

By default, most identifiers have external linkage. Constants are an exception. They have static linkage by default, which you learned in Chapter 3. Another exception are the special types of functions known as *inline functions*. These functions, which are similar to macros, are discussed in Chapter 5. Like constants, inline functions have static linkage by default. In all cases, you can override the default linkage with the appropriate **static** or **extern** keywords.

Tip

One way to reduce naming conflicts in multi-module programs is to declare as many identifiers as possible with static linkage.

Since the linkage attribute of an identifier helps determine its visibility, the linkage attribute is closely related to scope. We'll be discussing scope shortly, but first, let's look at operators, expressions, and statements. This will lead us into the subject of statement blocks, which directly affect the scoping of identifiers in a program.

Fix the problem in the following program, which is composed of two files to be linked together:

pay.cpp:

```
char signature[] = "Nobody's Paycheck Program";

double determine_pay(double wage, double hrs)
{
   return wage * hrs;
}
```

paychk.cpp:

```
#include <stdio.h>

extern double determine_pay(double wage, double hrs);

char signature[] = "Nobody's Paycheck Program";

main()
{
  printf("%s\n\n", signature);
  printf("Pay is: %6.2f\n", determine_pay(22.0, 40.0));
}
```

*The string **signature** is defined in both files. By default, identifiers defined outside any function have external linkage. The linker will see both declarations and determine that* *there is a duplicate definition. To fix the problem, declare signature external in* ***paychk.cpp,*** *but don't define it there:*

paychk.cpp:

```
extern char signature;
...
```

Operators and Expressions

Any worthwhile C or C++ program performs at least some action. Actions are represented by *expressions,* where expressions are made up of operators and data elements. C++ has all the operators that C does, and adds a few of its own. Table 4.4 shows all the operators in Turbo C++. Table 4.5 shows those that are specific to C++.

Table 4.4. The Operators in Turbo C++

[]	()	.	->	++	—
&	*	+	-	~	!
/	%	<<	>>	<	>
<=	>=	==	!=	^	|
&&	||	?:	=	*=	/=
%=	+=	-=	<<=	>>=	&=
^=	|=	,	#	##	sizeof
new	delete	::	.*	->*	

Table 4.5. Operators Specific to C++

Operator	Description
new	Memory allocation operator
delete	Memory deallocation operator
::	Scope operator
.*	Pointer to member operator
->*	Also a pointer to member operator

In this chapter, you'll learn what the scope operator, ::, is for. The **new** and **delete** operators provide new ways to allocate and deallocate dynamic memory that you'll learn about in Chapter 7. The other two new operators, .* and ->*, have to do with special types of pointers than can point to members of classes. These are of a more advanced nature and won't be discussed in this book.

Besides adding a few operators, a more important feature of C++ is that you can redefine, or overload, the built-in operators. Chapter 10 discusses operator overloading in depth.

Statements

Expressions are used to form other constructs called *statements*. A statement is an expression that ends with a semicolon. Statements come in many forms: assignments, declarations, **if** statements, **switch** statements, iteration statements, jump statements, and compound statements. Here are some examples:

```
int i; // A declaration
int j = 3;// A declaration with initialization
j = 5; // An assignment statement
if (j == 5) k = 3;  // An if statement

switch(c) { // A switch statement
  case '\n': numlines++; break;
  case ' ' : numspaces++; break;
}

// Here are some iteration statements

while(*s != 0) n++;
for (i=0; i<5; i++) putc(' ');
do { putc('\n'); } while(n--);

// And some jump statements

break; // Jump out of this block
continue; // Go to end of loop
return 5; // Return a value from a function
goto quit;// Go to some label
```

Blocks: Compound Statements

Compound statements are multiple statements enclosed by a pair of curly braces. A compound statement can be used anywhere a simple statement can be used. For instance, in

```
for (i=0; i<n; i++) {
  putc(' ');
  putc('*');
}
```

the two **putc()** statements represent a compound statement.

One of the things that compound statements do is block off the enclosing statements from the rest of the program. For that reason, compound statements are also called *blocks*. While you normally think of blocks in connection with function bodies, as well as **if**, **while**, and **switch** statements, you can use blocks anywhere statements can be used.

For example, we might have a sequence of statements such as:

```
int i;
i = 5;
{              // Start a block
  int i;       // A different i
  i = 7;
  printf("i = %d\n", i);
}
printf("i = %d\n", i); // What value is printed?
```

Here, we start a new block after the first two statements which lasts until the final **printf()** statement.

If you declare a variable inside a block that happens to have the same name as a variable declared outside the block, the innermost variable blocks or hides the outermost variable. In our example, the innermost **i** hides the outermost **i** inside the block. Thus the statement **i=7** sets the inner **i**, not the outer one. Because the two **i**'s are separate variables, assigning a value to one doesn't affect the other. Thus, the second **printf()** statement prints the number 5.

Scope, Visibility, and Name Space

As the example of the previous section shows, using compound statements brings up the issue of when an identifier is accessible to other parts of the program, and when it's legal to use the same name for different identifiers. The factors involved can be broken into three categories: *scope*, *visibility*, and *name space*.

The *scope* of an identifier is that part of a program in which the identifier is potentially available. Whether or not it is actually available depends on its *visibility*, which is determined by whether the identifier name is hidden by another identifier with the same name.

Identifiers in different scopes can have the same name, although the inner-most scope hides names from the outer scopes, as you saw in the last section. If two identifiers have the same scope, they can have the same name only if they belong to different *name spaces*. The different categories of identifiers make up the name spaces. For instance, tag names and function names belong to different name spaces, therefore, it's legal for a structure and a function in the same scope to have the same name.

We'll now study scopes, visibility, and name spaces in depth.

Scopes

There are five scopes in Turbo C++ as illustrated in Figure 4.2, and described in Table 4.6.

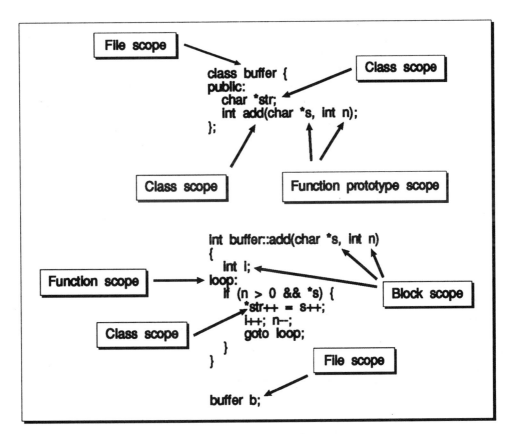

Figure 4.2. Scopes in Turbo C++

Table 4.6. The Five Scopes in Turbo C++

Scope	Description
Block	The area between the curly braces in a function
Function	Applies only to statement labels inside functions
Function prototype	The dummy arguments inside a function prototype
File	The areas outside function and class declarations
Class	Inside the curly braces of a class declaration

Identifiers declared inside blocks have block scope. The scope of an identifier in a block starts at the point the identifier is declared, and ends at the closing curly brace of the block. If the block has a nested block inside it, then the scope of identifiers in the outer block encompasses the inner block (as long as those identifiers were declared before the inner block).

Most identifiers in a function have block scope. This includes the formal parameters to the function. The only exception are statement labels. These have what is called *function scope*. The reason for the distinction is that labels have to be unique within a function, no matter what nested block they reside in. Thus, code such as the following is illegal:

```
void myfunc(int a)
{
 x:
    printf("At first label\n"):
    {// A nested block
     x: // Error: duplicate label
        printf("At second label\n");
    }
    if (--a > 0) goto x; // Which x?
}
```

Tip | Because labels have function scope, you can use the same label in more than one function. This never poses a problem, since you can't jump between functions using **goto**s anyway.

The names for parameters inside a function prototype have *function prototype scope*. The scope of these identifiers lasts only until the end of the function prototype. This gives you much freedom in choosing parameter names inside function prototypes.

Identifiers not residing in blocks, functions, or classes have *file scope*. The scope of an identifier in file scope begins at the point of declaration of the identifier and ends at the file completion. If an identifier appears in a header file, then the scope of the identifier extends to any files that include the header file. File scope encompasses all other scopes in a file.

The last scope is *class scope*. The members of a class are in the scope of that class and their names are hidden from the rest of the program. Since **structs** and **unions** are special forms of classes, then class scope also applies to the members of **structs** and **unions**. There are special rules about class scope when enumerated types are embedded in classes, as you'll see later in the chapter.

Note || Even though the members of a class are in class scope, the *name* of the class is not. Its scope is whatever scope the class is declared in.

Name the scopes of the identifiers in the following code:

```c
#include <stdio.h>

struct clock {
    int hr, min, sec;
};

extern int line_no;
static char line[80];

void *readline(FILE *g);

void *readline(FILE *f)
{
  loop:
    line = fgets(f);
    line_no++;
    printf("%d\n", line_no);
    if (line != NULL) goto loop;
}
```

The identifiers and their scopes are given in the following table

Identifier	Scope
clock	File scope
hr, min, sec	Class scope
line_no	File scope
line	File scope
readline	File scope
FILE	File scope

Identifier	Scope
g	Function prototype scope
f	Block scope
loop	Function scope
printf	File scope

Note that **line_no** and **line** both have file scope, even though one is declared **extern**, and the other **static**. These keywords don't control the scope, they control the linkage of the variables, as discussed earlier in the chapter.

Also, note that g has function prototype scope, but its counterpart f has block scope. The variable f is a local variable to **readline()**. In contrast, g doesn't really exist and is just a place holder for that variable.

The Scope Operator

The scope and visibility of an identifier are often the same, but not always. A variable may be in scope, but not be visible because another identifier with the same name is hiding it. We saw that in an earlier example, which we'll now repeat:

```
int i;
i - 5;
{ // Start a block
  int i; // A different i
  i - 7;
  printf("i - %d\n", i);
}
printf("i - %d\n", i); // What value is printed?
```

In this example, the outermost i has file scope, and the innermost i has block scope. The innermost i hides the outermost i.

With C, you have no way to access the file scoped i from within the innermost block. However, with C++, there is a way, through the use of the *scope operator*, ::. Here's an example of using the scope operator to access a variable with file scope:

```
int i; // Has file scope

main()
{ // Starting the main() block
  i - 5; // Setting the file scoped i
  { // Start another block
```

```
   int i;      // Block scoped i hides file scoped i
   i - 7;      // Sets the block scoped i to 7
   ::i - 12;   // Sets the file scoped i to 12
   }
   printf("i - %d\n");
   return 0;
}
```

In the prior example, the scope operator is being used in its unary form. (It has a binary form you'll see later in the chapter.) In its unary form, the scope operator forces the identifier it operates on to have file scope. Thus, in the statement

```
::i - 12;
```

the outermost **i** is accessed.

Why won't the following program compile?

```
main()
{ // Starting the main block
  int i;  // Block-scoped i
  i - 5;
  {  // Start another block
    int i;      // Hides outer i
    i - 7;      // Sets the block-scoped i to 7
    ::i - 12; // Can't do!
  }
  printf("i - %d\n");
  return 0;
}
```

We can't access the outermost i by using the scope resolution operator because that i has block scope, not file scope. Thus, you can't get arbitrary access to hidden variables in deeply nested blocks.

Name Spaces

The names used for identifiers in Turbo C++ are split into four different categories called *name spaces*. The four name spaces are

- Statement labels
- **Class, struct, union,** and **enum** tags

- Member names of class types (which include **class**, **struct**, and **union** members)
- Functions, variables, **typedef** names, and members of enumerations

Examples of each name space are given in Figure 4.3.

If two identifiers are in the same scope and belong to the same name space, they can't have the same name. For example, in the following function, the name **point** is illegally being used twice for both a **struct** and an **enum** declaration:

```
void func1(void)
{
  struct point {int x, y;};
  enum point {single, double}; // Illegal, duplicate name
  ...
}
```

This is illegal since **structs** and **enums** belong to the same name space. However, two identifiers *can* have the same name *and* belong to the same name space *if* they are in different scopes. For example, in the following code, **point** is declared in two different functions. This is valid since the bodies of the functions have different scope.

```
void func1(void)
{
  struct point {int x, y;};
  ...
}
```

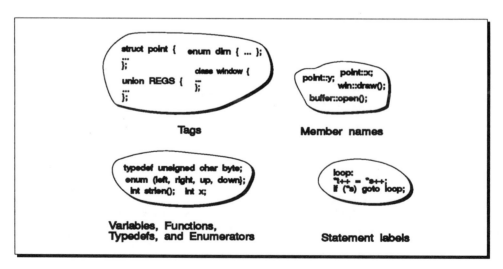

Figure 4.3. Name Spaces in C++

```
void func2(void)
{
  enum point {single, double}; // Okay, different scope.
  ...
}
```

If two identifiers have different name spaces, then it doesn't matter what scopes they have. In general, they can have the same name and not cause any problems. For example, you can name a label x and a variable x in the same function without a problem (although it's confusing). Thus, the following code is perfectly legal:

```
void myfunc(int x)
{
  if (x == 5) goto x;
  printf("Made it here");
x:
  printf("Leaving function");
}
```

1. Would the following code compile even though the name **num1** is being used for two different identifiers?

```
struct three_nums {
  int num1;
  int num2;
};

int num1;
```

2. Explain why we can use the name x for the two different identifiers in the following code:

```
int x;

void add5(int x)
{
  return x+5;
}
```

1. *Yes. Even though we're using the name **num1** twice, it's being used by identifiers belonging to different name spaces.*
2. *Even though x is being used for the names of identifiers with the same name space, the identifiers have different scopes.*

Nested Enumerations

In C, you can declare an enumerated type inside a structure, as in:

```
struct toolbox {
  enum tool { hammer, saw, screwdriver };
  enum tool tools[3];
  int num_screws, num_nails;
}
```

However, it doesn't do much good to declare **tool** inside **toolbox**. That's because the scope of an enumerated type declared inside a structure actually resides outside the structure. We might as well have written:

```
enum tool { hammer, saw, screwdriver };

struct toolbox {
  enum tool tools[3];
  int num_screws, num_nails;
};
```

This rule is slightly different in C++. Although the name of the **enum** is still scoped outside the structure, the *members* of the enumeration are not. This fact is illustrated in Figure 4.4. Given the prior **toolbox** structure, the second statement which follows is legal in C, but not in C++:

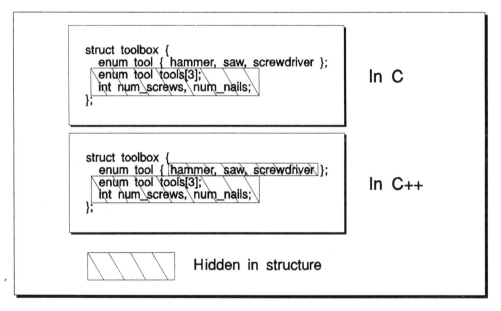

Figure 4.4. Hiding Enumerations in Structures

```
enum tool x;   // Legal both in C and C++
x - hammer;    // Legal in C, but not in C++
```

You can use the name **tool** outside the structure **toolbox** in C++, but you can't use any of the members of **tool** directly. To access those members, you must use the scope operator. You've seen the use of the unary scope operator to designate file scope. You can also use the scope operator as a binary operator. In this case the right operand designates the identifier, and the left operand designates the scope, which can be any **class, struct, union,** or **enum** tag name.

Thus, to access the **hammer** enumeration hidden by the **toolbox** structure, we can write

```
x - toolbox::hammer; // Access hammer from toolbox
```

Note || The rule about hiding enumerators applies to all class types, including those declared with the **class** and **union** keywords as well as the **struct** keyword.

What advantage would there be to hiding members of enumerations inside structures as C++ does?

Being able to hide members of enumerations inside structures (and all classes) helps reduce the number of global names in a program, minimizing conflicts between otherwise identical names. It also keeps the enumerations more closely associated with the classes they are defined in.

Nested Class Types

Just as you can't hide the name of an enumeration (you can only hide its members), likewise, you can't hide the name of a class inside another class. For instance, in the following code we've nested one structure inside the other. (Recall that structures are special forms of classes.)

```
structs phone_contact {
  char name[80];
  struct number { // A nested structure
    char area_code[3], prefix[3], num[4];
  };
  number phone_num;
};
```

Is **number** hidden from the outside? No. In general, the scope of a nested class is the same as the scope of the outer class. In our example, we might as well have written:

```
struct number {
  char area_code[3], prefix[3], num[4];
};

struct phone_contact {
  char name[80];
  number phone_num;
};
```

Even though you can't hide a class name inside another class, the names of objects you create from a class can be hidden inside a class. Thus, in both preceding examples, the name **phone_num** is hidden inside the structure **phone_contact**.

Remember that this scoping rule about nested classes applies not only to classes declared with the **struct** keyword, but also to classes declared with the **class** and **union** keywords.

Tip | Since there's no advantage to nesting class declarations, it's recommended that you always declare classes separately. It's much less misleading this way.

Tags and Type Names

Recall that **class, struct, union,** and **enum** tags are type names in C++. This allows you to declare variables of these types with or without the corresponding **class, struct, union,** or **enum** keywords. For example, in the following C++ code, you can choose to leave off **struct** keyword when declaring **part_data** objects:

```
struct part_data {
  int id, qty;
  float price;
};

struct part_data p; // Legal in C and C++
part_data q;        // Not legal in C, but legal in C++
```

Sometimes, though, you have no choice but to use the **class, struct, union,** and **enum** keywords in variable declarations, even in C++. The reason is to avoid potential ambiguities between structure tags and function names. To see how such problems can come about, consider the following code:

```
#include <stdio.h>

void status(FILE *fp)
{
  if (feof(fp)) printf("At end of file\n");
}

struct status {
  int opened, modified, failed;
};
```

Here, the identifier **status** is being used in two different guises: as a structure tag and as a function name. This is allowed because tags and function names belong to different name spaces. Even so, problems occur if you try to declare variables from the **status** structure:

```
status s;  // Compiler can't figure this out
```

In this declaration, the compiler gets confused and thinks we're using the function **status** rather than the structure **status**. The result is a syntax error. To fix this use the **struct** keyword so that there's no doubt which **status** should be used:

```
struct status s;  // Now the compiler knows which status to use
```

There's another problem with tag names in C++. Because they are type names, you can't give a tag the same name as some other type. This would be like trying to give two types the same name. For instance, the **typedef** in the following code leads to ambiguities:

```
struct word {
  int lowbyte, hibyte;
};

typedef int word; // Not legal in C++, but legal in C
```

You should note that the preceding **typedef** is legal in C. No ambiguities arise, because every time you used the **word** structure in C, you'd have to prefix it with the **struct** keyword.

1. Will the following code compile in C? In C++?

```
struct person {
  char name[80];
  struct date {
    int mo, day, yr;
  } birthday;
};
```

```
struct date {
  int mo, day, yr;
} cinco_de_mayo;
```

2. Given the structure declaration.

```
struct drawer { // File drawer
  int num_slots; // Number of file slots available
  int used_slots; // Number of slots used
};
```

which declaration below is illegal, the function declaration or the **typedef** declaration?

```
void drawer(int color)
// Draw using the specified color
{
  ...
}

typedef int drawer;
```

---

1. *It won't compile in either C or C++, because there is a duplication declaration for* **struct date**. *Even though one of the declarations appears hidden inside another structure, it's really not.*
2. *The* **typedef** *declaration is illegal.*

Declarations in C++

Another difference between C and C++ is where they allow declarations to be placed, which we'll investigate next. First, let's review what declarations are.

Declarations come in three forms:

1. Variable declarations
2. Type declarations
3. Function prototypes

The following are some sample declarations:

```
int i;     // Variable declaration
int j - 5; // Variable declaration and initialization

struct clock { // Type declaration
  int seconds;
```

```
    clock(int s);
    void hms(int &h, int &m, int &s);
};

int add(int a, int b); // Function prototype
```

As shown by the second declaration, a declaration can not only specify the type of a variable, it can initialize that variable as well. Declarations that perform initializations look like assignments, but they're not. You can always tell the difference because assignments never declare the type of a variable, they only assign values to it.

In C, declarations can be placed either inside blocks or outside them in file scope. Declarations placed in file scope can be placed anywhere in the file, although typically, they're placed at the top of the file. However, when placed in blocks, declarations *must* appear at the top of the block. No other statements can appear before the declarations in a block.

In C++, this placement rule has been modified. Now declarations can appear anywhere an assignment statement can. The following are some examples.

```
void compute(int a, int b)
{
  a = b+5;// Here's an assignment
  int c;  // Followed by a declaration, not legal in C
  c = a+b;
  int d = c + 7; // Another declaration and initialization
  return d;
}
```

Using Declarations Inside Loops

C++ relaxes the placement restrictions of declarations so that you can keep the use of variables more localized, rather than having to declare them in one place and use them somewhere else. For example, the following code shows a variable **q** which is used only inside the **do** loop, therefore, that's where we've declared it. In C we would have had to declare **q** at the top along with the node **p**.

```
void clear(list *x)
{
  node *p;
  p = x->last;
  if (p != 0) {
     do {
        node *q = p; // Declare and initialize q
        p = p->next;
        free(q);   // Free it
```

```
    } while (p != x->last);
  };
  x->last = 0;
}
```

You can also place declarations in the initialization section of a **for** loop. For instance:

```
// Note declaration for i in header of loop
for(int i = 0; i<10; i++) { printf("%d\n", i); }
```

However, watch out for consecutive loops such as the following:

```
for(int i = 0; i<10; i++) { printf("%s\n", names[i]); }
for(int i = 0; i<50; i++) { printf("%s\n", vars[i]); }
```

The variable **i** does not have the scope you might think it has. Its scope isn't in the **for** loops, but outside them. It's as though we wrote:

```
int i;
for (i = 0; i<10; i++) { ... }

int i;
for (i = 0; i<50; i++) { ... }
```

Now you can see where the trouble is, for we're declaring **i** twice.

In contrast, if we place declarations inside a loop (between the curly braces), then those declarations are in the scope of the loop's block. Thus, the following is legal (but not recommended:)

```
int i;
for (i = 0; i<10; i++) {
  int j;   // This j is in scope of the loop
  ...
}

// A different j
int j;
for (j = 0; j<10; j++) { ... }
```

1. In the following program, what scope do the variables **s, i,** and **p** have?

```
#include <conio.h>

main()
{
  char *s = "Turbo C++";

  for (int i = 0; i<9; i++) {
    char *p = s;
```

```
      putch(*p++);
    }
  }
```

2. What does the **for** loop in Question 1 print out? (Hint: Does **p** get reinitialized every time through the loop?)
3. Could we rearrange the **for** loop in Question 1 by moving the increment of **p** to the loop header, as follows?

```
    for (int i - 0; i<9; i++, p++) { // Move p++ to here?
        char *p - s;
        putch(*p);
    }
```

4. What's wrong with the following code:

```
    for(int i - 0, char *p - src; *p != 0; p++, i++) {
        int ns;
        if (*p -- ' ') ns++; // Count spaces
    }
    printf("The string has %d characters, %d spaces\n", i, ns);
```

---

1. *Their respective scopes are:*

```
    s  block scope (main)
    i  block scope (main)
    p  block scope (for loop)
```

2. *The variable p gets set to the beginning of the string "Turbo C++" every time through the loop. Thus, the loop prints out:*

   "TTTTTTTTT"

3. *No. The compiler will complain about p being undefined in the **for** loop header. That p is a different p than the one inside the loop.*
4. *The variable **ns** is in scope of the **for** loop and is thus not available to the **printf()** statement. However, the scope of the variable **i** begins just before the **for** loop, thus, it is available to the **printf()** statement.*

Duplicate Declarations

Another difference between C and C++ when it comes to declarations is the following: in certain cases, C allows you to declare variables twice, C++ never does. For instance, the following program is legal in C, but not in C++:

```
#include <stdio.h>

int i;  /* Declare i        */
int i;  /* Declare it again */

main()
{
  i - 42;
  printf("i - %d\n", i);
}
```

Which of the following groups of statements would be legal in C? In C++?

a. `int i - 42;`
   `int i;`

b. `int i;`
   `int i - 42;`

c. `int i - 42;`
   `int i - 55;`

Groups a and b are legal in C, but c is not. None are legal in C++.

Jumping Around Initializations

Now that you know you can place declarations almost anywhere, you'll probably start taking advantage of the freedom it buys you. However, you should exercise caution. Don't use a feature just because it's there, use it because it makes the program better. Moving declarations around can get you into trouble. One problem to watch out for is jumping around a variable initialization with a **goto**. For instance:

```
...
if (some_cond) goto x;
int i - 5;
x: if (i -- 5) printf("i is 5\n");
...
```

In C, skipping around initializations is merely bad style. In C++, it's illegal. The problem becomes particularly acute when initializing objects. That's because there are more powerful ways to initialize objects that involve calling special functions called *constructors* (see Chapter 7). These functions can do more than just initialize a value, they can cause all sorts of things to occur, such as opening files, drawing windows, and so on.

Summary

The different attributes that variables and identifiers can have were discussed in this chapter. In particular, you learned about storage classes, duration, linkage, scope, and name spaces. You've also learned how C++ handles declarations.
Perhaps the most important things were:

- Having tags as type names affects the scoping rules for C++
- C++ allows you to place declarations in more places than C does, letting you declare variables closer to where they are being used

We've now completed our study of the fundamental building blocks of Turbo C++ programs. In the next few chapters we'll move on to the study of C++ functions and classes.

Exercises

1. Using the scope resolution operator, fix the following function. (Hint: We want to call the **stdio** version of **fopen()** inside the other **fopen()** function. It's possible to use the same name twice for functions in C++. Such functions are called overloaded functions. See Chapter 5.)

```
FILE *fopen(char *myfile)
// Open file for read access, report any errors
{
  FILE *f;
  f = fopen(myfile, "r");  // Call stdio fopen()
  if (f == NULL) printf("Couldn't open file");
  return f;
}
```

2. Is the following function legal in C++?

```
void func(int x)
{
  x: // Start of loop
    x++;
    if (x > 25) return;
    goto x;
}
```

3. Would the following code compile okay in C++? What about C?

```
#include <stdio.h>

struct status { int opened, modified, failed; }

void status(char *fname, status *s)
{
   if (s->failed) printf("File %s is corrupted\n", fname);
}
```

4. Because tag names are in a different name space from function names, you can have a function with the same name as a tag. However, **typedef** names are also in a different name space from tag names, in fact, they are in the same space that function names are. Yet you can't have a **typedef** name the same as a tag name. If that's so, isn't there a flaw in the name space rules?

Answers

1. *The call to* **fopen()** *inside the function was meant to be a call to the standard library function. External functions by definition have file scope, thus we can fix the function call by prefixing it with :: as follows:*

```
FILE *fopen(char *myfile)
// Open file for read access, report any errors
{
   FILE *f;
   f = ::fopen(myfile, "r");  // Call stdio fopen()
   if (f == NULL) printf("Couldn't open file");
   return f;
}
```

2. *Yes, even though we're using the name x for two different identifiers, those identifiers have different name spaces.*

3. *The name* **status** *is being used two ways: as a tag name and as function name. Although the example is confusing, it will compile in C++. It won't compile in C because the parameter s needs the* **struct** *keyword.*

4. *Yes, there is a flaw, which came about due to historical reasons. C++ was given the same basic name space rules that C had. However, tag names were made type names in C++, which unfortunately made the name space rules inconsistent.*

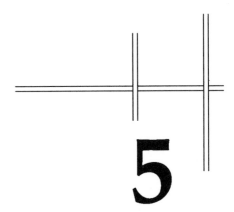

5

Functions in Turbo C++

In the previous chapters the basic building blocks of a C++ program, such as constants, types, variables, and expressions, were discussed. The next step is to learn how to define and use functions, and that's the focus of this chapter.

Although C and C++ functions have much in common, many new features are available in C++. For instance, there are new ways to pass arguments to functions, using *reference arguments* and *default arguments*. And there are new types of functions, such as *inline functions* and *overloaded functions*. In addition, C++ relies more heavily on the use of *function prototypes* than C does.

This chapter will discuss the following:

- The importance of function prototypes in C++
- What type-safe linkage is
- How C and C++ function prototype rules differ
- How to call C functions from C++ programs
- What default arguments are and how to use them
- What reference arguments are and how to use them
- What inline functions are and how to use them
- What overloaded functions are and how to use them

Function Prototypes

The basic difference between using functions in C and C++ is that in C++, you must declare all functions before using them. There are two ways to do this. You can simply define the functions before any calls to them are made. Or, more typically, you can use *function prototypes*.

A function prototype is a forward declaration that declares the number and type of arguments to a function. Figure 5.1 shows some examples of function prototypes.

The same syntax used for function prototypes is also used when defining functions. For example:

```
// Function prototype
void point_setlocn(point *p, double xs, double ys);

// Function definition
void point_setlocn(point *p, double xs, double ys)
{
   p->x = xs; p->y = ys;
}
```

Note You don't have to declare a function prototype before defining a function; the function definition itself can serve as the function prototype. Typically, though, you will use a function prototype and place it in a header file.

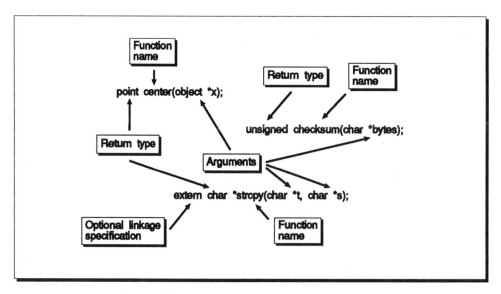

Figure 5.1. Function Prototypes

If you haven't been using one of the newer C compilers that support ANSI C (such as Turbo C 2.0), you may not be used to the new style of defining functions. Recall the old C style:

```
void point_setlocn(p, xs, ys)
point *p;
double xs, ys;
{
 p->x = xs; p->y = ys;
}
```

Besides the obvious simplification in syntax, the new style has one important difference: the parameters can be type checked at compile time. As you probably already know, having parameters type checked is invaluable for reducing frustrating and time-consuming errors. In the old C days, you had to run a separate lint program to get such type checking.

Another benefit of using function prototypes is that they can cause type conversions to take place when needed. For instance, if you have a function taking an **int** argument:

```
int add5toit(int n)
{
   return n + 5;
}
```

and pass that function a floating point number:

```
int k = add5toit(17.42);
```

the number is converted to an **int** before being passed. Without the function prototype, no conversion would take place, resulting in erroneous answers.

---

1. Rewrite the following function header using the new function prototype syntax:

```
int read(f, d, n)
FILE *f;
char *d;
int n;
{
   ...
}
```

2. Is the following a valid function prototype?

```
int read(FILE *, char *, int);
```

1.
```
int read(FILE *f, char *d, int n)
{
    ...
}
```

2. *Yes. Only the parameter types are required; the names of the parameters are optional. You should include the names anyway, to help document the function calling sequence.*

Unsafe Linkage in C

Even though both C and C++ have function prototypes, there are some differences between them. Function prototypes are required in C++, however, they're only strongly recommended in C. If you forget a function prototype in C, you may get a warning, but only if you have the warning turned on. In any case, the compiler defaults the arguments and the return type to **int**. This can lead to serious problems, especially with multifile programs. An example is:

myfile.c:

```
double absval(double x)
{
    if (x < 0) return -x; else return x;
}
```

myprog.c:

```
main() /* Forgot prototype for absval() */
{
    int am, m = -3;
    am = absval(m);
    return 0;
}
```

Since **absval()** doesn't have a prototype in **myprog.c**, the C compiler treats the argument and return type of **absval()** to be **int**. You can still run the program; however, the result is entirely erroneous. In contrast, with C++ you would get a compiler error, and you wouldn't be able to run the program.

Using function prototypes in C doesn't guarantee you won't have problems. For instance, what happens if you specify those prototypes incorrectly? Suppose you mistakenly code **myprog.c** from the previous example as follows:

myprog.c:

```
int absval(int x); /* Wrong argument and return type */

main()
{
   int am, m = -3;
   am = absval(m);
   return 0;
}
```

A C compiler would accept this, and would not even give you a warning. The compiler assumes that you've specified the correct parameter types.

You can help the compiler catch problems like this as follows: First, always place your function prototypes in header files. Then, include those header files both in the files where the functions are declared and in any files where the functions are called. In that manner, the same prototypes will be used throughout. Let's rewrite our program using this technique:

myfile.h:

```
double absval(double x);  /* Prototype goes in header */
```

myfile.c:

```
#include "myfile.h"

double absval(double x)
{
   if (x < 0) return -x; else return x;
}
```

myprog.c:

```
#include "myfile.h"

main()
{
   int am, m = -3;
   am = absval(m);  /* Error caught here */
   return 0;
}
```

In this case, the error would be caught.

You might think this approach is infallible, but it's not. Suppose we mistyped the function prototype in the header, and then used this prototype as a guide for writing our main program:

myfile.h:

```
double absval(int x); /* Wrong argument type */
```

myfile.c:

```
#include "myfile.h"

double absval(double x)
{
   if (x < 0) return -x; else return x;
}
```

myprog.c:

```
#include "myfile.h"

main()
{
   double am;
   int m = -3;
   am = absval(m);
   return 0;
}
```

A C compiler would not catch this error, not even inside **myfile.c** where **absval()** was declared. The compiler has no way of knowing that the prototype in the header file is related to the function in **myfile.c**. Also, the linker would happily link up the call to **absval()** in **main()** with the function **absval()** defined in **myfile.c**. The problem is that the linker only looks at the name of the function, and not the argument types. C++ provides a solution to this problem by using *type-safe linkage,* as we're going to discuss next.

Type-Safe Linkage

The linker in Turbo C++ performs type-safe linkage by checking argument types when linking a function call to the code for the function. The way the linker knows about argument types is through a technique called *name mangling*.

In Turbo C, the compiler prefixes your function names with underscores (at least, that's the default method), and uses these modified names when linking modules together. In Turbo C++, the names are encoded with type information. This encoding is sometimes referred to as *name mangling*. Let's compare how C and C++ handle function names with our **absval()** function from the previous section and its faulty prototype:

Declaration	C Name	Turbo C++ Name
double absval(double x);	_absval	@absval$qd
double absval(int x);	_absval	@absval$qi

It's easy to see why the linker can't tell the two **absval()** functions apart in Turbo C, since they both have the same internal name. In contrast, the last characters in each name in Turbo C++ indicate the argument types to the functions: **d** for **double** and **i** for **int**. Now, if we call **absval()** using the faulty prototype, we'll get an unresolved external reference in the linker, because the calling name, **@absval$qi**, is different from the name of the actual function **@absval$qd**.

Not Quite Safe Linkage in C++

Unfortunately, even C++ can't guarantee you won't have problems with erroneous function prototypes. If you look carefully at the mangled names in the previous section, you'll notice that the return types to the functions are not included in the name. This means that the following error, where the return type to **absval()** is mistyped, cannot be found:

myfile.h:

```
int absval(double x); /* Wrong return type */
```

myfile.cpp:

```
double absval(double x)
{
  if (x < 0) return -x; else return x;
}
```

myprog.cpp:

```
#include "myfile.h"

main()
{
  int am;
  double m = -3;
  am = absval(m); /* Error not found in C++ */
  return 0;
}
```

Note || If you don't specify a return type in a function prototype, C++ defaults the type to **int**, just as C does.

Keep in mind that the name mangling applies only to function names, not to variable names. Thus, programs such as the following will present problems:

myfile.cpp:

```
double area - 3.14;
```

myprog.cpp:

```
#include <stdio.h>
extern int area; // Wrong type

main(void)
{
  printf("Area - %d\n", area);
}
```

Using Unspecified Arguments or No Arguments

If you are mixing C and C++, or porting code from C to C++, be careful when declaring functions that have no arguments and functions that take any number of arguments. Recall that in C, the best way to declare these two types of functions is:

```
int f(void); /* f takes no arguments            */
int f(...);  /* f takes any number of arguments */
```

This syntax can also be used in C++. However, you'll encounter problems with declarations such as:

```
int f(); /* f takes any number of arguments in C, */
         /* but no arguments in C++                */
```

Unfortunately, this kind of prototype means exactly the opposite in the two languages. To be safe, always specify the number of arguments, either by giving actual parameters, or by using ... or **void**.

Tip || Use the **f(...)** style of prototype with caution, as it completely defeats the type checking on calls to the function.

1. Assuming all warnings are turned on, would Turbo C++ complain about the following program?

```
#include <stdio.h>

unsigned checksum(unsigned char *s)
{
  unsigned c = 0;
  while(*s) { c += s++; }
  return c;
}

main()
{
  printf("Checksum is: %u", checksum("Turbo C++"));
}
```

2. Find the mistake in the following code. Would the Turbo C++ compiler catch the error?

myheader.h:

```
deg_to_rad(double x);
```

myfile.cpp:

```
double deg_to_rad(double x)
{
  return x * 0.01745392
}
```

myprog.cpp:

```
main()
{
  double rad_angle = deg_to_rad(45.0);
  return 0;
}
```

1. *It depends on whether the -K option is turned on, which forces all characters to be unsigned. Literal strings are by default signed, so the function call would have a type mismatch unless -K is on.*
2. *In the header file, the return type is missing on the prototype, thus it defaults to **int**. Yet the return type should really be **double**. Since name mangling in C++ does not encode the return type, the error would not be caught in C++.*

Using C Functions in C++ Programs

Since C++ function names are mangled, but C function names aren't, you'll encounter problems if you try to link functions compiled in the two languages.

C++ provides a way of handling this by providing an external linkage declaration that specifies a function as being a C function. An example is:

```
extern "C" int printf(char *fmt, ...);
```

Recall that Turbo C++ has the **cdecl** and **pascal** function modifiers. For instance:

```
extern int cdecl printf(char *fmt, ...);

extern int pascal length(char *s);
```

However, the "C" declaration specifies something entirely different from **cdecl** and **pascal**. The **cdecl** and **pascal** keywords tell the compiler which parameter passing convention to use. The "C" declaration tells the compiler not to use a mangled name for the function.

The "C" modifier is used for all functions that don't require name mangling, no matter what language they are written in. This includes functions using Pascal calling conventions. To declare the latter, use the **pascal** modifier in conjunction with the "C" modifier. For instance,

```
extern "C" int pascal Length(char *s);
```

To specify a group of functions with the "C" modifier, you can enclose the functions in curly braces. For instance:

```
extern "C" {
  char *memcpy(char *t, char *s);
  int strlen(char *t);
}
```

Note It's possible to link C functions into C++ programs, but not the other way around, unless you declare all your external C++ functions with the "C" declaration. This includes the functions from any libraries you're using.

1. Turbo C++ uses the same standard library functions for both C and C++ programs. Explain how this is accomplished.
2. Suppose the following external function is written in assembly, using the standard underscore prefix in its name. How can you easily access this function in C++?

```
void *get_video_ptr_using_asm(int mode);
```

1. *Take a look at the **stdio.h** header file in your Turbo C++ include directory. You'll see that **#defines** are used to determine if the C++ compilation is in force. In such cases, all the function prototypes have an **extern "C" {}** wrapper around them so that the C++ compiler doesn't try to mangle their names. All of the standard header files are coded this way.*
2. *You can also use the "C" modifier for assembly language routines:*

```
extern "C" void *get_video_ptr_using_asm(int mode);
```

Using Default Arguments

A nice extension that C++ provides is support for default arguments. To declare a default argument, you specify its type and name as you would normally do, and then initialize it right in the function header. Figure 5.2 illustrates the technique.

The following is an example of using a default argument:

```
void set_pixel(int x, int y, int color = BLACK);

set_pixel(1, 1, RED);  // Set pixel to RED
set_pixel(1, 1);  // Set pixel to BLACK
```

Note || A default argument can only be initialized with a constant expression, that is, one that can be determined at compile time.

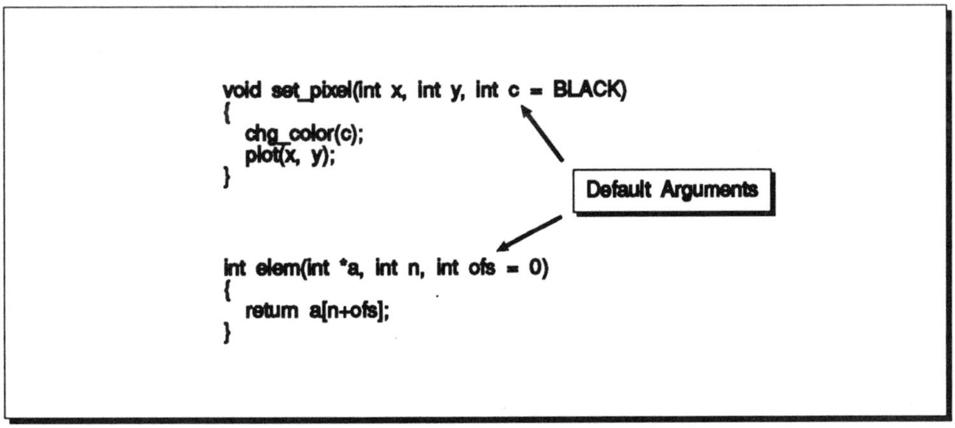

```
void set_pixel(int x, int y, int c = BLACK)
{
    chg_color(c);
    plot(x, y);
}
```

```
                                              Default Arguments
```

```
int elem(int *a, int n, int ofs = 0)
{
    return a[n+ofs];
}
```

Figure 5.2. Declaring Default Arguments

You can specify more than one default argument in a function. However, only trailing arguments may be made default, and you cannot alternate between normal arguments and default arguments. The following are some legal and illegal examples:

```
// Legal

void set_pixel(int x, int y=0, int color=BLACK);
void set_pixel(int x=0, int y=0, int color=BLACK);

// Illegal

void set_pixel(int x, int y=0, int color);
void set_pixel(int x=0, int y, int color);
void set_pixel(int x=0, int y, int color=BLACK);
```

One problem you'll encounter is declaring functions with default arguments in header files. C++ allows you to specify the default arguments only once, either in the function prototype, or when the function is defined. The best place is in the function prototype.

1. Suppose you want to have a function that does subscripting, but accepts offsets other than zero, even though zero is the default. Here's one attempt at declaring such a function. What's wrong with it? How can you fix it?

```
int elem(int *array, offset = 0, int indx)
{
    return array[indx + offset];
}
```

2. Which of the following function prototypes are illegal?

a. `char *buff(int sz = 80);`

b. `int maxsize = 100;`
   `char *make_table(int sz = maxsize);`

c. `const int maxsize = 100;`
   `char *make_table(int sz = maxsize);`

d. `struct part { ... };`
   `void file_init(int recsz = sizeof(part));`

e. `int open_file(char *f = "temp.dat");`

f. `struct part { ... };`
   `int open(char *f="temp.dat", int readonly,`
   `        int recsz = sizeof(part));`

3. Given the following function, what does the function call return?

```
int add(int x - 17, int y - 40)
{
   return x + y;
}

int result - add(2);
```

4. What's wrong with the following code? Suggest a way to fix it.

```
#include <stdio.h>

void report_error(char *msg);

void do_something(int action)
{
   if (action < 0) report_error();
}

void report_error(char *msg - "General error")
{
   printf("Error: %s\n", msg);
}
```

---

1. *The default argument was placed in the middle. Default arguments can only be trailing arguments. You can fix the function by moving the **offset** parameter to the end:*

```
int elem(int *array, int indx, offset - 0)
{
   return array[indx + offset];
}
```

2. *Prototypes a, c, d, and e are all legal, since they involve only constant expressions in the default initializers. Prototype b is illegal because we're trying to initialize the default parameter with a nonconstant integer. Prototype f is illegal because the default arguments are not consecutive and are not trailing arguments.*
3. *It returns 42. Parameter **x** gets assigned 2, and **y** defaults to 40.*
4. *The compiler complains when function **do_something()** calls **report_error()** without any arguments, because it doesn't know about the default argument until it sees the actual function definition for **report_error()**. The fix is to put the default argument specification in the prototype for **report_error()** and take it out of the function definition:*

```
#include <stdio.h>

void report_error(char *msg - "General error");
```

```
void do_something(int action)
{
  if (action < 0) report_error();
}

void report_error(char *msg)
{
  printf("Error: %s\n", msg);
}
```

Using Reference Arguments

Recall that C passes all parameters by value. That is, a copy of each parameter is made before it is passed to the function. Traditionally in C, you achieve the effects of pass-by-reference by using pointers. For instance, in the following function, **target** is passed-by-reference by way of a pointer, and **source** is passed by value:

```
void update1(int *target, int source)
{
  *target = source;
}
```

Using pointers to achieve pass-by-reference seems somewhat artificial doesn't it? In C++, there's another way: by using *reference arguments*. A reference argument is a parameter that's typed to be a reference variable. Figure 5.3 shows how to declare a reference argument. Let's rewrite our update function to use one:

```
void update2(int &target, int source)
// Target is a reference variable and is thus
// passed by reference.
{
  target = source; // Assignment sticks
}
```

Contrast this to the pointer method. It seems cleaner doesn't it? We don't have to explicitly dereference the reference to update the parameter. Not only that, but when we call the function it's much cleaner too. Study the following two function calls to see if you agree:

```
int i;

update1(&i, 25); // Had to take address of i
update2(i, 55); // Didn't have to take address here
```

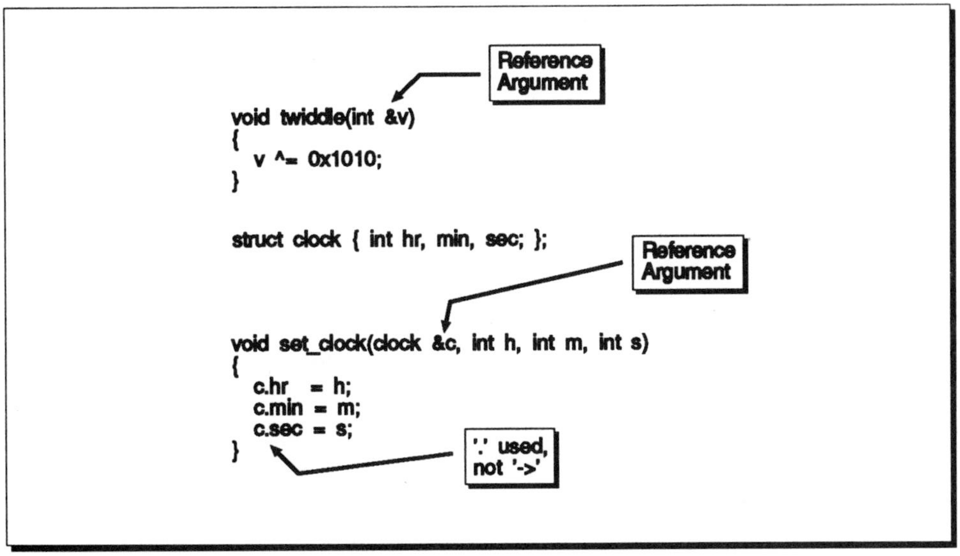

Figure 5.3. Declaring Reference Arguments

If you know Pascal, you'll immediately recognize that reference arguments are a lot like **var** parameters in Pascal.

Passing Constant References

Besides wanting to update a parameter while it's in a function, the main reason for using pass-by-reference is to pass large structures, and to avoid the over-head of copying the structures. In C, you would use pointers to the structures to achieve pass-by-reference. In C++, you could use reference arguments. For example, contrast the three methods shown next for passing a **clock** structure to a function:

```
#include <stdio.h>

struct clock {
  int hr, min, sec;
};

void say_time_ptr(clock *c)
// Using a pointer
{
  printf("The time is %02d:%02d:%02d\n",
          c->hr, c->min, c->sec);
}

void say_time_ref(clock &c)
// Using a reference
```

```
{
  printf("The time is %02d:%02d:%02d\n",
            c.hr, c.min, c.sec);
}
void say_time_val(clock c)
// Pass by value
{
  printf("The time is %02d:%02d:%02d\n",
            c.hr, c.min, c.sec);
}
```

Note how we access the **clock** members in **say_time_ref()**. Even though it's passed by reference, we use **c** in **say_time_ref()** just as though it were a structure, rather than a pointer to a structure. We don't use the pointer selector '->', we use the basic member selector '.'. The body of **say_time_ref()** looks like the body of **say_time_val()**, which passes the **clock** by value.

Now let's compare the way the three functions are called:

```
clock cuckoo;

say_time_ptr(&cuckoo); // Must take address
say_time_ref(cuckoo);  // Don't take address
say_time_val(cuckoo);  // Don't take address
```

Clearly, the calls to **say_time_ref()** and **say_time_val()** are cleaner than the call to **say_time_ptr()**. However, neither of the latter calls are exactly what we want. The clock isn't supposed to be modified, just read. If we use a reference argument, we risk accidentally changing the clock. If we use pass-by-value, we incur overhead in copying. Thus, what do we do?

We can use a **const** modifier to help us out. For instance, we could pass a reference to a constant, as follows:

```
void say_time_ref(clock const &c)
// Parameter c is a reference to a constant clock
{
  ...
}
```

With this technique, we have the best of both worlds. Even though the function call looks like pass-by-value, for efficiency's sake, it's really pass-by-reference. Yet it's completely safe. There's no way that the function will be modifying the clock inadvertently.

1. Modify the following function to use pass-by-reference for **employee**, by using a reference argument:

```
void set_info(employee *e, int i, int a, float w)
{
  e->id = i;
  e->age = a;
  e->wage = w;
}
```

2. Given the following function, what's wrong with the associated call?

```
void clear_num(int &n) { n = 0; }

int k = 55;

clear_num(&k);
```

3. Using the same function in Question 2, is the following call legal?

```
clear_num(5);
```

---

1. *Using a reference argument, our function looks like:*

```
void set_info(employee &e, int i, int a, float w)
{
  e.id = i;
  e.age = a;
  e.wage = w;
}
```

2. *We're trying to pass a pointer when a reference is required. We should take off the & in the function call.*
3. *Yes. What happens is that a temporary variable is created to hold the value 5. It's this temporary variable that is passed to the function and set to 0, not the constant literal 5 itself.*

Returning References

One interesting thing about reference types is that they can also be used when specifying the return type for a function. Let's first look at an example where using a reference return type would be useful, and then see how to declare it that way.

The following function does a subscripting operation. It takes an array of characters and returns a copy of the **nth** character:

```
char elem(char *s, int n)
{
  return s[n];
}
```

We can use this function in situations such as the following:

```
char c;
char *s = "Turbo C++";
c = elem(s, 6);
```

However, why use the **elem()** function when you could use the subscript operator directly? Well, for one thing, we could extend **elem()** to check the size of the array and disallow indexing beyond it. (We won't do that here.) However, since we're only passing back a copy of the **nth** character, we can't assign values to that element and have the array itself updated. For instance, the following code,

```
char c;
char *s = "Turbo C++";
c = elem(s,6);
c = 'A';
```

doesn't change **s** to be "Turbo A++" since **c** is merely a copy of the sixth element of **s**, and doesn't point directly to it.

We could correct this problem by modifying the function to return a pointer to a character:

```
char *elem(char *s, int n)
{
   return &s[n];
}
```

Now we could write:

```
char *c;
char *s = "Turbo C++";
c = elem(s, 6);
*c = 'A';    // Changes s to be "Turbo A++"
```

We could even combine the last two statements into one by putting the function call on the left-hand side of the assignment:

```
*elem(s,6) = 'A';
```

However, there's a more elegant approach. Instead of passing back a pointer, we could pass back a reference. Figure 5.4 illustrates the process. Let's rewrite our **elem()** function using a reference return type:

```
char &elem(char *s, int n)
// Function passes back a reference to a char
{
   return s[n];
}
...
elem(s,6) = 'A'; // Now s becomes "Turbo A++"
```

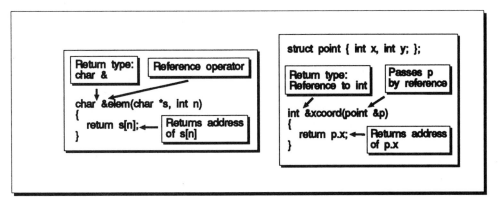

Figure 5.4. Declaring Reference Return Types

Even though the return statement looks like it's passing back **s[n]** by value (copying the nth character), because the return type is a reference, the address of **s[n]** is passed back instead. We can assign a value to the function result, and have it update the appropriate character in the array, as we've shown in our example.

Such use of reference variables may seem odd at first, but when you start using operator functions (discussed in Chapter 10) you'll see how handy they can be. As a sneak preview, we'll pretend that we know how to attach the subscript operator (denoted by square brackets **[]**), to our **elem()** function, and write code such as:

```
s[6] = 'A';
```

Although this may look like an ordinary subscripting operation, we could make it call **elem()**. If we made **elem()** do range checking on the index, we could in a sense make range checking be part of the language itself. (Recall that C does not normally do range checking on subscripts.) You'll have to wait until Chapter 10 to see how this is done. However, note that reference types play an important role in the process.

Illegal References
Like pointers, references can get you into trouble. For instance, the following code is a system crash just waiting to happen:

```
int &select_max(int a, int b)
{
  if (a > b) return a; else return b;
}

select_max(17, 42) = 500; // Boom!
```

Can you see what's wrong? Since **a** and **b** are passed by value, they reside on the stack. The function returns a reference to one of these stack locations, and then that location is set to 500. The trouble is, after the function return and before the assignment, the stack is reused for other things. Whatever the stack was reused for gets overwritten by the assignment. The result is a mangled stack that will most likely crash the program.

1. What does the following function do?

```
int &alias(int &k)
{
  return k;
}
```

2. Given the function in Question 1, what value does **i** have after the following code executes?

```
int i - 17;
alias(i) - 42;
```

3. Given the function in Question 1, is the following statement legal? If so, what does it do?

```
alias(i)++;
```

4. Suppose we changed **alias()** to pass **k** by value, but to still have pass-by-reference on the return:

```
int &not_quite_alias(int k)
// Note that k is passed in by value, but
// returned by reference
{
  return k
}
```

What value is returned from the call to **not_quite_alias()**?

```
int i - 55;
int j - not_quite_alias(i);
```

1. *The name of the function is suggestive. It's basically a transparent filter, passing back a reference to whatever integer it receives. You can use it like you would any other integer variable. (See Questions 2 and 3.)*
2. *It has the value 42.*

3. *A reference can be accessed just like any other variable. This includes references that are the result of a function call. In this case, we're simply incrementing the value of i.*
4. *You may or may not get the value 55 back. The parameter **k** is a local variable and resides on the stack. We're returning a reference to its stack location. It's not guaranteed what will be at this location after the function returns. Avoid such situations at all costs!*

   *In the original **alias()** function, where **k** was a reference variable, everything was okay. Even though in that case **k** was also a stack variable, we simply used it as a placeholder to pass along the address of the parameter i coming in. It's the address of i and not **k** itself that gets returned from the function.*

Inline Functions

You probably have, at one time or another, used macros to simulate function calls. Take for example, the following macro, and its invocation:

```
#define INC(i) i++
...
k - INC(j);
```

The trouble with using such macros is that they look like function calls, but they aren't. Parameters to macros are simply substituted inline, as is. In contrast, parameters to functions are type checked and passed using the proper scoping.

To see macro substitution in action, what do you suppose the following code produces?

```
k - INC(3+5);
```

That's right, it produces the following:

```
k - 3+5++;
```

What kind of syntax is that? It sure won't compile!

To help solve problems such as this, C++ provides *inline functions*. An inline function is basically a cross between a macro and a function. As with a macro, a call to an inline function is expanded and replaced with the body of the function. Unlike a macro, however, type checking is performed on the parameters, and the parameters are passed just as they are in regular function calls.

You can make any function an inline function by using the **inline** keyword in front of the function definition, as illustrated in Figure 5.5. Let's change the **INC()** macro to an inline function:

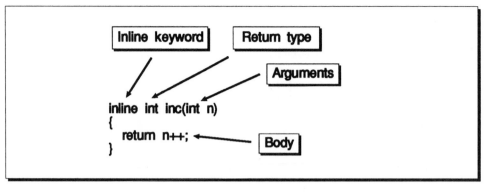

Figure 5.5. Components of an Inline Function

```
inline int inc(int n)
{
    return n++;
}
```

Note || The **inline** keyword is placed *before* the return type specification.

Let's make a call to **inc()** and see how it works:

```
int i;
i = inc(3+5);
```

When the compiler sees the call to **inc()**, it expands the function inline, but not before first adding 3 and 5 together and storing the result temporarily. The result is then incremented and assigned to **i**. In effect, the function call is transformed into:

```
int temp = 3+5;
i = temp++;
```

The function call completely disappears! Well, actually, it's not quite that simple.

Using the **inline** keyword does not guarantee that your function will be expanded inline when used. Like the **register** keyword, the **inline** keyword serves only as a hint to the compiler that you think the function is small enough to be expanded inline. The compiler may or may not choose to implement the function that way.

Tip || You can turn off inline function expansion altogether through the **-vi** compiler option. You may want to do this when debugging a program, as expanded inline functions are hard to trace through the debugger.

Inline Functions and Header Files

Inline functions are the function counterpart to constants. Recall that identifiers declared with the **const** keyword are initialized when declared. In a similar fashion, the bodies of inline functions are defined at the time the function is declared to be inline. In addition, **const** identifiers have internal linkage (recall the discussion in Chapter 4), as do inline functions. Also, constants are usually declared in header files, as are inline functions. Let's take a look at using inline functions in header files.

Suppose you have an inline function that prints the value of an integer that you wish to include in several files. The following is one erroneous attempt at including the function in a header:

header.h:

```
void showval(int v);  // Forgot inline keyword
```

file1.cpp:

```
#include <stdio.h>
#include "header.h"

inline void showval(int v)  // Now we remembered
{
  printf("The value is: %d\n", v);
}
```

prog.cpp:

```
#include "header.h"

void twiddle(int &v)
{
  v ^= 0x1010;
  showval(v);
}

main()
{
  int bits = 42;
  twiddle(bits);
}
```

Here we declared **showval()** to be inline inside **file1.cpp,** where we defined it, however, we forgot to use the **inline** keyword in the header file. The problem is that by declaring **showval()** inline, we also gave it internal linkage. This means it's not visible outside **file1.cpp.** Thus, although the program compiles, the linker will complain that it can't find the function **showval()** for **prog.cpp.**

If we had left off the inline keyword inside **file1.cpp,** then **showval()** would have external linkage, which is the default for normal functions. The program would have then compiled and linked okay, but **showval()** would not have been inline. Thus, how do we make it inline and still work properly?

The solution is to declare **showval()** inline in the header file, where it belongs. We can then remove **file1.cpp** altogether. Figure 5.6 shows the correct arrangement.

Tip || The easiest way to remember how to declare inline functions in header files is to treat them just as you would macros.

Fix the following inline declarations:

a. `inline void no_op(void);`

b. `int inline zero(void) { return 0; }`

*In a, we forgot to give the function body. In b we misplaced the **inline** keyword, which should have come before the return type. The fixes are:*

a. `inline void no_op(void) { ; } // Function does nothing`

b. `inline int zero(void) { return 0; }`

```
prog.cpp:                          header.h:

    #include "header.h"                #include <stdio.h>

    void twiddle(int &v)               inline void showval(int v)
    {                                  {
      v ^= 0x1010;                        printf("The value is: %d\n", v);
      showval(v);                      }
    }

    main()
    {
      int bits = 42;
      twiddle(bits);
    }
```

Figure 5.6. Using an Inline Function in a Header File

Creating Function Wrappers

One use of inline functions is to create high-level "wrappers" around other, more low-level functions. For instance, you might have a function that opens a file:

```
int file_open(char *fname, int create_flag);
```

The **create_flag** parameter is supposed to indicate whether you want the file created first (**create_flag** = 1), or whether it should already exist (**create_flag** = 0). For instance,

```
// Create myfile.dat
file_handle = file_open("myfile.dat", 1);
```

The trouble is that it's easy to forget whether to use a 1 or a 0 for **create_flag**. This could have disastrous consequences if you're trying to open an existing file that you spent hours building, only to wipe it out by mistakenly setting **create_flag** to one.

One solution to this problem is to create two inline functions called **file_create()** and **file_open_again()** which serve as wrappers around **file_open()**:

```
inline int file_create(char *fname)
{
   return file_open(fname, 1);
}

inline int file_open_again(char *fname)
{
   return file_open(fname, 0);
}
```

Using these two functions is more readable and intuitive than using the lower-level **file_open()** function. And, by making the functions inline, it doesn't cost us anything, either in execution time, or in code space!

Overloaded Functions

Turbo C++ allows you to have more than one function with the same name. Such functions are called *overloaded functions*. For example, we might have three **add()** functions, one that adds integers, one that adds doubles, and one that adds strings:

```
#include <string.h>

int add(int a, int b)
```

```
{
  return a + b;
}

double add(double a, double b)
{
  return a + b;
}

char *add(char *a, char *b)
{
  strcat(a, b);
  return a;
}

main()
{
  int i - add(42, 17);
  double d - add(42.0, 17.0);
  char s1[80] - "abc";
  char s2[80] - "xyz";
  add(s1, s2);
}
```

You don't have to specify the same number of arguments in a set of over-loaded functions. For instance, we could write yet another **add()** function that takes only one argument, as follows:

```
int add(int i)
{
  return i + 42;
}
```

How does the compiler know which **add()** function to call?

Resolving Ambiguities in Overloaded Functions

When the compiler sees a call to an overloaded function, it determines which function to call by looking at the argument types and trying to match them with the actual arguments used in the call. Figure 5.7 illustrates this process.

When the functions have different numbers of arguments, this matching is quite easy. All the compiler needs to do is match up the number of arguments. In general, however, the matching rules are quite complex.

For each argument in the function call, the compiler uses the set of match-ing rules shown in Figure 5.8 to try to find the best match. The rules are invoked in the order given. That is, those listed first are considered "better" than the later ones. The basic strategy is to look for an exact match, and if one can't be found, try to find simple type conversions that will lead to the "best" match.

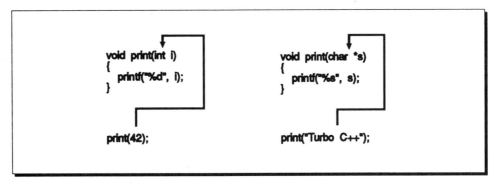

Figure 5.7. Matching Overloaded Functions

Note | The compiler looks only at the argument types. It does not look at the return type. Thus, two overloaded functions cannot differ only in the return type, or you'll get a compiler error.

1. Look for an exact match and use those if found. Also, look for matches involving *trivial conversions*. The trivial conversions are given in Table 5.1.

2. Look for conversions involving *integral promotions* or for conversions from **float** to **double**. The integral promotions include converting **char, short, enumerator,** and **int** bit fields to **int**.

3. Look for matches involving the standard arithmetic conversions (such as **int** to **double, unsigned** to **signed,** and so on.) Also, look for matches involving conversions from any pointer type to **void*,** and for converting the constant 0 to the null pointer. In addition, look for converting a derived class pointer to a base class pointer, and a derived class reference to a base class reference. (Derived and base classes are covered in Chapter 9.)

4. Look for conversions that require the creation of temporary objects, such as passing a constant object to a function requiring a nonconstant object.

5. Look for matching requiring user-defined conversions. (See Chapter 10 for examples of user-defined conversions.)

6. Finally, match with ellipses arguments, such as f(...).

Figure 5.8. Matching Rules for Overloaded Functions

Table 5.1. Trivial Argument Type Conversions

Actual Type	Formal Type	Description
T	T&	From an object of type T to a reference to an object of type T
T&	T	From a reference to an object of type T to an object of type T
T[]	*T	From an array of type T to a pointer to an object of type T
T	const T	From an object of type T to a constant object of type T
T	volatile T	From an object of type T to a volatile object of type T
F(args)	(*F)(args)	From a function with the given argument types to a pointer to a function with the same argument types

Although you might not think it, we've purposely simplified the definitions of the matching rules. The exact rules are very complex and would require much explanation.

Tip You should use explicit type conversions in the arguments to function calls whenever possible to help the compiler resolve any function overloading ambiguities. When in doubt, try out simple examples and let the compiler show you indirectly what its rules are by the error messages you receive.

You'll notice that many of the matching rules involve performing some kind of type conversion. In some cases, the compiler might do multiple conversions looking for a match. For instance, it might convert a **char** to an **int** to a **const int**. In general, though, there is a limit to how many conversions the compiler will do before giving up on finding a match. Again, the best policy is to design your overloaded functions to not rely on such conversions.

Note It's legal to have potentially ambiguous function calls as long as you either don't call the functions at all, or that all calls to the functions can be resolved. That is, you won't receive a compiler error until you make an ambiguous call.

1. Match up the following overloaded functions with the function calls given:

```
void f(char c);
void f(int i);
void f(double d);
...
```

a. f('A');
b. f(76.2);
c. f(0);

2. Given the two overloaded functions below and a call to one of the functions, which function is called?

```
void f(char c);
void f(const char c);
...
f('\n');
```

3. Are the following overloaded functions and function call legal?

```
void h(void *p);
void h(double d);
...
h(0.0);
```

4. What if we change the call in Question 3 to the following:

```
h(0);
```

Is the code now legal?

5. The following program contains two ambiguous f() functions. Will it compile anyway?

```
#include <stdio.h>

void f(int x)       { printf("integer is: %d\n", x);  }
void f(const int x) { printf("constant is: %d\n", x); }

main()
{
  printf("Hello\n");
}
```

1. *The answers are:*

   a. *calls f(char c)*
   b. *calls f(double d)*
   c. *calls f(int i)*

2. *Neither function is called. You'll actually get an error stating that the functions can't be overloaded. As far as matching arguments for overloaded functions goes, the compiler doesn't distinguish between an argument of type **T** and an argument of type const **T**.*

3. *Yes. The compiler uses **h(double d)** for the call.*

4. *Surprisingly, no. The compiler can't decide whether to convert the constant 0 to a null pointer, or whether to convert it to a **double**.*

5. *Yes. Even though the overloaded functions are ambiguous, the compiler won't give us an error since the ambiguous functions are never called.*

Summary

You should now have a solid understanding of how functions are used in Turbo C++. The most important thing you should have learned is how important function prototypes are in Turbo C++ programming. Without them, type-safe linkage and overloaded functions would not be possible.

However, even though C++ has type-safe linkage to help catch argument typing mistakes, it's still not totally safe when it comes to return types. A good rule to remember is to always include function prototypes, and always be careful when specifying return types.

This chapter shows some of the extra power that C++ gives to functions in the form of reference arguments, reference return types, default arguments, inline functions, and overloaded functions. However, the real power behind C++ functions has yet to be expounded upon. Later chapters will show you the power of virtual functions and operator functions.

Exercises

1. Is the following code legal in C? What about C++?

```
extern void write();

main()
{
  char cmd[] = "Make it so.";

  write(cmd);
}
```

2. Would it be possible to declare overloaded functions as C functions? (Hint: think about the absence of name mangling on C functions.)

3. There's a serious error in the following function. What is it and how can it be fixed?

```
int &select_max(int a, int b)
{
    if (a > b) return a; return b;
}
```

4. Two overloaded functions can't differ only in their return types. Given what you've learned about type-safe linkage, can you guess why?
5. Given the following overloaded functions and calls, which of the calls is illegal?

```
void f(int x, int y = 0); // y is a default argument
void f(int x);

f(25);
f(17, 42);
```

Answers

1. *Using C interpretation, the prototype for **write()** indicates that the function accepts any number and type of arguments, so the call to **write()** is legal. Using C++ interpretation, the prototype means that **write()** takes no arguments, so the call to **write()** is illegal.*
2. *No. Without name mangling, the overloaded functions would look alike to the linker, since no type information is included in the otherwise duplicate names. You'll get a duplicate function definition error.*
3. *The function returns a reference to a stack location, where either **a** or **b** resides. The fix is to pass **a** and **b** by reference rather than by value:*

```
int &select_max(int &a, int &b)
{
    if (a > b) return a; else return b;
}
```

4. *In type-safe linkage, the return types are not encoded in the mangled function names. Thus, two overloaded functions that differ only in their return types would have identically mangled names, and would look the same to the linker.*
5. *The call **f(25)** is ambiguous. The compiler doesn't know whether to call the function with one argument, or whether to use a default for the second argument. In the call **f(17,42)** it's clear which function to call, since only one of the functions passes two arguments.*

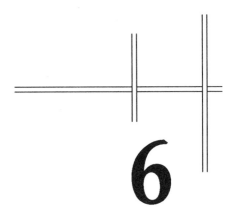

6

Learning about Classes

Virtually every program you have ever written or will ever write has two main ingredients: data and operations used to process that data. You specify how data is to be represented through the use of data types. You specify how data is to be processed through the use of functions. Up until now, we've kept these two ingredients separate. In this chapter we'll discuss how to merge data and functions together through the use of *classes*.

In this chapter, you'll learn:

- What abstract data types are, and how classes relate to them
- How to declare classes
- How to create objects from classes
- How to declare member functions
- How member functions access other class members
- How to hide the details of your classes
- How to use inline member functions

Classes: Implementations of Abstract Data Types

An important feature of any good programming language is the ability to create user-defined types. While you can create your own types in C, using the **typedef** and **struct** keywords, the resulting types can't easily be integrated into the rest of the program. You can only define types in terms of the data making up those types. The functions used to operate on those types aren't a part of the type definition. Also, there's no way to *encapsulate*, or hide, the details of how the type is implemented.

A type definition that includes both data and functions, and the means to encapsulate the details, is referred to as an *abstract data type*. In C++, you can implement abstract data types through the use of *classes*. A class is a type definition that merges data and functions together in a single framework. In equation form, we might write

```
Class = Data + Related operations
```

By using the class construct, you can create your own abstract data types that are as convenient to work with as the built-in types. Let's look at an example of an abstract data type and see what problems we encounter when trying to define the abstract data type in C. Then we'll see how the class construct can come to the rescue.

Sample Abstract Data Type

An example of an abstract data type is a "circular number," as shown in Figure 6.1. A circular number has a range of values, and if you try to increment the number past its range, the number wraps around back to its minimum value. In a similar fashion, decrementing past the beginning of the range causes the number to wrap around to its maximum value. An example of a circular number is a geometric angle that ranges in value from 0 to 359 degrees. If you try to set the angle to 360 degrees, it gets changed to 0, since 360 degrees and 0 degrees are the same angle.

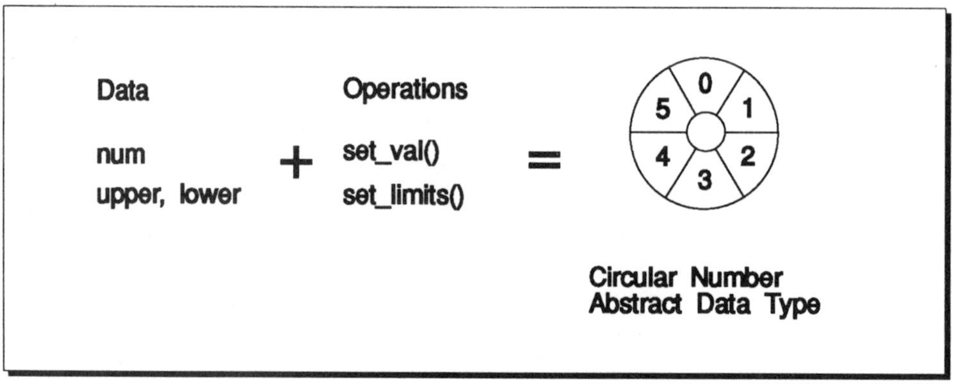

Figure 6.1. An Abstract Data Type

How could you implement a circular number? You might implement it as a collection of three data items: the current value of the number, and the upper and lower limits of the number. In C, you might use a structure to group these data items together, as in:

```
struct circular_num {
    int num;            /* The actual value */
    int upper, lower;  /* The limits */
};
```

However, something is missing. How do you operate on this structure? That is, how do you set the value of the circular number? How do you set its limits?

In C, you would code up a set of functions to do the job. These functions could all take a **circular_num** structure as a parameter and perform operations on that structure. For instance:

```
void set_limits(struct circular_num *c, int l, int u)
{
    c->lower = l; c->upper = u;
}

int set_val(struct circular_num *c, int v)
/* Set the value, wrapping to keep it in range */
{
    int range = c->upper - c->lower + 1;
    while(v > c->upper) v -= range;
    while(v < c->lower) v += range;
    return c->num = v; /* Record and return result */
}
```

You might then declare some **circular_num** variables and operate on them:

```
main()
{
    struct circular_num angle, x_coord;

    /* Set limits used for angles */
    set_limits(&angle, 0, 359);
    set_val(&angle, 570);
    printf("The angle is: %3d\n", angle.num);

    /* Set limits used for the x coordinate on the screen */
    set_limits(&x_coord, 0, 79);
    set_val(&x_coord, -15);
    printf("The x coordinate is %3d\n", x_coord.num);
}
```

If you turned all this code into a proper C program and compiled and ran it, the output would be:

```
The angle is: 210
The x coordinate is 65
```

While the program works, it has problems. Really, the structure **circular_num** and the functions **set_limits()** and **set_val()** are all part of the same thing: a circular number abstract data type. We have data, and we have functions to operate on that data. However, besides the fact that our two functions take **circular_num** structures as parameters, nowhere is it indicated that the structure and the functions belong together.

Worse yet, nothing forces you to use the functions in the proper sequence. You must set the limits of the circular number before setting its value, otherwise you'll get erroneous results. And what's to stop you from just setting the structure member **num** directly, bypassing the steps to keep it in range?

The problem with our structure and functions is that they do very little *encapsulation*. That is, we haven't bundled the structures and functions together so that they work cohesively as a whole.

An important feature of abstract data types is encapsulation. In the next section, we'll see how we can turn our circular number structure and its functions into a C++ class.

 A user-interface window could be represented as an abstract data type. Give some examples of what data and operations could be associated with a window abstract data type.

A window has some location that you could specify with an (x,y) coordinate pair. It also has a width and height. In addition, the window might have a set of colors associated with it, and a frame style. For operations, you need some way to draw, resize, move, and erase the window. You also might have some routines to write text or draw graphics in the window.

A Sample Class

Let's rewrite our circular number abstract data type as a C++ class. The easiest way to do this is to move the function prototypes for **set_limits()** and **set_val()** into the structure declaration itself. In the new class terminology, the data members are known as *instance variables* and the class functions are known as *member functions*. The following program shows what our new class looks like:

```
#include <stdio.h>

// Class declaration

struct circular_num {
    int num;                      // Instance variable
    int upper, lower;             // Instance variables
    void set_limits(int l, int u); // Member function
    int set_val(int v);           // Member function
};

// Class implementation

void circular_num::set_limits(int l, int u)
{
    lower = l; upper = u;
}

int circular_num::set_val(int v)
// Set the value, wrapping to keep it in range
{
    int range = upper - lower + 1;
    while(v > upper) v -= range;
    while(v < lower) v += range;
    return num = v; // Record and return result
}

main()
{
    circular_num angle, x_coord;

    angle.set_limits(0, 359);
    angle.set_val(570);
    printf("The angle is: %3d\n", angle.num);

    x_coord.set_limits(0, 79);
    x_coord.set_val(-15);
    printf("The x coordinate is %3d\n", x_coord.num);
}
```

As the comments suggest, a class definition consists of two parts: a *declaration* and an *implementation*. The declaration lists the members of the class. The implementation defines the functions for the class. Figure 6.2 illustrates these two parts.

Note that only the function prototypes for **set_limit()** and **set_val()** are placed in the class declaration. The function bodies are defined after the class.

In the implementation section, the class name is attached to each of the member functions, and the **circular_num** structure is no longer passed to these functions. The member functions have direct access to the instance variables of the class.

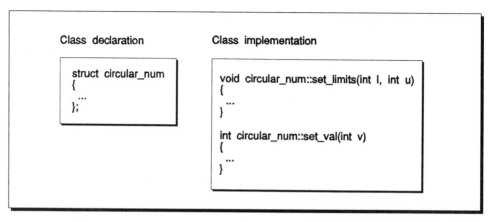

Figure 6.2. Components of a Class Definition

Since the functions are members, we access them just as we would any structure member: using the . operator, as in

```
angle.set_val(570);
```

The key to understanding how classes work is to understand how member functions work. We need to discover the "glue" that binds member functions and instance variables together. Before we continue our discussion on abstract data types and encapsulation, let's see if we can find this glue by studying member functions.

Declaring Member Functions

What sets C++ classes apart from C structures is the ability to include functions as well as data. You indicate that a function belongs to a class by placing its prototype inside the class declaration. Typically, the actual definition of the function (i.e., its body) is declared outside the class, although it is possible to include the body inside the class declaration. (Such functions are called *inline member functions*, as you'll see later on.)

You indicate that a function belongs to a class by attaching the class name to the function using the scoping operator. For example, the following is the **set_limits()** member function of our **circular_num** class:

```
void circular_num::set_limits(int 1, int u)
{
   upper = u; lower = 1;
}
```

Using **set_limits()** as a model, Figure 6.3 illustrates the different components that make up a member function declaration, such as its return type, class, scoping operator, name, arguments, and body.

Besides indicating what class the function belongs to, the scoping operator does one other important thing: it brings the function into the scope of the class, so that all the class members are directly accessible to the function. In the next section we'll discuss this further.

Like any function, member functions can be overloaded, and they can have default arguments. An example of providing two **set_val** functions in the **circular_num** class, and using default arguments for **set_limits()** is:

```
struct circular_num {
  int num;
  int upper, lower;
  void set_limits(int l=0, int u=9); // Note default arguments
  int set_val(int v); // One version
  int set_val(void);  // Another version
};

void circular_num::set_limits(int l, int u)
{
  lower = l; upper = u;
}

int circular_num::set_val(int v)
{
  int range = upper-lower+1;
  while(v > upper) v -= range;
  while(v < lower) v += range;
  return num = v;
}
```

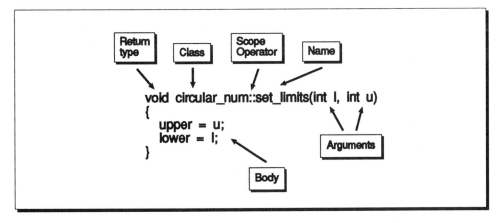

Figure 6.3. Components of a Member Function

```
int circular_num::set_val(void)    // Sets value to the lower limit
{
  set_val(lower); // Call other set_val() version
}
```

Note that the default arguments for **set_limits()** are specified in the class declaration, and not in the function implementation. Also, note how the second **set_val()** function calls the first to set the value to the lower limit.

Given the following class, what's wrong with the member function declaration?

```
struct reversed_num {
  int num;
  void set(int n);
};

void set(int n)
{
  num = ((n >> 8) & 0x00ff) | ((n << 8) & 0xff00);
}
```

The function set() wasn't scoped to be part of the class. Because of this, set() becomes an ordinary normal function, and the function reversed_num::set() is left undefined. We need to include the class name in the function definition:

```
void reversed_num::set(int n)
{
  num = ((n >> 8) & 0x00ff) | ((n << 8) & 0xff00);
}
```

It's very easy to forget to include the class name in a member function declaration. If you do forget, you'll get a number of confusing compiler errors.

Scoping in Member Functions

Recall from Chapter 4 that class members have class scope. This includes member functions too, which means the functions can access other members of the class directly. For example, take our **set_limits()** function, which directly accesses the class members **lower** and **upper**:

```
void circular_num::set_limits(int l, int u)
{
  lower = l; upper = u; // Note direct access
}
```

Actually, there are three scopes that interact inside a member function, as Figure 6.4 illustrates: the scope of the class, the block scope of the function, and the global file scope. The rules for the interaction of these scopes are as follows:

1. Variables in block scope (that is, local variables to the function such as parameters) hide the names of both class members and global variables.
2. Class member names hide the names of global variable names.

Since parameter names hide the names of members, one problem that occurs is when you give a parameter the same name as a member. For example, suppose we changed **set_limits()** to have its parameters named **lower** and **upper**:

```
void circular_num::set_limits(int lower, int upper)
{
   lower = ??; upper = ?? // What do we do here?
}
```

How do we go about accessing the members **lower** and **upper**? The answer is to use the binary scope operator, as follows:

```
void circular_num::set_limits(int lower, int upper)
{
   circular_num::lower = lower;
   circular_num::upper = upper;
}
```

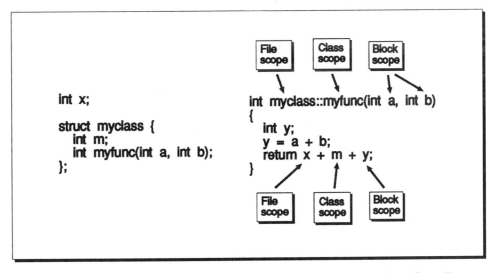

Figure 6.4. Interacting Scopes Inside a Member Function

In a similar fashion, if you have a member name hiding a global name, you can access the global name with the unary scope operator, as in the following window class:

```
#include <conio.h>

struct win { // A window class
  int xul, yul, wd, ht;
  void set_size(int w, int h);
  void open(int x, int y);
  void draw(void);
  void close(void);
  void gotoxy(int x, int y);
};

// Other member functions here ...

void win::gotoxy(int x, int y)
// Move cursor given relative window coordinates
{
  x += xul; y += yul; // Translate to screen coordinates
  ::gotoxy(x, y);      // Call gotoxy() from conio.h
}
```

By using the unary scope operator, the **gotoxy()** function that's called inside **win::gotoxy()** has file scope. This causes the **gotoxy()** function in Turbo C++'s **conio** library to be used. If the scope operator was left off, an infinitely recursive call to **win::gotoxy()** would be created.

What does the following program output?

```
#include <stdio.h>

int a = 1, b = 2, c = 42; // Some global variables

struct two_nums {
  int a, b; // Some instance variables
  void do_something(int b);
};

void two_nums::do_something(int b)
{
  a = 17; // Who is set here?
  b = 55; // Who is set here?
  c = 3;  // Who is set here?
}

main()
{
  two_nums dos_numbres;
```

```
    dos_numbres.do_something(36);
    printf("%d %d %d\n", a, b, c);
}
```

---

*In the function **do_something()**, the member name **a** hides the global variable by the same name. Thus, the assignment to **a** is for the object member **a**; the global one stays untouched. Parameter **b** hides both the global variable **b** and the member **b**. Thus, the assignment to **b** sets the value of the local copy of the parameter on the stack. The global **b** and the member **b** remain unaffected. The assignment to **c** sets the global **c**. Thus, the program outputs*

    1 2 3

Inside Member Functions

Now that you understand about the scoping of member functions, let's see how this scoping is implemented.

It turns out that every member function has a hidden argument, called **this,** which is passed automatically to the function by the compiler. The argument **this** is a pointer to the object that called the function.

As an example, consider the **set_limits()** function from our earlier **circular_num** class:

```
void circular_num::set_limits(int l, int u)
{
  lower = l; upper = u;
}
```

As given in the function definition, it looks as though **set_limits()** takes two arguments: **l** and **u**—the limits for the circular number. However, when compiled, the function actually takes three arguments. The hidden argument, **this,** is added to the front of the argument list, and the members **lower** and **upper** are accessed through this argument. An equivalent C version of **set_limits()** might be written as:

```
/* Equivalent C version */
void set_limits(struct circular_num *this, int l, int u)
{
  this->lower = l; this->upper = u;
}
```

Notice that we have come full circle in defining the **set_limits()** function. When we first wrote **set_limits()** in C, it looked like:

```
void set_limits(struct circular_num *c, int l, int u)
{
  c->lower = l; c->upper = u;
}
```

All we've done for the C++ member function is to change the name of the structure pointer argument to **this**, and then hide it.

Note | The **this** pointer is actually typed to be a constant pointer. That is, for some class T, **this** is typed to be **T *const**.

Suppose you have a **circular_num** object **c**. The following shows how a call to the C++ version of **set_limits()** might be translated into an equivalent C function:

C++ version	C version
`c.set_limits(0,359);`	`set_limits(&c, 0, 359);`

Note that it's the address of **c** that is passed through the **this** pointer.

The **this** pointer is the magic glue of C++ encapsulation. It's what ties together the members of a class and the functions used to operate on those members. Understanding the **this** pointer can be quite useful if you get confused about how a member function works. For that reason, we've provided Figure 6.5 which illustrates how member functions can be translated to C. This translation shows the role that **this** plays.

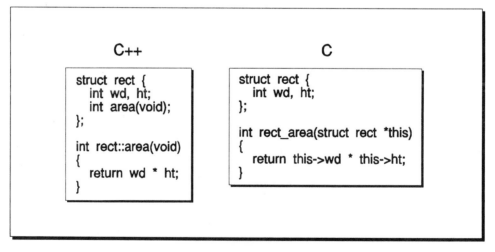

Figure 6.5. Translating Member Functions to C

Using the "this" Pointer

Although it's rarely necessary, you can use the **this** pointer explicitly in a member function. For instance, we could have written our **set_limits()** function as:

```
void circular_num::set_limits(int 1, int u)
{
  this->lower = 1; this->upper = u;
}
```

Such use of the **this** pointer is redundant, and clutters up the code for a member function. There are, however, legitimate times when you do need to use **this** explicitly. Suppose, for example, that you wished to have a window object attach itself to a window stack. The object might do that by passing its own address, using **this**, to a stack function. For instance:

```
struct window { ... };

void push_window(window *w); // Some push routine

void window::open(int x, int y)
// Draw window at (x,y), push onto window stack
{
  draw(x,y);
  push_window(this); // Pass pointer to this object
}
```

Given the following class and its member function, can you think of not one, but two ways to remove the ambiguity between the parameter named **len** and the class member named **len**? Try doing it without renaming either variable. (Hint: Use what you've learned in the last few sections about **this**.)

```
struct int_array {
  int data[100];
  int len;
  void set_length(int len);
};

void int_array::set_length(int len)
{
  len = len; // Fix this two ways
}
```

*You can use the scoping operator, or you can use the **this** pointer, as follows:*

```
void int_array::set_length(int len)
```

```
{
  int_array::len = len; // Fixed using scoping operator
}

void int_array::set_length(int len)
{
  this->len = len; // Fixed using the this pointer
}
```

*Of the two methods, using the scoping operator is preferred. It doesn't rely on the low-level implementation of the **this** pointer.*

Data Hiding

Now that you know how member functions work, let's continue our discussion about encapsulation. Encapsulation involves more than just packaging together data and functions. It also has to do with *hiding* the data. One ability that C++ classes have that C structures don't is a means to restrict access to the members of the class.

Note ‖ Even though we use the term data hiding here, we're really talking about internal functions as well as data. It's just that most of the time, it's the data that gets hidden.

By restricting access to certain members, you can hide the details of how a class operates. For instance, recall the **circular_num** class:

```
struct circular_num {
  int num;                   // Instance variable
  int upper, lower;          // Instance variables
  void set_limits(int l, int u) // Member function
  int set_val(int v);        // Member function
};
```

You should set the member **num** through the function **set_val()**. That way, **num**'s value is guaranteed to be in the proper range. However, nothing stops you from setting **num** directly, as in

```
circular_num c;

c.set_limits(0, 17); // Define limits
c.num = 42;          // Out of range!
```

The same situation applies to the members **upper** and **lower**. They're supposed to be set only through the function **set_limits()**. In this case, though, accessing them directly is relatively harmless. Even so, we're not hiding them as well as we could. Suppose the limits are implemented some other way. (Maybe they're tied directly to some hardware, and aren't normal variables at all.)

The way to fix this problem is to make the instance variables accessible only to members of the class. We want **num, upper,** and **lower** to be accessible only to the functions **set_limits()** and **set_val()**. Of course, we still want access to the functions themselves. That is, we want to make the data *private* to the class, but the functions *public*. We can do this through the use of the **private** and **public** keywords. The following modified **circular_num** class declaration shows how:

```
struct circular_num {
private:  // Makes the following members private
  int num;
  int upper, lower;
public:   // Makes the following members public
  void set_limits(int l, int u);
  int set_val(int v);
};
```

Now, the only class members we can use directly are **set_limits()** and **set_val()**. If we try to access **num, upper,** and **lower** directly, we'll get compiler errors:

```
circular_num c;

c.set_limit(0, 10); // Okay
c.set_val(42);      // Okay
c.num = 42;         // Can't do
c.upper = -1;       // Can't do
c.lower = 1000;     // Can't do
```

Access Functions

Since we've declared **num, upper,** and **lower** private, we can no longer inspect their values. We might want to add some other functions to our **circular_num** class to access them. To serve that purpose, let's add functions **get_val()**, **high_val()**, and **low_val()**:

```
struct circular_num {
private: // Makes the following members private
  int num;
  int upper, lower;
public: // Makes the following members public
  void set_limits(int l, int u);
  int set_val(int v);
```

```
int get_val(void);   // New function
int high_val(void);  // New function
int low_val(void);   // New function
};
```

In addition, we need to add the new function bodies:

```
int circular_num::get_val(void)
{
  return num;
}

int circular_num::high_val(void)
{
  return upper;
}

int circular_num::low_val(void)
{
  return lower;
}
```

Functions such as these, which do nothing except return the values of private variables, are sometimes called *access functions*. Access functions are useful because they allow you to examine the contents of private variables, yet you can't change these private variables unless the functions let us. The **num** variable is a case in point. You can read the value of **num** through **get_val()**, but you can only set **num** through **set_val()**, which ensures that **num** stays in range. Figure 6.6 illustrates this concept.

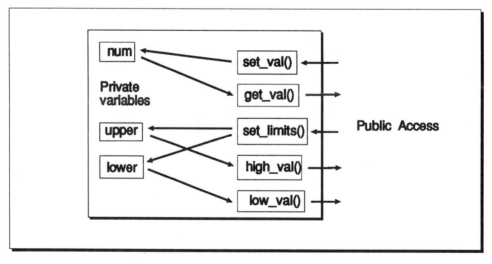

Figure 6.6. Accessing Private Data

Before, when we declared our class without any **private** or **public** keywords, all of our members were public. That's because we used the **struct** keyword when declaring our class. There are actually other ways to declare classes. In the next section we'll see just what those ways are.

1. How can you simulate data hiding in C? (Hint: Think about external and internal linkage of identifiers in multiple-module programs.)
2. Given what you discovered in Question 1, comment on the difference between data hiding in C versus data hiding in C++.

1. Suppose you had the following class:

```
struct piggy_bank {
private:
  float savings;
public:
  void open(void);
  void deposit(float amt);
  float withdraw(float amt);
  float balance(void);
};
```

You could simulate this class in C using two files as follows:

piggy.h:

```
/* Header file for public access */

extern void open(void);
extern void deposit(float amt);
extern float withdraw(float amt);
extern float balance(void);
```

piggy.c:

```
/* Implementation file */

static float savings;  /* Declared internal */

void open(void)             { savings = 0; }
void deposit(float amt)     { savings += amt; }
float withdraw(float amt)   { return savings -= amt; }
float balance(void)         { return savings; }
```

*The trick is in making the variable **savings** static, and thus local to the implementation file. Only the functions can be accessed outside the file **piggy.c**, by virtue of having external linkage.*

2. *Simulating data hiding in C is clumsy. With our piggy bank example, the C version works fine for one piggy bank, but what if we wanted multiple piggy banks? The problem is that the C version works on too coarse a level—the file level. The C++ version works on a much finer grained level—individual structures.*

Inside Class Declarations

Thus far, we have used only the **struct**, **public**, and **private** keywords when declaring classes. There are other keywords you can use too, which you'll learn about in this section.

Classes can be declared using any of three keywords: **class**, **struct**, and **union**. The basic syntax is:

```
<class-specifier> <class_name> {
private:
  <private members go here>
protected:
  <protected members go here>
public:
  <public members go here>
} obj1, obj2, ...;
```

The list of members in a class is organized into sections, each section having its own access level. The access levels are **private**, **protected**, and **public**. Table 6.1 summarizes these different access levels.

We've already talked about private and public access. The protected level of access has to do with *derived classes*, which is the subject of Chapter 9. We won't explain the **protected** keyword until then.

Some examples of class declarations are:

```
class clock {  // A clock class
private:
  long seconds;
public:
  clock(int h, int m, int s);
  void tick(void);
  void hms(int &h, int &m, int &s);
};

union token {  // A token class
  int op_type;
  double number;
  void set_op(int op);
  void set_num(double num);
};
```

Table 6.1. The Different Access Levels

Level	Description
private	The member is only accessible by the member functions of the class.
protected	Like private, but in addition, the member is accessible to the functions of any class derived from this one.
public	The member is accessible to any function.

```
struct point {  // A point class
   int x, y;
} p1, p2;       // Optional object declarations p1 and p2
```

Tip || Remember that C-like structures and unions are considered classes in C++.

Take a closer look at the **point** class declaration. Recall that a class declaration is a template from which objects are created, just as a structure declaration in C is a template from which C structure variables are created. It's possible to create objects of a class at the time you declare the class, as we've done with the **point** class.

Typically, though, you won't be declaring objects with your class declarations, because class declarations usually go in header files, and you shouldn't be declaring variables in header files.

Tip || Most of the time, you'll be leaving out the optional variable declarations in a class declaration. However, don't forget the semicolon after the last curly brace in the class declaration!

Setting Access Levels for Class Members

There's a lot of flexibility in how you specify the access sections of a class. You may have more than one of the same kind of section in a class. For instance, we could rewrite the **circular_num** class to have multiple private and public sections as in:

```
struct circular_num {
private:
   int num;
public:
```

```
  void set_limits(int l, int u);
private:
  int upper;
public:
  int set_val(int v);
  int get_val(void);
private:
  int lower;
public:
  int high_val(void);
  int low_val(void);
};
```

You don't have to use any particular order when specifying the different sections of a class. It's best to stick to some convention, such as listing the private members first.

You may choose to leave out the access keywords altogether in a class and not specify different access sections. In that case, the members of the class receive a default access level, which depends on the kind of class it is. The default access levels are listed in Table 6.2.

Note ‖ Unions cannot have **private** or **protected** sections. Their members are always public.

For example, in the following class, all the members are public since the class was declared using the **struct** keyword:

```
struct dynarray {
  int *data; // All members public
  int size, len;
  dynarray(int sz);
  int &elem(int n);
};
```

By having **struct** members default to **public**, upward compatibility with C is maintained.

Table 6.2. Default Access Levels of Classes

Keyword:	Default Access Level
class	Private
struct	Public
union	Public

In a similar fashion, if you do not specify the access level for the first section of a class, then the members in that section receive the default access level for that kind of class. For instance, we could rewrite our **circular_num** class declaration as follows:

```
struct circular_num {
  void set_limits(int l, int u);  // Public by default
  int set_val(int v);             // Public by default
  int get_val(void);              // Public by default
  int high_val(void);             // Public by default
  int low_val(void);              // Public by default
private:
  int num;
  int upper, lower;
};
```

You may want to always declare the **public** and **private** members of classes explicitly. That way, you and the reader of your code won't forget that there might be private members. This is particularly true with classes declared using the **class** keyword, since they can have default private members.

1. Restate the following structure declaration as a class declaration, keeping the access levels of the members the same:

```
struct button {
  char *label;
  int action_code;
};
```

2. Restate the **circular_num** class declaration we gave a few paragraphs back into one using the **class** keyword. Be sure to keep the same access levels.
3. Given the following class and object declaration, what happens when we try to call **init()**?

```
class file_mgr {
  FILE *fp;
  char *name;
  int reclen;
  void init(int rlen);
};

file_mgr f;

f.init(80);  // What happens here?
```

4. What's wrong with the following class declaration?

```
union float_bytes {
private:
  char mantissa[3], char exponent;
public:
  float num;
  char exp(void);
  char *mant(void);
};
```

1. *The class should declare all members public:*

```
class button {
public:
  char *label;
  int action_code;
};
```

2. *You could write it a number of ways. Two are:*

```
class circular_num {
private:
  int num;
  int upper, lower;
public:
  void set_limits(int l, int u);
  int set_val(int v);
  int get_val(void);
  int high_val(void);
  int low_val(void);
};
```

```
class circular_num {
  int num;            // Private by default
  int upper, lower; // Private by default
public:
  void set_limits(int l, int u);
  int set_val(int v);
  int get_val(void);
  int high_val(void);
  int low_val(void);
};
```

3. *The compiler will give you an error, since **init()** is private and can't be accessed outside the class. In fact, all the members are private, which makes the class rather useless.*

4. *Unions can't have private members. It is legal, however, for unions to have member functions, just like any class.*

Inline Member Functions

In typical cases, you access the data members of a class indirectly through special access functions, as you've seen with the **get_val()**, **high_val()**, and **low_val()** functions of the **circular_num** class. While this achieves the proper encapsulation, it unfortunately comes at a cost. Calling a function is generally more inefficient than accessing a structure member. To refresh your memory, here is the **get_val()** function:

```
int circular_num::get_val(void)
{
  return num;
}
```

It seems a bit ridiculous to go to all the trouble of creating such a simple function that does nothing but return a value. And there is certainly more overhead involved. So what do we do? Can we get the best of both worlds, having encapsulation, but efficient encapsulation? In many cases, we can, by using *inline member functions*.

Recall that inline functions have the efficiency of macros, but the safety of functions. They seem like just the ticket for our access functions. Indeed they are. Let's take a look at how we can declare inline member functions.

Declaring Inline Member Functions

One way to declare inline member functions is to include the whole function right in the class declaration, body and all. Such functions are implicitly considered inline functions. For example, we could write our **circular_num** class as:

```
class circular_num {
private:
  int num;
  int upper, lower;
public:
  void set_limits(int l, int u);
  int set_val(int v);
  int get_val(void)  { return num;   } // Inline
  int high_val(void) { return upper; } // Inline
  int low_val(void)  { return lower; } // Inline
};
```

Another way is to explicitly use the **inline** keyword when implementing the functions outside the class:

```
class circular_num {
private:
  int num;
  int upper, lower;
public:
  void set_limits(int l, int u);
  int set_val(int v);
  int get_val(void);
  int high_val(void);
  int low_val(void);
};

// Note where inline keyword goes in relation to
// the return type and the class specifier.

inline int circular_num::get_val(void)
{
  return num;
}

inline int circular_num::high_val(void)
{
  return upper;
}

inline int circular_num::low_val(void)
{
  return lower;
}
```

You must be careful about using explicit inline member declarations. The problem is this: In order to expand an inline function, the compiler must have the body of the function. In the preceding inline functions, the compiler doesn't have the bodies of the functions until their actual definitions are encountered.

To illustrate why this is a problem, suppose we add another member function that returns the range of the circular number. The range is computed by making calls to **high_val()** and **low_val()**:

```
class circular_num {
  ...
  int high_val(void);
  int low_val(void);
  int range(void);
};

int circular_num::range(void)
{
  return high_val() - low_val() + 1; // What happens here?
}
```

```
inline int circular_num::high_val(void) { ... }
inline int circular_num::low_val(void)  { ... }
```

If you try to compile this code, Turbo C++ will complain that **high_val()** and **low_val()** are being declared twice. In **range()**, the compiler sets up the calls to **high_val()** and **low_val()** as normal function calls, only to find out later that the calls should have been expanded inline.

The problem of not discovering that a function is inline until it's too late does not occur with functions declared implicitly inline. Turbo C++ first scans the class declaration for implicit inline functions before further processing.

Note ‖ If you have inline expansion turned off, you may not encounter the problems described in this section. However, they are problems just waiting to happen if you should turn inline expansion on.

1. What's wrong with the following class definition?

```
#include <string.h>

struct buffer {
  char data[255];
  int cursor;
  void init(char *s);
  inline int len(void);
  char *contents(void);
};

void buffer::init(char *s)
{
  strcpy(data, s); cursor = 0;
}

char *buffer::contents(void)
{
  if (len()) return data; else return 0;
}

inline int buffer::len(void) { return cursor; }
```

2. Suppose we rewrote the class in Question 2 to use the **inline** keyword for **contents()** as well. Will the code work now?

```
#include <string.h>

struct buffer {
  char data[255];
  int cursor;
```

```
    void init(char *s);
    inline int len(void);
    inline char *contents(void); // Now declared inline
};

void buffer::init(char *s)
{
  strcpy(data, s); cursor = 0;
}

inline char *buffer::contents(void)
{
  if (len()) return data; else return 0;
}

inline int buffer::len(void) { return cursor; }
```

1. *There is an error here, but it might not be what you think. We forgot to include the body for* **len()** *inside the class declaration when we declared* **len()** *inline, even though we provided the body later. Surprisingly, Turbo C++ won't care about that until we actually try to use* **len()** *inside* **contents().** *There, it can't find the body to expand in the call.*

   Had we not called **len()** *in* **contents(),** *the class would have compiled fine. It would have also worked had we switched around the two functions, and given the full definition of* **len()** *before* **contents().**

2. *This will work. Even though you're supposed to define the body of an inline function when you declare it, here's a case where you can get away with not doing so. That's because* **len()** *and* **contents()** *were both declared inline. Turbo C++ is able to expand the call to* **len()** *inside* **contents()** *in this case. However, it's probably better to re-write the class as follows:*

```
#include <string.h>

struct buffer {
  char data[255];
  int cursor;
  void init(char *s);
  int len(void) { return cursor; }
  char *contents(void) {
    if (len()) return data; else return 0;
  }
};

void buffer::init(char *s)
{
  strcpy(data, s); cursor = 0;
}
```

You might complain that class declarations can get too crowded this way, because the inline functions inside them might take a lot of code. If that's the case, the functions shouldn't be inline anyway.

Sample Class Revisited

To summarize what has been discussed in this chapter, let's make a few improvements to our **circular_num** class, and write a complete example using it. Listings 6.1, 6.2, and 6.3 give the program.

The program uses a **circular_num** object to cause portions of a character string to be repeated. You input a string, and then specify what portion of the string you'd like repeated, and how many characters to output. The program then builds the appropriate **circular_num** object to use as an index for the string. Figure 6.7 shows this index in action. To keep our program simple, no error checking is done on the values input.

To make our **circular_num** class a little more high level, we've added three more member functions: **add()**, **inc()**, and **dec()**. It turns out that these functions are really just special cases of calling **set()**. As such, they make great candidates as inline functions.

Listing 6.1. The circular.h File

```
// circular.h: circular number class declaration

#ifndef H_CIRCULAR
#define H_CIRCULAR
```

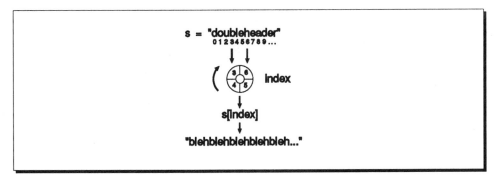

Figure 6.7. A Circular Number in Action

```
class circular_num {
private:
  int num;
  int upper, lower, range;
public:
  void set_limits(int l, int u);
  int set_val(int v);
  int get_val(void)  { return num; }
  int high_val(void) { return upper; }
  int low_val(void)  { return lower; }
  int add(int v)     { return set_val(num + v); }
  int inc(void)      { return add(1); }
  int dec(void)      { return add(-1); }
};

#endif
```

Listing 6.2. The circular.cpp File

```
// circular.cpp: circular number class implementation

#include "circular.h"

void circular_num::set_limits(int l, int u)
{
  upper = u; lower = l;
  range = u - l + 1;
}

int circular_num::set_val(int v)
// Set the value, wrapping to keep it in range
{
  while(v > upper) v -= range;
  while(v < lower) v += range;
  return num = v; // Record and return result
}
```

Listing 6.3. The cnumtst.cpp Program

```
// cnumtst.cpp: test program for circular number class

#include <stdio.h>
#include "circular.h"

main()
{
  circular_num index;
  char s[80];
```

```
int start, fin, n;

printf("Enter string: ");
gets(s);
printf("Enter starting and ending index of substring: ");
scanf("%d %d", &start, &fin);
index.set_limits(start, fin);
index.set_val(start);
printf("Enter number of spaces you need to fill: ");
scanf("%d", &n);
for (; n>0; n--) { // Do the repeated substring fill
    putchar(s[index.get_val()]);
    index.inc();
}
putchar('\n');
}
```

Summary

This chapter is probably the most important chapter in this book, because it introduces you to classes. It's with classes that C++ programs start to diverge from C programs in significant ways. We've discussed how classes allow you to elegantly express and work with abstract data types in ways that a C programmer can only dream about.

Part of what makes classes hard to emulate in C is the encapsulation. It's difficult to control access to members of structures in C, but it's easy in C++ through the use of private members and access functions. Many times in C, you'll forgo using access functions because the overhead is too great. However, C++ allows for efficient encapsulation through the use of inline member functions, giving you the the best of both worlds.

Now that you know the basics of defining classes, in Chapter 7 you'll learn how to take those classes and create and initialize objects from them.

Exercises

1. Consider a stack as an abstract data type. Define a simple class implementing a stack of 100 characters. What are the two operations that every stack should perform? Try to implement the class as efficiently as possible using inline member functions where appropriate.
2. Turn your stack class in Question 1 into an equivalent C program. Don't worry about using data hiding or inline functions.
3. Rewrite the stack class to use a linked list instead of an array. (Hint: Use another class to represent list nodes.) Make sure the member functions of the

list-based stack class have the same prototypes they have in the array-based version. Using this case as an example, what can you say about the benefits of encapsulation?

Answers

1. *The two basic stack operations are push() and pop(). Here's one way to define the stack class:*

```
class cstack { // A stack of characters
private:
  char data[100];  // Array holding stack data
  int top;         // Top of stack
public:
  void init(void)   { top = -1; }
  void push(char n);
  int pop(void);
  int isempty(void) { return top == -1; }
  int isfull(void)  { return top >= 99; }
};

void cstack::push(char n)
// If stack full, ignore the operation
{
  if (top < 99) data[++top] = n;
}

int cstack::pop(void)
// If stack is empty, return -1
{
  if (top == -1) return -1;
  return data[top--];
}
```

2. *Here's how we might code cstack in C:*

```
typedef struct {  /* A stack of characters      */
  char data[100]; /* Array holding stack data */
  int top;        /* Top of stack               */
} cstack;

void cstack_init(cstack *cs)
{
  cs->top = -1;
}

void cstack_push(cstack *cs, char n)
/* If stack full, ignore the operation */
```

```
{
  if (cs->top < 99) cs->data[++cs->top] = n;
}

int cstack_pop(cstack *cs)
/* If stack is empty, return -1 */
{
  if (cs->top == -1) return -1;
  return cs->data[cs->top--];
}

int cstack_isempty(cstack *cs)
{
  return cs->top == -1;
}
int cstack_isfull(cstack *cs)
{
  return cs->top >= 99;
}
```

3. *Even though the internal details of how the stack is implemented is completely different, the list-based stack appears the same to the user as the array-based stack. Thus, you have more freedom in redesigning the stack class without the risk of breaking any existing code using the stack class. Here is the list-based stack class.*

```
#include <alloc.h>

struct cnode { // Create character list node
  char c;
  cnode *prev;
};

class cstack { // A stack of characters
private:
  cnode *top;  // Top of stack
public:
  void init(void)   { top = 0; } // Make stack empty
  void push(char n);
  int pop(void);
  int isempty(void) { return top == 0; }
  // Stack never full (unless we run out of heap,
  // which we won't deal with here)
  int isfull(void)  { return 0; }
};

void cstack::push(char n)
{
  cnode *p = (cnode *)malloc(sizeof(cnode));
  p->c = n; p->prev = top; // Initialize node
  top = p;                 // Make new node the top
}
```

```
int cstack::pop(void)
{
  if (top) {
     cnode *p = top;   // Point to top
     int c = top->c;   // Retrieve character
     top = top->prev;  // Set top to prev node
     free(p); // Delete old node
     return c;
  }
  else return -1;
}
```

*We used **malloc()** and **free()** to allocate and deallocate the stack nodes. A better way is to use the operators **new** and **delete**. Chapter 7 describes how to use these operators.*

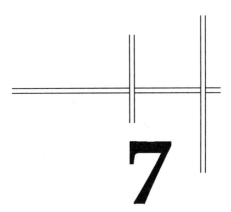

7

Creating and Initializing Objects

In Chapter 6, you learned what classes are and how to declare them. Now it's time to take the next step and learn how to declare objects from classes. Related to this process is the initialization of objects. C++ has special member functions called *constructors* that can handle such initializations automatically. Constructors have counterparts, called *destructors*, that can perform cleanup tasks when the object is to be destroyed. C++ provides two new operators to help manage objects created dynamically: **new** and **delete**. These operators work hand in hand with constructors and destructors.

There's also another way to initialize objects: use initializer lists like you can for structures and arrays in C. We'll start this chapter by discussing how to initialize objects using initializer lists, and then move on to the more powerful method of using constructors and destructors.

After completing this chapter, we'll have discussed:

- How to use C-style initializer lists
- How to use constructors and destructors
- What the special types of constructors are
- How to initialize and destroy objects composed of other objects
- How to create and initialize arrays of objects
- How to create and initialize dynamic objects

Using Initializer Lists

Recall that in C, you can initialize structures and arrays by using initializer lists. You can also use this same technique in C++. Initializer lists are enclosed in curly braces and specify the initial values for each member of a structure or array. Some examples are:

```
struct rect { int wd, ht; };
struct rect r = { 3, 5 };      /* Initializer list */

int numbers[3] = { 1, 2, 3 }; /* Another initializer list */
```

Initializer lists also work with unions, but you can only initialize the first member of a union. For example:

```
union ident { int id; char *a; };

ident x = { 1 };          /* Ok    */
ident x = { "C++"; }      /* Error */
ident x = { 1, "C++"; } /* Error */
```

In C++, you can also use initializer lists to initialize objects. However, there are some restrictions as to what type of object can be initialized with an initializer list:

1. The object can't have private members
2. The object can't have constructors
3. The object can't have virtual functions (see Chapter 9)
4. The object can't be from a derived class (see Chapter 9)

Let's look at the first restriction. If we changed the **rect** structure we gave earlier to have private members, then we couldn't use an initializer list on **rect** objects. For example:

```
struct rect {
private:
  int wd, ht;
public:
  void set(int w, int h);
};

rect r = { 3, 5 }; // Illegal, because rect has private members
```

The second restriction states that if an object has constructors, then you can't initialize the object with an initializer list. Because constructors are a new way to initialize objects, the second restriction is really a suggestion and invitation to use the new type of initialization provided by constructors. In the next section, we'll take a look at constructors.

1. Given the following **file_data** class, which of three variable declarations are legal?

```
#include <stdio.h>

struct file_data {
  FILE *f;
  char fname[80];
  int reclen;
};

file_data fd = { stdin, "file.bin", 80 };
file_data gd = { stdin, "file.bin", 80, 72 };
file_data hd = { stdout };
```

2. What if the **struct** keyword in Question 1 was replaced with the **class** keyword. Could you still use an initializer list for **fd**?

1. *The first declaration is legal. The second list has too many initializers, and the third is legal, even though it doesn't have enough initializers. For the latter declaration, the file pointer would be set to **stdout**, and the other members of the structure would be set to a default value of zero.*
2. *Only if we explicitly declared the class members public, as in:*

```
class file_data {
public:
  FILE *f;
  char fname[80];
  int reclen;
};

file_data fd = { stdin, "mytest.dat", 80 };
```

Constructors

Constructors are C++'s answer to initializer lists. They provide a more powerful, more general way to initialize an object. Constructors can not only set values for the members of the object, they can perform other kinds of operations as well, such as allocate dynamic memory, open files, and so on.

A constructor is a special member function that has the same name as the class it's a member of. Figure 7.1 shows the components of a constructor. As you can see from Figure 7.1, a constructor has all the elements that any member function has, except it has no return type.

Let's take the **circular_num** class from Chapter 6 and give it a constructor:

```
class circular_num {
private:
  int num;
  int upper, lower, range;
public:
  circular_num(int v, int l, int u); // Constructor
  int set_val(int v);
  int get_val(void)   { return num; }
  int high_val(void)  { return upper; }
  int low_val(void)   { return lower; }
  int add(int v)      { return set_val(num + v); }
  int inc(void)       { return add(1); }
  int dec(void)       { return add(-1); }
};

circular_num::circular_num(int v, int l, int u)
// Body of constructor: sets value and limits of number
{
  upper = u; lower = l; // Initialize limits first
  range = u - l + 1;    // Compute range
  set_val(v);           // Then set value
}

int circular_num::set_val(int v)
// Set the value, wrapping to keep it in range
{
```

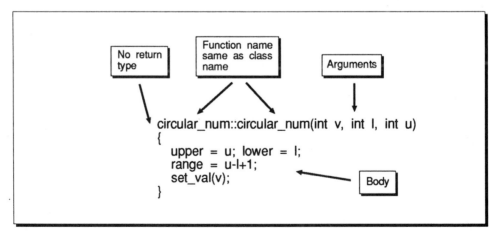

Figure 7.1. Components of a Constructor

```
    while(v > upper) v -= range;
    while(v < lower) v += range;
    return num - v; // Record and return result
}
```

Note that we've replaced the **set_limits()** function with the new constructor. This constructor initializes both the range and value of the number. A constructor can not only have assignment statements, it can also call other functions, as we did when calling **set_val()**.

Tip || Don't try to perform too many tasks with a constructor. A constructor should only be concerned with initializing values for an object. It shouldn't be performing the main task of the object.

Calling Constructors

Constructors are called when objects are declared. One way to use a constructor is to make a direct call to it, as in:

```
circular_num cn = circular_num(0, 0, 9);
```

Here, **cn** is declared to be a **circular_num** object, and is then initialized to have its value set to 0 and its limits set to 0 and 9. The initialization takes place in the call to the **circular_num()** constructor.

There is actually a shorter way to call the **circular_num** constructor:

```
circular_num cn(0, 0, 9);
```

With this syntax, it looks as though we're calling the function **cn()**, but we're not. Instead, the **circular_num** constructor is called with the arguments given in the argument list. Figure 7.2 illustrates what is happening.

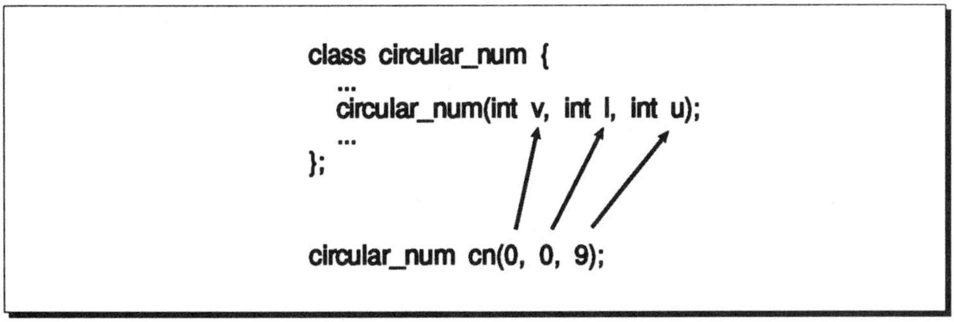

```
class circular_num {
    ...
    circular_num(int v, int l, int u);
    ...
};

circular_num cn(0, 0, 9);
```

Figure 7.2. Shorter Method for Calling Constructors

You might wonder when constructors are actually called. The constructor for an object is called when the declaration for the object is encountered during program execution. The constructor for a global object is called when the program starts, just before **main()** is entered.

If you have multiple global objects in your program, it can be tricky figuring out what order the objects' constructors are called. When your program is a single file, the constructors are executed in the order the object declarations appear in the file. However, when your program is composed of multiple files, each containing constructor calls, there is no guarantee which set of constructors is called first.

Tip || It's best not to rely on the order that global objects' constructors are called. In particular, try not to have one global object constructor use objects created from another global constructor.

Having constructors coupled with object declarations makes your objects more robust. For instance, since we gave the **circular_num** class a constructor, we can now guarantee that a **circular_num** object will be initialized properly before being used. It's no longer possible to set the value of a **circular_num** object before defining what its limits are.

Constructors with Default Arguments

Like any function, a constructor can have default arguments. For example, let's modify the **circular_num** constructor to use default limits of (0, 9):

```
class circular_num {
  ...
  circular_num(int v, int l=0, int u=9);
  ...
};

void circular_num::circular_num(int v, int l, int u)
// Body of constructor: sets value and limits of number
{
  upper = u; lower = l; // Initialize limits first
  range = u - l + 1;    // Compute range
  set_val(v);           // Then set value
}
```

As with any member function having default arguments, note that we specify the default arguments in the class declaration, but not in the implementation of the function itself.

Here's how you can call the new constructor having default arguments:

```
circular_num cn(0); // Set num = 0, use default limits
```

There's actually an alternate syntax available:

```
circular_num cn = 0; // Set num = 0, use default limits
```

This declaration looks like an ordinary initialization, such as one we might use to initialize an integer. However, as Figure 7.3 illustrates, what's really happening is that the **circular_num** constructor is called with the first argument set to 0, and the other two set to their defaults.

You can use this alternate syntax any time your constructor requires only one argument to be specified. That is, you can use it on constructors taking only one argument, constructors taking all default arguments, or as in the case just shown, constructors taking one nondefault argument followed by a set of default arguments.

If you have a constructor taking all default arguments, then you may drop the parenthesis when making an implicit constructor call. For instance, if we change our constructor to

```
class circular_num {
  ...
  circular_num(int v=0, int l=0, int u=9); // All default
  ...
};
```

then we can declare a **circular_num** object as follows:

```
circular_num cn; // Use all defaults
```

You may also drop the parenthesis for constructors that take no arguments at all.

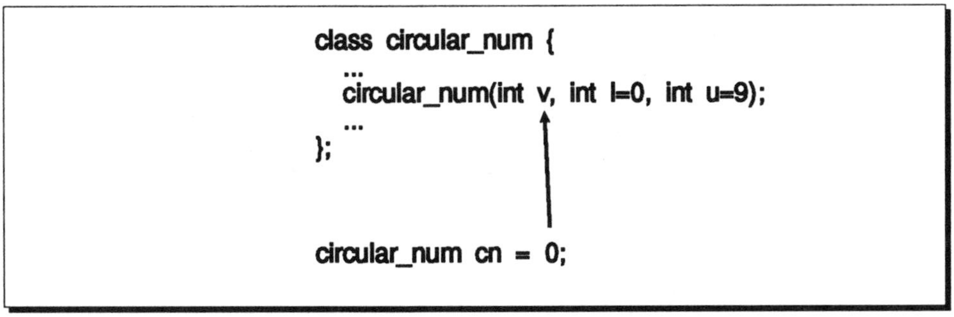

Figure 7.3. Calling a Constructor With One Required Argument

Dropping the parenthesis only works for short-hand declarations. For full declarations, the parenthesis must still be used:

```
circular_num cn;                      // Doesn't need parenthesis
circular_num cn = circular_num(); // Needs parenthesis
```

Restrictions on Constructors

There are two basic restrictions on the use of constructors:

- Constructors cannot have a return type, not even **void**
- Constructors cannot be virtual

Note that the **circular_num** constructors presented earlier don't have a return type. In order to understand the second rule, you need to learn about virtual functions, which we'll discuss in Chapter 9.

There is another caveat about using constructors. In almost all cases, you'll want to make your constructors public. There are only two ways a private constructor can be called: by another member function of the class itself, and by *friend functions* of the class. Thus, only members and friends can create objects from a class with private constructors. Because of this, classes with private constructors are called *private classes*. You'll learn how to use friend functions and private classes in Chapter 8.

Overloaded Constructors

A class may have more than one constructor. For example, suppose we have a **clock** class that stores the time in seconds. We could have a **clock** constructor that takes a single argument for the desired seconds, and a another constructor that accepts hours, minutes, and seconds. The following **clock** class provides an example:

```
// clock.h: Clock header file

#ifndef H_CLOCK
#define H_CLOCK

class clock {
private:
  long seconds;
```

```
public:
  clock(long s);                   // One constructor
  clock(int h, int m, int s);      // Another constructor
  void set(int h, int m, int s);   // Set hours, min, sec
  void tick(void) { seconds++; }   // Tick the clock
  void hms(int &h, int &m, int &s); // Convert back to hms
};

#endif

// clock.cpp: Clock implementation file

#include "clock.h"

clock::clock(long s)
// Initialize the clock with specified seconds
{
  seconds = s;
}

clock::clock(int h, int m, int s)
// Initialize the clock to the specified hours,
// minutes and seconds
{
  set(h, m, s);
}

void clock::set(int h, int m, int s)
// Set the clock by storing the time in seconds
{
  seconds = (long)h*3600L + (long)m*60L + (long)s;
}

void clock::hms(int &h, int &m, int &s)
// Function to convert internal seconds back to
// (h,m,s) format
{
  long th = seconds / 3600L;
  h = int(th);
  long ts = seconds - th*3600L;
  long tm = ts / 60L;
  m = int(tm);
  ts -= tm*60L;
  s = int(ts);
}
```

Note that each constructor has the same name: **clock()**. Recall that functions with the same name are called *overloaded functions*. It's perfectly legal to have overloaded constructors. As with any overloaded function, the arguments to overloaded constructors must be different enough so that the compiler can distinguish between the various constructors. Figure 7.4 illustrates this point.

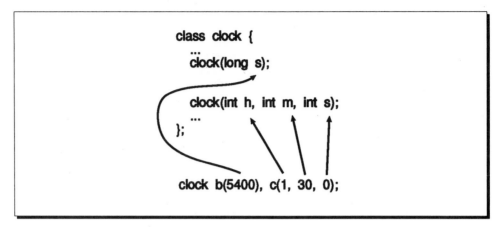

Figure 7.4. Calling Overloaded Constructors

The following program shows examples of using the two **clock** constructors:

```
#include <stdio.h>
#include "clock.h"

main()
{
  int h, m, s;
  clock b(5400);  // Set to 5400 seconds
  clock c(1,30,0); // Set to 1:30:00 (which = 5400 seconds)

  b.tick();        // Tick both clocks
  c.tick();

  b.hms(h, m, s);
  printf("Clock b's time is: %02d:%02d:%02d\n", h, m, s);
  c.hms(h, m, s);
  printf("Clock c's time is: %02d:%02d:%02d\n", h, m, s);
  return 0;
}
```

The output from this program is:

```
Clock b's time is: 01:30:01
Clock c's time is: 01:30:01
```

Using Constructors with Unions

Recall that initializing unions using an initializer list is limited, since only the first member of the union can be initialized. However, it's possible to initialize any member of the union using constructors.

How do you specify which member is to be initialized? The trick is to use overloaded constructors, one for each member of the union. For example, the following is an integer list node class that holds either a pointer to the next node in the list, or an integer:

```
union intnode {
  intnode *next;
  int n;
  intnode(intnode *n) { next = n; }
  intnode(int i) { n = i; }
};
```

In the following, we have two constructors, one taking an **intnode** pointer, and one taking an **int**. Depending on which constructor is called, the corresponding member will be initialized:

```
intnode inode(42);      // Initialize member n
intnode jnode(&inode);  // Initialize member next
```

1. Fix the following class declaration:

```
class point {
  int x, y;
  void point(int xi, int yi) { x = xi; y = yi; }
};
```

2. Given the following program, do you think the statement in **main()** is legal?

```
struct point {
  int x, int y;
  point(int xi, int yi) { x = xi; y = yi; }
};

main()
{
  point(25, 14); // Is this legal?
}
```

3. Given what you just learned in Question 2, what does the following program print out?

```
#include <stdio.h>

struct point {
  int x, int y;
  point(int xi, int yi) { x = xi; y = yi; }
  point(int z)          { point(z, z); }
};
```

```
main()
{
  point p(25);
  printf("x - %d, y - %d\n", p.x, p.y);
}
```

---

1. *There are two problems. First, the constructor has a **void** return type, but it shouldn't have any return type. Second, the class has no public members. Even the constructor is private. No object can be created from the class because the constructor can never be called. A valid declaration for **point** is:*

```
class point {
public: // Need public members
  int x, y;
  point(int xi, int yi); // No return type
};
```

2. *Yes. An unnamed temporary **point** object is created.*
3. *Surprisingly, the output is unpredictable. The call to the two-argument constructor inside the one-argument constructor creates a unnamed **point** object, as you learned in Question 2. This object has nothing to do with the object **p**, so the **x** and **y** variables for **p** never get initialized.*

   *A rule emerges from this example: Don't call constructors by themselves as you would other functions. Constructors calls should only be used in conjunction with object declarations. To fix the problem in the **point** class, you could introduce another member function that sets the coordinates. This function is to be used by both constructors:*

```
struct point {
  int x, int y;
  point(int xi, int yi)    { set(xi, yi); }
  point(int z)             { set(z, z);   }
  void set(int xi, int yi) { x - xi; y - yi; }
};
```

Special Constructors

You've seen how constructors can take a variety of argument types. Constructors can be classified into four different groups, depending on the type of arguments they have. Table 7.1 lists the four basic kinds of constructors. In the table, **X** stands for some class name (i.e., a type), and **T** stands for a type different from **X**.

Table 7.1. The Different Types of Constructors

Prototype	Description
X(void)	Default constructor
X(X&,...), X(const X&,...)	Copy constructor, if other arguments have defaults
X(T, ...), X(T&, ...) X(const T, ...) X(const T&, ...)	Type conversion constructor, if other arguments have defaults
X(T1, T2, ...)	General constructor

The first three constructor types have special uses. Let's now take a look at the default, copy, and type conversion constructors.

Default Constructors

A *default constructor* is a constructor that takes no arguments. Note that a constructor in which all the arguments are default arguments is not a default constructor. For example:

```
clock::clock(void)        // Default constructor
clock::clock(long s = 0); // Not a default constructor
```

Default constructors are useful when you wish to be able to implicitly initialize objects of the class. For example:

```
clock c; // Uses default constructor
```

Tip || Default constructors are useful when declaring arrays of objects, as you'll see later in this chapter.

Copy Constructors

A *copy constructor* is a constructor whose first argument is a reference to the same type as the class itself. (It can be a constant reference, too.) If more arguments are present, then they must all be default arguments in order for the constructor to be a copy constructor. Some copy constructors are:

```
clock::clock(clock &c);            // A copy constructor
clock::clock(const clock &c);      // A copy constructor
clock::clock(clock &c, int h=12);  // A copy constructor
```

Copy constructors are used to initialize one object with another object of the same class. For instance, a copy constructor for our **clock** class is:

```
clock::clock(clock &c)
// A copy constructor
{
  seconds = c.seconds;
}
```

Here's how you might call it:

```
clock c1(3, 30, 0); // Set c1 to 3:30
clock c2 = c1;      // Call copy constructor to set
                    // c2 to same time as c1
```

As Figure 7.5 shows, **c2** is initialized through the copy constructor, and is set to the same time as **c1**.

If you have a class without a copy constructor, and you initialize an object from that class with another object of the same class, then a default copy constructor will be generated for you. This constructor will do a memberwise copy of the source object. That is, the members are copied one at a time, in the order they are declared in the class. For instance, if you initialize one **circular_num** object with another, as in:

```
circular_num cn1(180, 0, 359);
circular_num cn2 = cn1; // Use default copy constructor
```

then code such as the following is generated:

```
cn2.num = cn1.num;   // Do a memberwise copy
cn2.upper = cn1.upper;
```

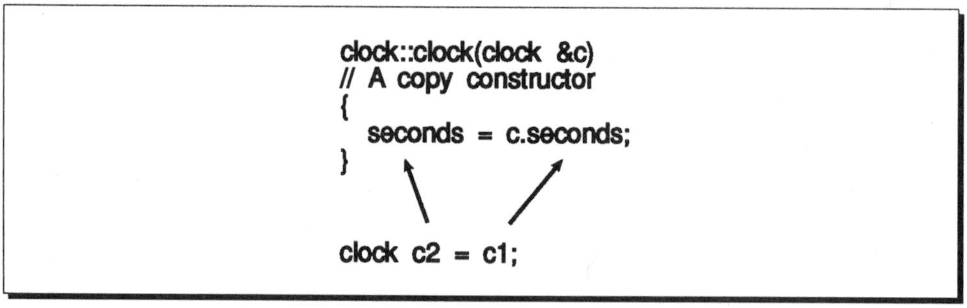

Figure 7.5. Calling a Copy Constructor

```
cn2.lower = cn1.lower;
cn2.range = cn1.range;
```

Recall that objects can be passed by reference or by value to functions. If you pass an object by value, a temporary copy of the object is made by calling the copy constructor for the object. If the object's class has no copy constructor, then a default copy constructor is used.

For example, in the following function, the copy constructor for **clock** is called twice, once when passing the clock argument, and once when returning the clock value. Thus, two temporary objects are created.

```
clock set_ahead(clock c, int seconds)
// Clock passed by value, and returned by value
{
  for (int i = 0; i<seconds; i++) c.tick();
  return c;
}
```

Type Conversion Constructors

A *type conversion constructor* is a constructor whose first argument is of a type different from the class itself. If other arguments are present, then they must all be default arguments in order for the constructor to be a type conversion constructor. One of our **clock** constructors does a type conversion:

```
clock::clock(long s) { seconds = s; }
```

In this case, the constructor converts a **long** integer into a **clock** object. For example:

```
clock c;  // Declare a clock

c = clock(3600L); // Convert a long integer to a clock
                  // object, and initialize c with it
```

In addition, our **circular_num** class has a type conversion constructor. Even though its constructor takes three arguments, the last two are defaults, thus qualifying the constructor as a type conversion constructor:

```
class circular_num {
  ...
  circular_num(int v, int l = 0, int u = 9);
};

circular_num cn = 17;
```

The **circular_num** constructor converts an integer into a **circular_num** object. (In this case, the value 17 gets changed to 7, in order to keep the number in range between 0 and 9.)

1. Classify the following constructors, based on their prototypes:

   a. rect::rect(int w, int h);
   b. node::node(void);
   c. calculator::calculator(float *ival = 0.0);
   d. string::string(string &s);
   e. bcd::bcd(float f);

2. How many times would the **clock** copy constructor be called for a call to the following function?

   ```
   clock &set_ahead(clock &c, int seconds)
   {
     for (int i = 0; i<seconds; i++) c.tick();
     return c;
   }
   ```

3. Given a **clock** object **c** with a constructor taking a long integer as an argument, do you suppose the following syntax is legal? (Hint: look where the parentheses are placed.)

   ```
   c = (clock)(4576L); // Is this legal?
   ```

1. *The answers are:*

   a. *general constructor*
   b. *default constructor*
   c. *type conversion constructor*
   d. *copy constructor*
   e. *type conversion constructor*

   *Note that the **calculator** constructor in c is a type conversion constructor, not a default constructor. Default constructors take no arguments, not even default arguments. The **calculator** constructor converts a floating point number into a calculator object.*

2. *None. The **clock** object is passed by reference and returned by reference.*

3. *Yes. Since the constructor takes one argument that isn't of the same type as the class, then it is a type conversion constructor. Recall that you can specify type conversions in one of two ways in C++:*

```
(new_type)(old_data); // C style type conversion
```

or

```
new_type(old_data);   // New C++ style type conversion
```

Destructors

Destructors are the counterpart to constructors. They are used to perform cleanup activities for an object that's no longer needed. Typically, destructors are used to deallocate dynamic memory that might have been allocated by a constructor, although they can be used for anything you wish.

A destructor has the same name as the class it belongs to, except the name is preceded by a tilde '~' character. Figure 7.6 shows the components of a destructor. As an example, let's create a **string** class that stores a character array dynamically. The array is allocated by a constructor and deallocated by a destructor:

```
class string {
private:
  char *text;                 // Pointer to character array
  int len;                    // Allocated size
public:
  string(char *s, int ofs = 0); // Constructor
  ~string(void);              // Destructor
```

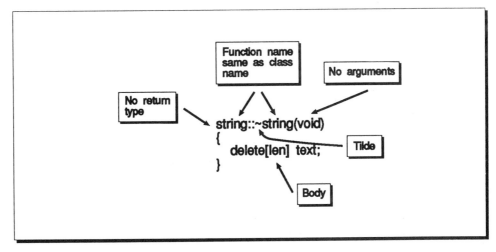

Figure 7.6. Components of a Destructor

```
  char *contents(void);           // Access function to text
};

string::string(char *s, int ofs = 0)
// Converts a null-terminated C string into a string
{
  s += ofs;
  len = strlen(s) + 1;
  text = new char[len]; // Call new to allocate space
  char *p = text;
  while(1) { // Copies null byte too
   *p++ = *s;
   if (*s) break; else s++;
  }
}


string::~string(void)
// Destructor to de-allocate memory allocated by
// the constructor
{
  delete[len] text; // Note use of delete
}
```

In this example, **new** is used to allocate space for the string in the constructor, and **delete** is used to de-allocate the space for the string in the destructor. These two special dynamic memory management operators will be discussed shortly.

Note ‖ Destructors are used mainly to de-allocate any dynamic memory allocated by ‖ an object.

The destructor for an object is called when the program execution leaves the scope of the object. For instance, an object declared local to a function has its destructor called just before the function returns. The destructor of a static object is called just before the program exits. The order is the reverse that the constructors were called. Different rules exist for objects created dynamically on the heap, as you'll learn later in this chapter.

There are three basic restrictions in declaring destructors:

- A class can't have more than one destructor
- Destructors can't have any arguments
- Destructors can't have a return type, not even **void**

As with constructors, you almost always want to make your destructors public. If the destructor of a class is private (thus making the class a private class), then only member functions or friend functions of the class can use objects from the class. (See Chapter 8 for an example.)

1. Can you spot three mistakes with the destructor in the following class declaration?

```
class image {
  char *bits;
  int wd, ht;
  image(int w, int h);
  void ~image(char *destruct_msg);
};
```

2. Given what you've learned about overloaded functions, can you guess why a class can't have more than one destructor?

1. *The destructor can't have a return type, it can't have arguments, and it is private. (No public keyword was used in the class, thus all the members are private.)*
2. *Since destructors can't have arguments, there's no way to overload a destructor. Remember that the compiler uses argument types to determine which overloaded function to call. Thus, how can the compiler tell two overloaded destructors apart?*

Creating and Destroying Complex Objects

The examples we've shown thus far involved simple objects that had built-in types for instance variables, such as integers and characters. You can, however, have classes whose members are other objects. For these more complex classes, there is the issue of how to initialize and destroy the member objects. In this section, we'll learn how this can be done.

Using Member Initialization Lists

There are actually two ways to initialize the members of an object when using a constructor. You've seen how to initialize members of an object by using assignment statements in the body of the constructor. However, there's another way by using *member initialization lists*. You can use such lists to not only initialize simple members, but also to initialize member objects having constructors. We'll start by first showing how simple members are initialized.

A member initialization list, which contains a list of members to be initialized, appears after the argument list of a constructor and before the constructor body. The list is denoted using the : operator as shown in Figure 7.7. Here's an example using our familiar **point** class:

```
struct point {
  int x, y;
  point(int xi, int yi);
};

point::point(int xi, int yi)
: x(xi), y(yi) // Member initialization list
{
  return; // Nothing else to do
}
```

The second line of the constructor is the member initialization list. Note how we call out each member by name, and pass an argument to it. The arguments represent what values to assign to the members. That is, we're assigning **xi** to **x**, and **yi** to **y**. Since we initialized both members of the **point** class in the member initialization list, there's nothing left for the body of the constructor to do, so it simply returns.

You can also use member initialization lists with constructors declared inline. For instance,

```
struct point {
  int x, y;
  point(int xi, int yi) : x(xi), y(yi) { return; }
};
```

This example shows that you don't need to place the member initialization list on a separate line. All you need to do is use the : operator and place the list between the arguments and the constructor body.

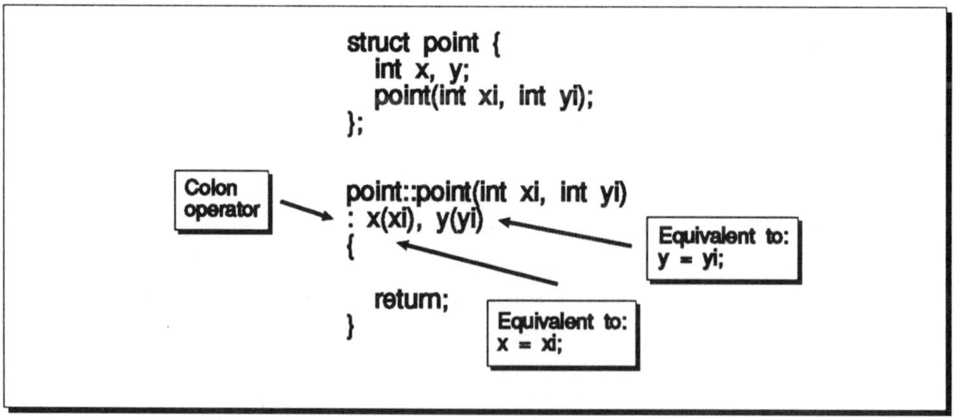

Figure 7.7. A Member Initialization List

In these examples, **x** and **y** were initialized with simple expressions: the values of the arguments **xi** and **yi** passed to the constructor. However, you can initialize members using virtually any expression. For instance, we might modify our **point** constructor to handle a different convention for the origin, where the origin starts at (1,1) instead of (0,0):

```
point::point(int xi, int yi) : x(xi+1), y(yi+1) { return; }
```

Or, we might simply have a default constructor and initialize the coordinates to (0,0):

```
point::point(void) : x(0), y(0) { return; }
```

Initialization Order

You can initialize a member with the value of another member in a member initialization list. For instance, we might initialize **y** with the value of **x** in our **point** constructor:

```
point::point(void)
: x(0), y(x) // Initialize y with x
{
    return;
}
```

While this works here, it is not recommended in most cases. The reason is that you have to rely on the order that the members are initialized. For instance, we have to be sure that x is initialized before y. But just what order are members initialized?

It turns out that the initialization order depends on the order that the members are declared in the class, not in the order that they are specified in the member initialization list. That is, had we said:

```
point::point(void)
: y(x), x(0) // x is still initialized first
{
    return;
}
```

where **y** was specified first, it would not have made a difference. Member **x** would still be initialized first, since it was declared first in the class.

Tip

Try not to rely on the order that member objects are initialized when using member initialization lists. If you find yourself relying on that order, you might want to rethink the design of your class. Chances are there is a better way to design it.

Another case where initialization order is important is when you have some members initialized in the member initialization list, and others in the body of the constructor. For example:

```
point::point(int xi, int yi)
: x(xi)    // Initialize x here
{
   y = yi; // Initialize y here
}
```

You might wonder: Does it matter where we specify the initialization of a member? Yes. The difference lies in when the initialization takes place. It's important to realize that the member initialization list is executed after the arguments have been passed, but *before* the body of the constructor executes. In this example, therefore, x is initialized first, and y second.

In many cases, you don't need to use a member initializer list at all. However, there are times when you do, as you'll now learn.

Chaining Constructor Calls

If the members of a class are more than just simple types, and instead are objects belonging to classes with constructors, then the constructors for these objects must be called. Member initialization lists provide a way to call these constructors.

Let's see an example. Suppose we take our **point** class and build a rectangle class from it. We'll use two nested **point** objects to specify the upper-left- and lower-right-hand corners of the rectangle:

```
struct point {
   int x, int y;
   point(int xi, int yi) { x = xi; y = yi; }
};

struct rect {
   point ulc; // Upper-left-hand corner
   point lrc; // Lower-right-hand corner
   rect(int xul, int yul, int xlr, int ylr);
};

rect::rect(int xul, int yul, int xlr, int ylr)
: ulc(xul, yul), lrc(xlr, ylr) // Initialize embedded objects
{
   return;
}
```

Note how the constructors are called in the member initialization list for each nested point. Figure 7.8 illustrates the process.

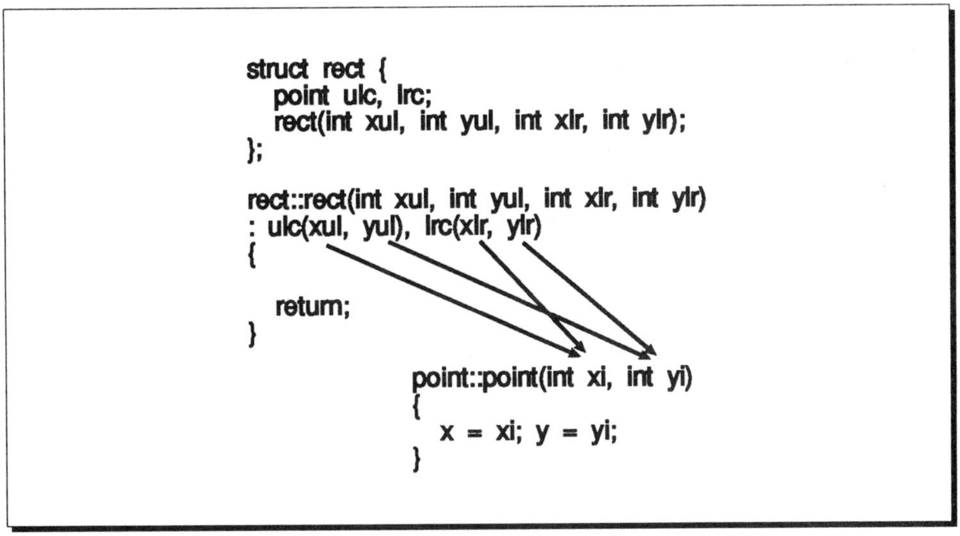

```
struct rect {
    point ulc, lrc;
    rect(int xul, int yul, int xlr, int ylr);
};

rect::rect(int xul, int yul, int xlr, int ylr)
: ulc(xul, yul), lrc(xlr, ylr)
{

    return;
}

                    point::point(int xi, int yi)
                    {
                        x = xi; y = yi;
                    }
```

Figure 7.8. Calling Constructors for Member Objects

As was the case with the initialization of simple members, the order that constructors in member initialization lists are called depends on the order that the member objects are declared in the class, and not in the order of the constructor calls in the list.

There are certain times when you don't need to explicitly call the constructor for a member object: If one of the constructors is a default constructor, or a constructor with all default arguments, then you don't have to initialize the object in the member initialization list. The constructor requiring no arguments will be called for you.

Pointers, References, and Constants as Members

If a member is a pointer to an object, rather than an object itself, you don't call the constructor for that member in the member initialization list. Constructors aren't called for pointers to objects, they are called for objects. Of course, somewhere there has to be an object for the pointer to reference. This object will have its constructor called when it is created. Later on, you'll see how to use pointers in conjunction with constructors.

It's possible for a member to be a reference to another object. In this case, the reference *must* be initialized at the time the object containing the reference is created. The way to do this (in fact, the *only* way) is by initializing the reference in the member initialization list. For example:

```
struct bizarre_type {
  int real_mcoy;
  int &just_a_shadow;
  bizarre_type(int rm);
};

bizarre_type::bizarre_type(int rm)
: real_mcoy(rm), just_a_shadow(real_mcoy)
{
  return;
}
```

In this example, the integer reference **just_a_shadow** is initialized to refer to another member, **real_mcoy**, which was itself initialized with the argument **rm**.

A similar situation occurs when you have members that are declared constant. Like references, constants must be initialized when they are declared. Again, the way to do this is in the member initialization list, as shown here:

```
struct array {
  char *text;
  const int size;   // Constant member
  array(int sz);
  ~array(void) { delete[size] text; }
};

array::array(int sz)
: size(sz) // Initialize constant
{
  text = new char[size];
}
```

The **array** constructor takes advantage of the fact that **size** is initialized before the constructor body executes, since the member initialization list is executed before the body. Thus, it's safe to use **size** when allocating space for the text array.

Note | Since constant and reference members must be initialized in the member initialization list, this implies that a class with constant or reference members must have a constructor.

Chaining Destructor Calls

If your member objects have destructors, then those destructors must be called when the object they are contained in is destroyed. Luckily, this is done for you by the compiler.

Destructors are always called in reverse order to the way constructors are called. This means two things:

1. Member object destructors are called after the destructor of the main object has executed. If the member object is composed of other objects, this process takes place recursively.
2. Member object destructors are called in the reverse order of how the objects are declared in the class.

1. Type in and run the following program. What does it print out?

```
#include <stdio.h>

struct num {
  int n;
  num(int i) { printf("num() called: %d\n", n=i); }
  ~num(void) { printf("~num() called: %d\n", n);  }
};

struct bunch_o_nums {
  num a, b, c;
  bunch_o_nums(int x, int y, int z);
  ~bunch_o_nums(void);
};

bunch_o_nums::bunch_o_nums(int x, int y, int z)
: c(z), a(x), b(y)
{
  printf("Body of bunch_o_nums constructor called\n");
}

bunch_o_nums::~bunch_o_nums(void)
{
  printf("Body of bunch_o_nums destructor called\n");
}

main()
{
  bunch_o_nums bon(1, 2, 3);
  return 0;
}
```

2. Type in and run this program. What does it print out?

```
#include <stdio.h>

struct chatty_class {
  chatty_class(void)  { printf("Constructor called\n"); }
  ~chatty_class(void) { printf("Destructor called\n"); }
};
```

```
struct another_class { chatty_class *cc; };

main()
{
  another_class ac;
}
```

1.

```
num() called: 1
num() called: 2
num() called: 3
Body of bunch_o_nums constructor called
Body of bunch_o_nums destructor called
~num() called: 3
~num() called: 2
~num() called: 1
```

*2. Nothing is printed. The constructor and destructor are not called for member cc, because cc is not a **chatty_class** object, it is a pointer to a **chatty_class** object.*

Creating Arrays of Objects

Just as you can create arrays of structures in C, you can create arrays of objects in C++. For instance, you can create an array of **point** objects:

```
struct point { int x, y; };
point triangle[3];
```

You can even initialize the array of **point** objects at the time of declaration, using a nested initializer list:

```
point triangle[3] = { {0, 0}, {5, 5}, {10, 0} };
```

The rule for determining when you can use a nested initializer list is the following: If you can use an initializer list to initialize a single object of a class, then you can also use a nested initialization list to initialize an array of objects from that class.

In the first part of the chapter we gave you the rules for determining when you could use an initializer list to initialize an object. To recap:

1. The object can't have private members
2. The object can't have constructors
3. The object can't have virtual functions
4. The object can't be from a derived class

If you're trying to create and initialize an array of objects that have at least one of the four properties listed, then you can't use an initializer list unless the objects have a constructor. In that case, you can initialize each object in the array by calling a constructor in the initializer list.

For example, suppose our **point** class has a constructor:

```
struct point {
  int x, int y;
    point(int xi, int yi) { x = xi; y = yi; }
};
```

We could initialize an array of **point** objects as follows:

```
point triangle[3] = { point(0, 0), point(5, 5), point(10, 0) };
```

Figure 7.9 contrasts the C and C++ methods for initializing arrays of points.

In the case that our class has a constructor taking a single argument, we can use a shorter syntax for each constructor call in the initializer list that specifies just the argument. For example, suppose we add another **point** constructor taking a single argument:

```
struct point {
  int x, int y;
    point(int xi, int yi) { x = xi; y = yi; }
    point(int c) { x = c; y = c; } // New constructor
};
```

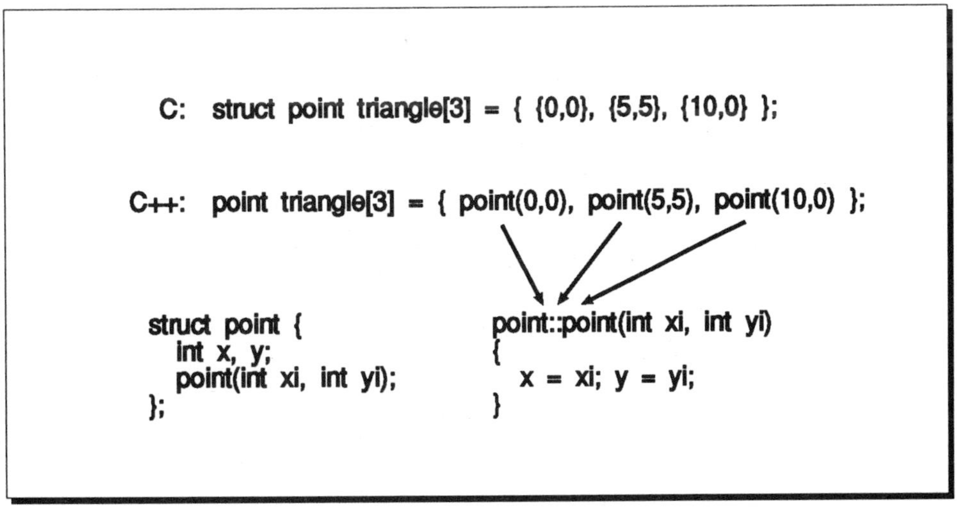

```
C:   struct point triangle[3] = { {0,0}, {5,5}, {10,0} };


C++:  point triangle[3] = { point(0,0), point(5,5), point(10,0) };




struct point {                       point::point(int xi, int yi)
  int x, y;                          {
    point(int xi, int yi);              x = xi; y = yi;
};                                   }
```

Figure 7.9. C versus C++ Method of Initializing Points

This constructor sets both **x** and **y** to the same value. Now we can initialize an array of **point** objects lying on a 45-degree angle as in the following:

```
point line45[3] = { 0, 1, 2 };
```

The numbers 0, 1, and 2 are interpreted as arguments to our single-argument **point** constructor.

You can even mix calls to both **point** constructors, as in:

```
point triangle[3] = {
    0,             // Calls point(0)
    5,             // Calls point(5)
    point(10, 0) // Calls point(10, 0)
};
```

Destructors and Arrays of Objects

If the objects in an array have destructors, then the destructors get into the act as well. Just as a constructor is called for each element when the array is built, the destructor is called for each element when the array is destroyed.

The following program illustrates this creation and destruction process. It sets up an array of objects that say hello and goodbye to you.

```
// person.cpp: Sample program illustrating arrays of objects

#include <stdio.h>
#include <string.h>

class person {
private:
   char name[20];
public:
    person(char *n);
    ~person(void) { printf("%s says goodbye\n", name); }
};

person::person(char *n)
{
   strcpy(name, n);
   printf("%s says hello\n", name);
}

main()
{
   person people[3] = { "Frank", "Katy", "Joe" };
}
```

If you run this program, you'll get the following output:

```
Frank says hello
Katy says hello
Joe says hello
Frank says goodbye
Katy says goodbye
Joe says goodbye
```

Note

The C++ 2.0 specification states that the destructors for arrays of objects should be called in reverse order to their construction. The version of Turbo C++ used for this book does not follow this rule. Otherwise, the above output would be:

```
Frank says hello
Katy says hello
Joe says hello
Joe says goodbye
Katy says goodbye
Frank says goodbye
```

Implicit Array Initialization

If your class has a default constructor, then you can have an array of objects initialized implicitly. For example:

```
struct point {
  int x, int y;
  point(void) { x = 0; y = 0; } // Default constructor
};

point pt_arr[3]; // Array elements implicitly initialized
```

In this case, the default constructor is called for each element in the array, initializing each **point** object to (0,0).

Since there's no way to specify arguments to a constructor in an implicit array initialization, you'll get a compiler error if you attempt to implicitly initialize an array of objects that have a constructor, unless the constructor is a default constructor.

Partial Array Initialization

You can have partial array initializations. For instance, in the declaration

```
int numbers[5] = { 602, 992, 5617 }
```

the fourth and fifth elements are initialized to 0, since no initializers are given for them.

Similarly, if an array of objects that have a default constructor is only partially initialized, then the default constructor is called for any elements not explicitly initialized. Given the code,

```
struct point {
  int x, y;
  point(int xi, int yi) { x = xi; y = yi; }
  point(void) { x = 0; y = 0; } // Default constructor
};

point pt_arr[4] = { point(40, 12), point(3, 5) }
```

the third and fourth elements of **pt_arr** are initialized to (0,0) by calls to the default **point** constructor.

It's an error to use a partial array initialization for an array of objects unless the object has either a default constructor, or no constructor at all. In the latter case the members of the unspecified objects are set to zero.

1. Given the following class declaration and array, why can't the array be built?

```
struct point {
  int x, int y;
  point(int a, int b) { x = a; y = b; }
};

point triangle[3]; // Why can't you do this?
```

2. Suppose we changed the constructor in Question 2 to take default arguments as given in the following declaration. Now can the array be built?

```
struct point {
  int x, int y;
  point(int a=0, int b=0) { x = a; y = b; }
};

point triangle[3]; // Can you do this?
```

3. Suppose we took out the **point** constructor in Question 2, as shown in the following class declaration. Can the array be built now?

```
struct point { int x, int y; };

point triangle[3]; // Can you do this?
```

1. *The declaration for **triangle** is invalid because the **point** class doesn't have a default constructor.*
2. *No. A constructor having default arguments is not a default constructor. You still can't build the array.*
3. *Yes. If your class has no constructors, then you can build an array of objects from it, just like you can build an array of C structures. The objects will be uninitialized, though.*

Creating Dynamic Objects

You can create objects allocated on the heap. Such objects are called dynamic objects. To manage the allocation and deallocation of dynamic objects, you use the operators **new** and **delete**. These operators go hand in hand with constructors and destructors, allowing you to write fairly robust programs involving dynamic memory. Let's take a closer look at **new** and **delete**.

The new Operator

The **new** operator can be used to allocate memory dynamically in C++. It takes the place of the C **malloc()** function. The **new** operator is superior to **malloc()** for two reasons: First, **new** knows how much memory to allocate for each type of variable; **malloc()** must be told how much to allocate. Second, **new** can cause a constructor to be called for the object to be allocated; **malloc()** cannot.

Let's look at the first case. Figure 7.10 shows equivalent uses of **new** and **malloc()**. Note how much cleaner using **new** is compared with using **malloc()**.

With **malloc()**, you have to explicitly declare how much memory to allocate, and you must use a type cast as well. Because of this, it's very easy to make mistakes with **malloc()**. With **new**, you simply specify the type of object you're creating, and **new** takes care of the rest.

Although **new** is an operator, you can call it like a function:

```
int *p = new(int);  // Called as a function
```

You can use **new** to declare arrays dynamically, as in:

```
int *p = new int[10];  // Declare array of 10 integers
```

Here's how you might declare an array of integer pointers:

```
int **p = new int*[10];  // An array of integer pointers
```

```
C method:

int *p = (int *)malloc(sizeof(int));
```

```
C++ method:

int *p = new int;
```

Figure 7.10. Using **malloc()** versus **new**

Although **new** is useful for allocating memory for variables of built-in types, its real power is in allocating dynamic objects that have constructors. When **new** is used for such objects, then one of the constructors is automatically called. For instance, here's an example of creating a dynamic **clock** object:

```
clock *c = new clock(12, 30, 45); // Allocate and initialize
```

Note how the **clock** constructor is called in conjunction with using **new**. The order of operation is: First, memory for the clock is allocated, then, the clock constructor is called.

You can allocate arrays of objects dynamically as well. For instance, we could create a dynamic array of **clocks**:

```
// Allocate 10 clocks
clock *time_pieces = new clock[10];
```

When using **new** for arrays of objects, you can't initialize the elements of the array using an initializer list. If, however, the objects have a default constructor, then the objects will be implicitly initialized by having the default constructor called for each object in the array.

As a matter of fact, if you declare an array of objects dynamically, then the objects must either have a default constructor, or no constructor at all. Otherwise, you'll get a compiler error. The reason is that there is no way to pass arguments to the constructor of the objects in the array.

The delete Operator

The **delete** operator is the counterpart to **new**, and takes the place of the C function **free()**. The **delete** operator is used to deallocate dynamic memory allocated by **new**. Here's an example of allocating and deallocating some dynamic objects:

```
int *p = new int; // Allocate integer
delete p;          // Deallocate integer
clock *c = new clock(4, 15, 55);  // Allocate clock
delete clock;                      // Deallocate clock
```

Just as **new** causes a constructor to be called for an object (if it has one), **delete** causes the destructor to be called. The order is this: first, the destructor is called, then, the memory is freed.

Tip ‖ Use **new** and **delete** rather than **malloc()** and **free()** whenever possible. The **new** and **delete** operators use type checking, and also work in conjunction with constructors and destructors.

Using **delete** is safer than using **free()** because it protects you from trying to free up memory pointed to by a null pointer. If you pass **delete** a null pointer, it simply does nothing. Try passing **free()** a null pointer, and you'll most likely mangle the heap.

Unfortunately, though, **delete** isn't as robust as it could be. The problem comes about when allocating and deallocating arrays. For instance:

```
int *my_arr = new int[10]; // Allocate 10 integers
delete my_arr; // Only one integer deallocated
```

When **new** allocates memory for an array, it does not store the size of that array. Thus, **delete** does not know how big the array is. When **delete** sees the array name **my_arr**, it treats it like a pointer, and thinks that it points to one integer. The result is that only one integer is deallocated.

To delete all the elements in an array, you must specify the array size in brackets, immediately following the **delete** keyword. For example:

```
delete[10] my_arr; // Delete array of 10 elements
```

Regrettably, this means that you must keep track of the size of the array yourself. And errors will occur if you specify the wrong size. However, the problem is mitigated by the fact that you can conveniently keep track of the size by wrapping the array up inside a class. Figure 7.11 shows an example.

```
struct int_array {
  int *data;
  int size;  // Keep track of allocated size
  int_array(int sz) { data = new int[size = sz]; }
  ~int_array(void)  { delete[size] data; }
};
```

```
                                              ┌──────────────────────┐
                                              │  Constructor sets size│
                                              │  and allocates space  │
                        struct int_array {    └──────────┬───────────┘
  ┌─────────┐             int *data;                     │
  │ Stored  │─────────▶   int size;                       ▼
  │ size    │             int_array(int sz)  { data = new int[size=sz]; }
  └─────────┘             ~int_array(void)   { delete[size] data; }
                        };
                                              ┌──────────────────────┐
                                              │  Destructor deallocates│
                                              │  space using stored size│
                                              └──────────────────────┘
```

Figure 7.11. Managing a Dynamic Array

1. Type in and run the following program. What does it output? Suggest a better way to code it.

```
#include <stdio.h>
#include <alloc.h>

class number_five {
private:
  int n;
public:
  number_five(void) { n = 5; }
  int val(void)     { return n; }
};

main()
{
  number_five *nf = (number_five *)malloc(sizeof(number_five));
  if (nf->val() == 5) printf("yes\n"); else printf("no\n");
}
```

2. If you compile the following program, what happens?

```
#include <stdio.h>

main()
{
  int *p = new char;
  *p = 15;
  printf("%d\n", *p);
}
```

1. *The output is unpredictable since the constructor for* *nf* *is never called. A better way would be to use* *new* *instead of* *malloc()*:

```
main()
{
  number_five *nf = new number_five;
  ...
}
```

Then the output would be "yes."

2. *You'll get a compiler error because we're trying to point an integer pointer to a dynamically allocated character. The* *new* *operator is smart enough to know that the types don't match.*

A Simple Window Class

It's now time to utilize what you've learned in this chapter. The program **winex.cpp**, given in Listing 7.1, creates a simple windowing system that uses many of the features of constructors and destructors.

The program builds an array of windows on the screen that you can select and type into. A separate cursor is maintained for each window. As you type into a window, the characters are displayed and the window automatically wraps the characters to the next line if needed. You can move between windows by pressing the TAB key. If you press ESC, the windows are removed and the program ends. Figure 7.12 shows how the screen looks when the program is running.

The windowing system consists of two classes: **textbuff** and **win**. These classes use many of the features you've learned about. Specifically, they use constructors, destructors, and dynamic memory. Also, the program uses another feature we've talked about: arrays of objects.

The **textbuff** class maintains a buffer used to save the image underneath each window. This class is a typical example of using dynamic memory. The class definition is:

```
class textbuff { // Class for a text image buffer
private:
  int *text;   // Pointer to buffer
  int wd, ht;  // Buffer size
public:
  textbuff(int w, int h);
  ~textbuff(void) { delete[wd*ht] text; } // Deallocate buffer
```

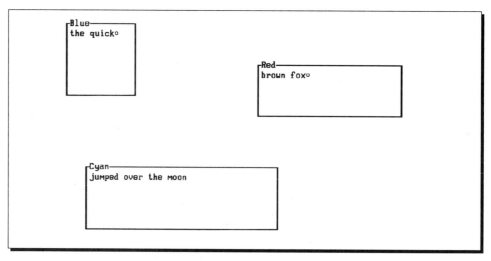

Figure 7.12. Screen from the **winex.cpp** Program

```
void get(int x, int y) { gettext(x, y, x+wd-1, y+ht-1, text); }
void put(int x, int y) { puttext(x, y, x+wd-1, y+ht-1, text); }
};
```

The text buffer is typed as an array of integers. We use integers because each element on the screen consists of two bytes: a character and an attribute. The text buffer is allocated dynamically, and is managed by the **textbuff** constructor and destructor. The size is stored in the instance variables **wd** and **ht** so that the destructor knows how much memory to delete. Two additional routines, **get()** and **put()**, are used to read and write to the screen. These routines call the Turbo C++ routines **gettext()** and **puttext()** to do the actual reading and writing.

The **win** class defines a window. It has the instance variables as illustrated in Figure 7.13. The definition for **win** is:

```
class win {    // A type-in window class
private:
  char title[40];      // Title of window
  int x, y, wd, ht;    // Location and size
  int xc, yc, color;   // Cursor coordinates, and window color
  textbuff image;      // Image save buffer
public:                // Public member
  win(char *n, int xi, int yi, int w, int h, int tcolor);
  ~win(void) { image.put(x, y); }
  void draw(void);
  void select(void);
  int type_into(void);
};
```

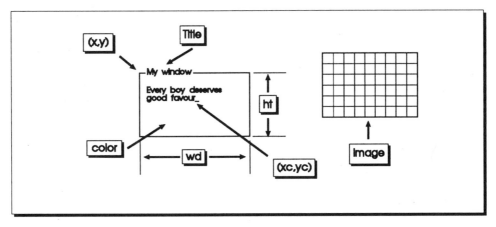

Figure 7.13. Instance Variables of a Window

The **win** class stores a title, size, location, and color for the window. In addition, the current cursor coordinates are maintained. The **win** class also contains a **textbuff** object. There are five member functions: a constructor, a destructor, and then the functions **draw()**, **select()**, and **type_into()**.

The constructor and destructor functions for **win** are:

```
win::win(char *n, int xi, int yi, int w, int h, int tcolor)
: image(w, h) // Initialize save buffer
{
  strcpy(title, n); // Copy title name
  x = xi;  y = yi;  // Set position
  wd = w; ht = h;   // Set size
  color = tcolor;   // Set color
  xc = 0; yc = 0;   // Initialize cursor
  image.get(x, y);  // Save image underneath window
  draw();           // Draw the window
  select();         // Then select it
}

win::~win(void) { image.put(x, y); }
```

The constructor first initializes the text buffer **image** by calling the **textbuff** constructor in the member initialization list. The **win** constructor then proceeds to initialize the other window variables in the body of the constructor. This is followed by a call to **image.get()** which saves the image underneath the window on the screen. The window is drawn (with a box and title) and then selected. The selection process consists of using Turbo C++'s **window()** function to change to the relative coordinates of the window.

The destructor is simple. It calls **image.put()** to restore the screen image underneath the screen. Note that the destructor for **image** is also called to deallocate the memory set aside for it. However, this happens implicitly, and only *after* the text in the image has been put back on the screen. Now you can see why the ordering of destructor calls is important for member objects.

The **main()** function is interesting, especially how it handles the construction and destruction of the array of window objects. The array is constructed with the following statement:

```
// Create an array of windows, draw them on the screen
win windows[3] = {
  win("Blue", 1, 1, 15, 8, 0x17), // 0x17 = white on blue
  win("Red", 40, 5, 30, 6, 0x40), // 0x40 = black on red
  win("Cyan", 5, 15, 40, 7, 0x30) // 0x30 = black on cyan
};
```

Note how the constructor is called for each element in the array. Since the constructor also draws as well as initializes, each window is drawn as it is created. Also, the image buffer for each window is allocated and the screen image is saved. Thus, there's more going on in the array declaration than meets the eye.

Even more interesting is how the windows are erased. If you look at **main()**, you'll note that nowhere do we explicitly erase the windows. The windows are erased when the destructor is called for each of them. Those destructor calls happen automatically at the end of the program, just before the program exits.

Listing 7.1. Example of a simple window class

```
// winex.cpp: A window class example

#include <string.h>
#include <conio.h>

const int TAB = 9;  // Some keyboard character constants
const int ESC = 27;

void fillhz(int xi, int yi, int ch, int len);
void fillvt(int xi, int yi, int ch, int len);
void putxy(int xi, int yi, int ch);

class textbuff { // Class for a text image buffer
private:
  int *text;   // Pointer to buffer
  int wd, ht;  // Buffer size
public:
  textbuff(int w, int h);
  ~textbuff(void) { delete[wd*ht] text; } // Deallocate buffer
```

```
    void get(int x, int y) { gettext(x, y, x+wd-1, y+ht-1, text); }
    void put(int x, int y) { puttext(x, y, x+wd-1, y+ht-1, text); }
};

class win {    // A type-in window class
private:
  char title[40];       // Title of window
  int x, y, wd, ht;     // Location and size
  int xc, yc, color;    // Cursor coordinates, and window color
  textbuff image;       // Image save buffer
public:                 // Public member
  win(char *n, int xi, int yi, int w, int h, int tcolor);
  ~win(void) { image.put(x, y); }
  void draw(void);
  void select(void);
  int type_into(void);
};


// Implementation for textbuff class

textbuff::textbuff(int w, int h)
// Size and allocate a text buffer
{
  wd = w; ht = h;  text = new int[wd*ht];
}


// Implementation for win class

win::win(char *n, int xi, int yi, int w, int h, int tcolor)
: image(w, h) // Initialize save buffer
{
  strcpy(title, n); // Copy title name
  x = xi;  y = yi;  // Set position
  wd = w; ht = h;   // Set size
  color = tcolor;   // Set color
  xc = 0; yc = 0;   // Initialize cursor
  image.get(x, y);  // Save image underneath window
  draw();           // Draw the window
  select();         // Then select it
}

void win::draw(void)
// Draw the window
{
  int xlr = x+wd-1;               // Compute lower-right-hand coordinates
  int ylr = y+ht-1;
  window(1, 1, 80, 25);          // Switch to absolute coordinates
  textattr(color);               // Set window color
  for (int i = 0; i<ht; i++)     // Blank window
      fillhz(x, y+i, ' ', wd);
  fillhz(x, y, 0xc4, wd);         // Draw top
  fillhz(x, ylr, 0xc4, wd);       // And bottom
  fillvt(x, y, 0xb3, ht);         // And left
```

```
    fillvt(xlr, y, 0xb3, ht);      // And right
    putxy(x, y, 0xda);             // And upper-left corner
    putxy(x, ylr, 0xc0);           // And lower-left corner
    putxy(xlr, y, 0xbf);           // And upper-right corner
    putxy(xlr, ylr, 0xd9);         // And lower-right corner
    gotoxy(x+1, y);  cputs(title); // Write title of window
}

void win::select(void)
// Change coordinates to interior of window
{
  window(x+1, y+1, x+wd-2, y+ht-2);
  gotoxy(xc, yc);    // Restore local cursor
  textattr(color); // Set window color
}

int win::type_into(void)
// Type into window until TAB or ESC key pressed
{
  int ch;
  while (1) {
    ch = getche();
    if (ch == TAB || ch == ESC) break;
  }
  xc = wherex(); // Save x cursor position
  yc = wherey(); // Save y cursor position
  return ch;      // Return last character pressed
}

// Some auxiliary nonmember functions

void fillhz(int xi, int yi, int ch, int len)
// Fill in horizontal direction
{
  gotoxy(xi, yi);  for (int i=0; i<len; i++) putch(ch);
}

void fillvt(int xi, int yi, int ch, int len)
// Fill in vertical direction
{
  for (int i=0; i<len; i++) { gotoxy(xi, yi+i); putch(ch); }
}

void putxy(int xi, int yi, int ch)
// Put a character at a given location
{
  gotoxy(xi, yi); putch(ch);
}

main()
{
    textattr(0x07); clrscr(); // Clear whole screen to white on black
```

```
// Create an array of windows, draw them on the screen
win windows[3] = {
  win("Blue", 1, 1, 15, 8, 0x17), // 0x17 = white on blue
  win("Red", 40, 5, 30, 6, 0x40), // 0x40 = black on red
  win("Cyan", 5, 15, 40, 7, 0x30) // 0x30 = black on cyan
};

// Select and type into windows until ESC pressed
for(int i = 0;;) {
  windows[i].select();
  if (windows[i].type_into() == ESC) break;
  if (i<2) i++; else i = 0; // Next window
}

textattr(0x07); // Back to white on black color
}
```

Summary

As you've seen in this chapter, constructors and destructors provide a powerful way to handle the creation and destruction of objects. At the same time, though, the old C style of initializer lists is still available in C++. The initializer lists have been extended, however, to allow constructor calls to be placed in the lists.

Constructors and destructors go hand in hand with the new memory management features of C++: specifically, the **new** and **delete** operators. These operators provide a much safer and more robust way of using dynamic memory, since they provide automatic type checking when called, and they can be used in conjunction with constructors and destructors.

Exercises

1. Given the following class and object declaration, which constructor is called?

```
class funny_num {
private:
  int num;
public:
  funny_num(void)      { num = 0;    }
  funny_num(int n = 0) { num = n;    }
  int val(void)        { return num; }
};

funny_num f;
```

2. Given the following class declaration and function, which constructors are called in the numbered statements?

```
class clock {
private:
  long seconds;
public:
  clock(void);
  clock(int h, int m, int s=0);
  clock(clock &c);
};
...
main()
{
  clock a(9, 30); // (1)
  clock b = a;    // (2)
  clock c;        // (3)
  c = b;          // (4)
}
```

3. Take the following C++ program and write an equivalent C program. Create equivalent C functions for the constructor and destructor, and be sure to call these functions at the appropriate times in the program.

```
#include <stdio.h>

class calculator {
public:
  float memory;
  calculator(void);
  ~calculator(void);
  float add(float f);
};

calculator::calculator(void)
{
  printf("Turning on calculator\n");
  memory = 0.0;
}

calculator::~calculator(void)
{
  printf("Turning off calculator\n");
}

float calculator::add(float f)
{
  memory += f;
  return memory;
}
```

```
main()
{
  calculator c;

  c.add(10.0);
  c.add(30.0);
  c.add(2.0);
  printf("The answer is %f\n", c.memory);
}
```

Answers

1. *Actually, neither constructor is called. You'll get a compiler error because the two overloaded constructors are ambiguous. To fix this, you must change the constructor taking a default argument to have no default, as in:*

   ```
   funny_num(int n);
   ```

2. *The answers are:*

   a. *The three-argument constructor is called, with the* **seconds** *argument defaulting to 0.*
   b. *The copy constructor is called.*
   c. *The default constructor is called.*
   d. *No constructor is called. This is an assignment, not an initialization. Constructors are only called during variable initializations.*

3. *Here's one way. Note where the C equivalents of the constructor and destructor are called:*

   ```
   #include <stdio.h>

   typedef struct { float memory; } calculator;

   void calculator_init(calculator *c)
   /* "Constructor" */
   {
     printf("Turning on calculator\n");
     c->memory = 0.0;
   }

   void calculator_done(calculator *c)
   /* "Destructor" */
   {
     printf("Turning off calculator\n");
   }
   ```

```
float calculator_add(calculator *c, float f)
{
  c->memory += f;
  return c->memory;
}

main()
{
  calculator c;          /* Declare */
  calculator_init(&c); /* Initialize (constructor call) */

  calculator_add(&c, 10.0);
  calculator_add(&c, 30.0);
  calculator_add(&c, 2.0);
  printf("The answer is %f\n", c.memory);

  calculator_done(&c); /* Cleanup (destructor call)*/
}
```

8

More Class Features

In this chapter, we'll continue our discussion of classes and talk about some of their additional features. We'll begin by discussing *static* and *const* members, which allow classes to solve a wider range of problems. In addition, we'll talk about another type of function that's almost a member function, but it isn't. This type of function is a called *friend function*. Friend functions are useful in creating classes that work in tandem. You'll learn about such *cooperating classes*, and see how they can be used to build *iterator objects*. These are special types of objects that are used to abstract the process of sequencing through a collection of objects.

After completing this chapter, the following will have been discussed.

- What static data members are and how to use them
- What static member functions are and how to use them
- What const member functions are and how to use them
- What friend functions are and how to use them
- What cooperating classes are and how to use them
- What iterator objects are and how to use them

Static Data Members

Normally, each object of a class has its own copy of the instance variables of the class. However, it's possible to define members that are shared between all

objects of the class. Such members are called *static data members*, and are declared using the **static** keyword. For example, in the following class,

```
struct string {
  char *buff;         // String buffer
  int size;           // Size of buffer
  static char eos;    // Code for end of string
  string(int sz);     // String constructor
  ~string(void);      // String destructor
  void copy(string &s); // String copy function
  void print(void);   // String print function
};
```

each object of *string* has its own array of bytes (**buff**), and its own size and
length (**size** and **len**), but all string objects share the same terminator byte code
(**eos**), since it is declared **static**. This is illustrated in Figure 8.1.

Note ‖ The use of the **static** keyword for static class members has nothing to do with
its other uses as a storage and linkage specifier. Don't be confused.

How do we set the static member **eos**? One way is to set it via some string
object, as in:

```
string s(80); // Declare 80 byte string
s.eos = '$'; // Use '$' to terminate string
```

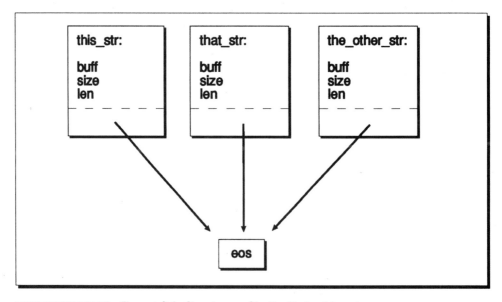

Figure 8.1. Sharing a Static Data Member

However, setting a static member through some object is somewhat misleading, since we're indirectly changing the member for all objects of the class, not just the object involved in the assignment. A better way to set a static member is by not specifying any object at all during an assignment to it. We can do this as follows:

```
string::eos = '$'; // Set string terminator
```

In this notation, we qualify the static member with the scope operator, and specify the name of the class, **string**. Note that we're using the class name, not an object name. That way, someone reading the code knows that we're changing the value for all objects of the class, and not just for one particular object.

The preceding example shows how to make an assignment to a static member. However, suppose you want the static member initialized before the program begins? You can do this by initializing the static member through a declaration. You might think this declaration would go right in the class itself, as in:

```
struct string {
  static char eos = '$';  // Illegal
  ...
};
```

but it doesn't. Instead, you make a separate declaration for the static member, outside the class. This declaration looks like an ordinary variable declaration, except the variable name is qualified with the class name. For instance,

```
struct string {          // Declare class
  static char eos;
  ...
};

char string::eos = '$';  // Initialize static member
```

As the example shows, you must specify the type of the static member in the declaration (in this case **char**), just as you would for any variable declaration.

Note || When initializing a static data member, you do not use the **static** keyword in the initialization.

Where should static declarations be placed? Just as you wouldn't put a normal variable declaration in a header file, neither should you put a static member declaration in a header file. The place you should put it is in the source file that implements the member functions of the class.

Static members do not follow the normal access rules of member functions. You can assign to and initialize a static member even if it is declared private. A private static member can't be accessed through an object, though.

1. Why not simply use global variables instead of static data members? Wouldn't they serve the same purpose?
2. What's wrong with the following initialization of the static members **xo** and **yo**?

```
struct graph_obj {
  static int xo, yo;  // Common origin
  int x, y;           // Location of object relative to origin
  graph_obj(int xi, int yi);
};

graph_obj::xo = 42;
static int yo = 17;
```

3. Suppose you placed the structure definition in Question 2, along with the (corrected) static member initializations in a header file. Explain what would happen if you included that header file in more than one source file in a multiple-file program.
4. If you made the static members in Question 2 constant, as in:

```
struct graph_obj {
  static const int xo, yo; // Common origin
  int x, y;                // Location of object relative to origin
  graph_obj(int xi, int yi);
  ...
};

const int graph_obj::xo = 42;
const int graph_obj::yo = 17;
```

do you think it would now be okay to place the static member declarations in a header file?

1. *Global variables would serve the same purpose, except their names would not be hidden inside the class, and would thus contribute to "global name-space pollution." By using static data members, you're basically getting the best of both worlds. The data members are global, but only to the objects created from the class they belong to.*
2. *In the initialization of **xo**, we forgot to specify the type of **xo**. In the initialization of **yo**, we forgot to specify the class name, and we incorrectly used the static keyword. In effect, what we did was to create a statically linked variable **yo**, instead of initializing the static data member **graph_obj::yo**. The correct initializations should read:*

```
int graph_obj::xo = 42;
int graph_obj::yo = 17;
```

3. *You would get duplicate definition errors in the linker.*
4. *Yes. Constant static member declarations can safely be placed in header files just as all constant declarations can.*

Static Member Functions

To go along with static data members, C++ provides static member functions too. Figure 8.2 shows an example. Like static data members, static member functions can be accessed both with objects, and without reference to any particular object. For example, we might add a static member function to set the origin in the **graph_obj** class given in the last section:

```
struct graph_obj {
    static int xo, yo; // Common origin
    int x, y;          // Location of object relative to origin
    graph_obj(int xi, int yi); { x = xi; y = yi; }
    // Static member function
    static void set_origin(int xs, int ys);
    void abs_coords(int &xa, int &ya);
};
```

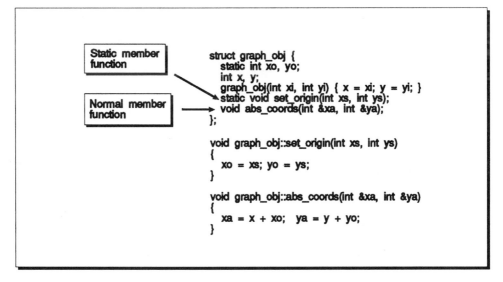

Figure 8.2. Declaring a Static Member Function

```
void graph_obj::set_origin(int xs, int ys)
{
  xo = xs; yo = ys;
}

void graph_obj::abs_coords(int &xa, int &ya)
{
  xa = x + xo;   ya = y + yo;
}

main()
{
  // Set origin for all graphic objects
  graph_obj::set_origin(0, 0);

  // Declare graphic object at location relative to origin
  graph_obj g(3, 5);
}
```

Static member functions are unlike ordinary member functions in that they have no hidden **this** argument. A side effect of this is that a static member function can directly access only other static members of the class. That's because it doesn't have any **this** pointer to access the regular members. The only way static member functions can access regular data or function members is by passing objects of the class as arguments, and accessing the members from these objects.

Even though they have no hidden **this** argument, you can still call a static function from an object, just like you can access a static data member from an object. For example:

```
graph_obj g(42, 17);

g.set_origin(12, 55); // Call static function through an object
```

You can call a static member function using the scope operator even if it is declared private. A private static member function can't be called through an object though.

---

1. What's wrong with the static member function in the following code?

```
struct array
  int data[10];
  static int first_elem(void); // Static member function
};

int array::first_elem(void)
{
  return data[0]; // Return first element of array
}
```

2. Suggest ways to get around the problem described in Question 1.
3. If a class has all static members, is it possible to use the class without ever declaring any objects from it?

---

1. *The static member function **first_elem()** is trying to access the nonstatic data member **data**.*
2. *There are two ways to fix the problem in Question 1: Either declare the function as a regular member, or pass in an array object to the function, as in:*

```
int array::first_elem(array &x)
{
    return x[0];
}
```

*Of course, declaring **first_elem()** static serves little purpose. It would be better to declare it as a regular member function.*
3. *Yes. Since static data members belong to no particular object, and static member functions can be called without using an object as well, it would be possible to use the class without ever declaring objects from it.*

Constant Member Functions

Recall that you can declare constant variables, such as:

```
const int tabsize = 8;
```

You can also declare constant objects as well, such as:

```
const clock c(12, 0, 0); // Declare clock at 12 noon
```

One problem that occurs when you can call functions from a constant object is that nothing stops those functions from changing the instance variables of the object. However, this violates the object being constant! Because of this problem, if you declare an object constant, then it is illegal to call any functions from that object, unless those functions are declared as *constant member functions*.

A constant member function is declared by placing the **const** keyword after the closing parenthesis of the argument list, as shown in Figure 8.3. In the following class, the function **val()** is a constant member function. It can be called safely from a constant object, but **twiddle()** can't.

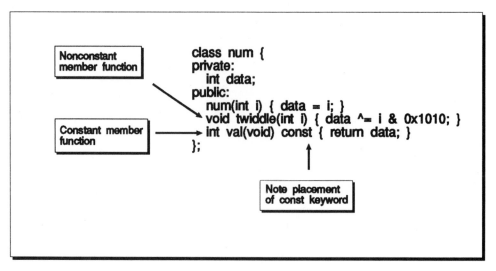

Figure 8.3. Declaring a Constant Member Function

```c
#include <stdio.h>

class num {
private:
  int data;
public:
  num(int i) { data = i; }
  void twiddle(int i) { data ^= i & 0x1010; }
  int val(void) const { return data; }
};

main()
{
  const num x(42); // Declare constant object

  x.twiddle(17);   // Illegal!
  int k = x.val(); // Okay
  printf("The num's value is %d\n", k);
}
```

You might wonder what's to stop a constant member function from modifying the instance variables of an object. As it turns out, the compiler checks for such activity inside a constant member function, and won't allow it.

Tip | You don't have to declare constructors and destructors as constant member functions. It's always legal to call constructors and destructors for constant objects.

1. Would the following class declaration compile?

```
struct num {
  int data;
  num(int i) { data = i; }
  int set(int i) const { return data = i; }
};
```

2. Suppose we modified the class in Question 1 by making **set()** nonconstant, and then adding a constant function **val()** that calls **set()**. Is the class legal now?

```
struct num {
  int data;
  num(int i)        { data = i; }
  void set(int i)   { data = i; }
  int val(void) const { return set(25); }
};
```

3. Describe what the member function **contents()** does in the following class:

```
class string {
private:
  char buffer[80];
  int len;
public:
  string(void);
  const char *contents(void) const { return buffer; }
};
```

4. What do you suppose happens when you pass a constant object to a function requiring a nonconstant object as an argument? For example:

```
class clock { ... };

void setclock(clock &c) { ... }

const clock c; // Declare constant clock

setclock(c);   // Modify the clock?
```

1. *The member function set() was declared constant, but it modifies the instance variable **data**. The compiler will flag this as an error.*
2. *No. Constant member functions cannot call nonconstant member functions of the class, as **val()** tries to do when it calls **set()**. However, constant member functions can call other constant member functions of the class.*

3. *The function* **contents()** *is a constant member function that returns a pointer to a constant character. Note how the keyword* **const** *is being used in two different places here. Not only is the function guaranteed not to change the instance variable* **buffer** *(because it's declared* **const***), no statements using the pointer returned by the function can modify* **buffer** *either.*

4. *A temporary* **clock** *object is created, and the contents of* **clock c** *are copied into this temporary object. The temporary object is then passed to the function. Even though the temporary* **clock** *is modified,* **clock c** *isn't.*

Friend Functions

Another type of function associated with classes are *friend functions*. These are functions that can bypass the access functions of a class and use the private members, even though they are not members themselves. Friend functions are meant for cases where a function works closely with a class, but for some reason, can't be a member. The most common use of friends is to make the member functions of one class friends with another class. In this manner, the first class can use the private members of the other class.

As Figure 8.4 shows, a friend function is declared much like a member function, with its prototype placed inside the class declaration. However, the prototype is preceded by the keyword **friend**. As an example, suppose we take our ever-familiar **point** class, and add a friend function to it that compares two points:

```
class point {
private:
   int x, int y; // Coordinates are private
public:
   point(int xi, yi)         { x = xi; y = yi; }
   friend int compare(point &a, point &b); // Friend function
};

int compare(point &a, point &b)
// Returns < 0 if point a is closer to the origin
// than point b, 0 if the points are equal, and > 0 if
// point a is further from the origin than point b
{
   return a.x * a.x + a.y * a.y - b.x * b.x - b.y * b.y;
}
```

Even though friend functions appear in the class declarations, they are not member functions. They have access to private members, but they're not in scope of the respective classes. Thus, the class members can't be accessed

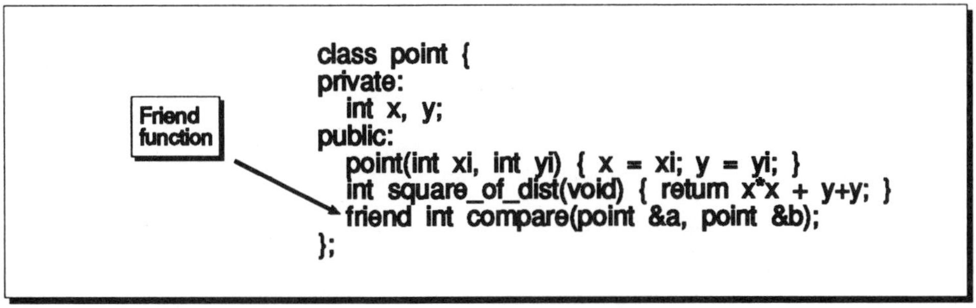

Figure 8.4. Declaring a Friend Function

directly, but rather must be accessed through objects. Note how our **compare()** function is implemented as a standard function (no class name or scoping operator), and can only access the **point** members **x** and **y** through the **point** objects **a** and **b**.

Note ‖ A class determines who its friend functions are, the functions themselves don't. Therefore, once you've defined a class and compiled it, it is no longer possible to add more friends to the class without changing the class declaration and recompiling it.

Although we've shown the friend declaration in the public section of the class, it could also be placed in the private section. However, friends don't follow the access rules of class members. Friends can't be made private even if they are declared to be private. They are always public.

The following is an example of using our **compare()** friend function:

```
main()
{
  point p(14, 17), q(25, 66);

  if (compare(p, q)) // Call friend function
     printf("p is closer to origin\n");
     else printf("q is closer to origin\n");
}
```

As the **if** statement shows, since **compare()** is not a member function, it is called directly, rather than through some object.

However, why bother with friend functions? Couldn't we write our **compare()** function as a member? We could. Here's how it would look:

```
#include <stdio.h>

class point {
private:
```

```
  int x, y;
public:
  point(int xi, yi);
  int compare(point &b); // Now a member
};

int point::compare(point &b)
{
  return x * x + y * y - b.x * b.x - b.y * b.y;
}

main()
{
  point p(14, 17), q(25, 66);

  if (p.compare(q))
     printf("p is closer to origin\n");
     else printf("q is closer to origin\n");
}
```

Look closely at how the modified **compare()** function is implemented. Instead of passing two **point** objects, one is passed. Actually, another **point** object *is* passed through the hidden **this** argument. Note how the **point a** has been replaced by the hidden argument. That is, instead of writing:

```
return a.x * a.x + a.y * a.y - b.x * b.x - b.y * b.y;
```

we write

```
return x * x + y * y - b.x * b.x - b.y * b.y;
```

Doesn't this seem a little awkward? Yes, it does. And so does the call to **compare()** in **main()**:

```
if (p.compare(q)) ...
```

However, besides these aesthetic reasons, there are cases when friend functions are the only solution. Let's see an example.

When to Use Friends

Suppose we had an array of points that we wish to sort using the standard library function **qsort()**. This sorting function implements quick sort in a generic way. The prototype for **qsort()** is:

```
void qsort(void *base, size_t nelem, size_t width,
       int (*fcmp)(const void *a, const void *b));
```

The last argument of **qsort()** is a pointer to a compare function that you must supply. This compare function takes two arguments which are **void** pointers to the variables (or objects) to compare.

If we tried to use a regular member function for **compare()**, we would run into problems. Regular member functions have a hidden **this** argument, which is typed as **T***, where T is the class type. The argument is not a **void** pointer. Even if the explicit arguments to the member function were **void** pointers, the hidden argument would still get in the way, as shown in Figure 8.5. However, if we tried to use a nonmember function, we'd get into trouble too, since we need to access the private variables x and y to do the comparison.

One solution to this problem is to use a friend function. Since it's not a member, it doesn't have the hidden **this** argument. As an example, the program given in Listing 8.1 uses a friend function **compare()** in conjunction with **qsort()** to sort an array of points. The points are sorted with those closest to the origin appearing first in the array.

Listing 8.1. Sample Point Sorting Program

```
// ptsort.cpp: Sample program that sorts points

#include <stdio.h>
#include <stdlib.h>

class point {
private:
  int x, y;
```

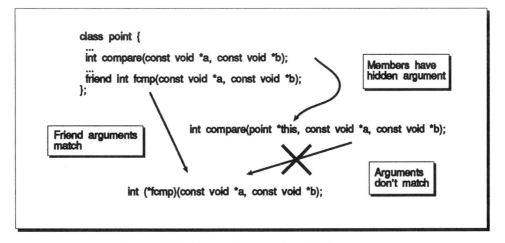

Figure 8.5. Where Friends Can Help

```
public:
  point(int xi, int yi) { x = xi; y = yi; }
  friend int compare(const void *a, const void *b);
  friend void print_points(point *p, int n);
};

int compare(const void *a, const void *b)
// Friend function to compare points
{
  point *pa = (point *)a; // Need to typecast to point objects
  point *pb = (point *)b;
  return pa->x * pa->x + pa->y * pa->y -
         pb->x * pb->x - pb->y * pb->y;
}

void print_points(point *p, int n)
// Another friend function
{
  printf("The sorted points are:\n\n");
  for(int i = 0; i<n; i++) {
    printf("%d: point(%02d, %02d)\n", i, p[i].x, p[i].y);
  }
}

main()
{
  point pt_arr[3] = { point(42, 15), point(3, 5), point(17, 12) };
  qsort(pt_arr, 3, sizeof(point), compare);
  print_points(pt_arr, 3);
}
```

The output to this sorting program is:

```
0: point(03, 05)
1: point(17, 12)
2: point(42, 15)
```

Not only is **compare()** a friend function, but we snuck in another friend function as well. The function **print_points()** prints out the list of points, as shown in the output.

Note that we had to use typecasting in **compare()**, since **qsort()** requires us to pass void pointers, even though we're addressing **point** objects:

```
int compare(const void *a, const void *b)
// Friend function to compare points
{
  point *pa = (point *)a; // Need to typecast to point objects
  point *pb = (point *)b;
  return pa->x * pa->x + pa->y * pa->y -
         pb->x * pb->x - pb->y * pb->y;
}
```

Of course, such typecasts are not safe. There's no guarantee that **a** and **b** are really addressing **point** objects. This not a problem of C++, but rather one of C. The **qsort()** function was designed for C programs, not C++ programs, so it can't take advantage of more powerful features that might make it safer.

However, there's another problem with our approach anyway. The friend function **print_points()** has to be passed the size of the **point** array. It would be easy to make mistakes here and pass the wrong size. What's needed is a way to encapsulate this function, and to encapsulate the call to **qsort()**. In the next section, you'll see how using another class that cooperates with the **point** class helps. You'll see that friend functions enter into the picture for this class as well.

Our problem with **compare()** not only has to do with trying to use it for **qsort()**, but also because the function passes two objects of the same type. In general, any time you have a function passing two or more objects of the same type, and that function needs to access private members, then that function quite likely would be better as a friend function.

A common example of this is with *operator functions*. These functions are associated with overloaded operators, such as + and <, and they are discussed in Chapter 10. Operators like + and < are binary, and take two objects as operands. It turns out that declaring binary operator functions to be friends is often very helpful.

There is one other type of function that has access to private class members that we could use as the **compare()** function for **qsort()**. Can you guess what kind of function that is? (Hint: Think about what you've learned in this chapter about special member functions.)

You could use a static member function. Recall that static member functions don't have the hidden **this** *argument. Thus, we could make both* compare() *and* print_points() *static members:*

```
class point {
  ...
  // Make these two functions static instead of friends
  static int compare(const void *a, const void *b);
  static void print_points(point *p, int n);
};

int point::compare(const void *a, const void *b) { ... }

void point::print_points(point *p, int n) { ... }
```

```
main()
{
  point pt_arr[3] = { point(3, 5), point(17, 12), point(42, 15) };

  // Note how we must use the scope operator on compare()
  qsort(pt_arr, 3, sizeof(point), point::compare);
  point::print_points(pt_arr, 3);
}
```

Using Member Functions as Friends

You've seen where a nonmember function can be made a friend of a class. But it's also possible to make member functions of one class be friends of another class. By doing this, we're basically indicating that the two classes cooperate with each other in some way.

There are two ways to make a member function a friend of another class. One way is to specifically call out the function as a friend. Another way is to make the whole class a friend, and thus make all of its member functions friends. Figure 8.6 shows both approaches. In both methods, we'll have to use a forward declaration for one of the classes, since each class refers to the other, and we can't define them both at the same time.

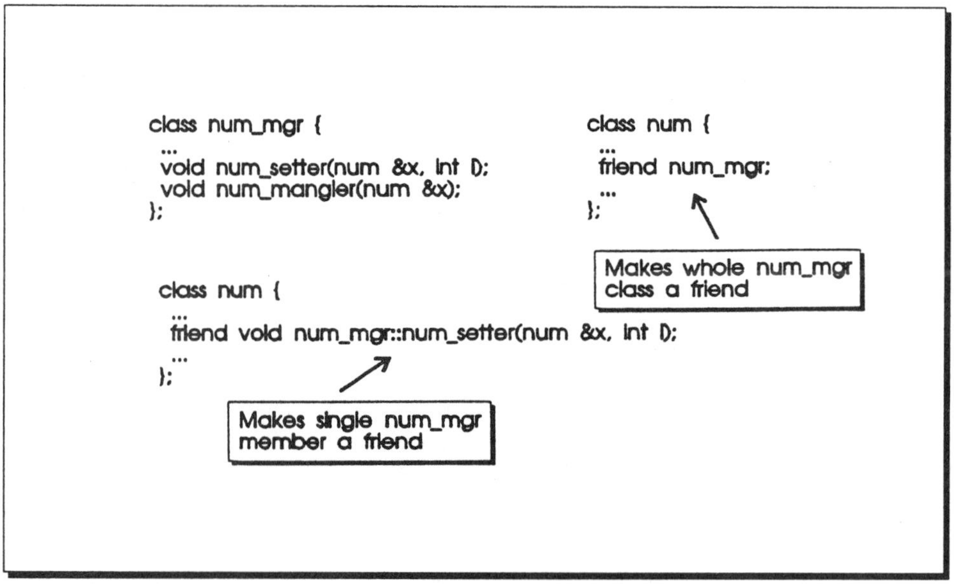

```
class num_mgr {                          class num {
  ...                                      ...
  void num_setter(num &x, int i);          friend num_mgr;
  void num_mangler(num &x);                ...
};                                        };
```

Makes whole num_mgr class a friend

```
class num {
  ...
  friend void num_mgr::num_setter(num &x, int i);
  ...
};
```

Makes single num_mgr member a friend

Figure 8.6. Ways of Making Friends

An example of making individual member functions friends of another class is:

```
class num_mgr; // We need forward declaration

class num {
private:
  int n;
public:
  num(int i) { n = i; }
  friend void num_mgr::num_setter(int i); // Friend
};

class num_mgr {
private:
  num x; // Holds a num object
public:
  num_mgr(void) : x(0)   { return;        }
  void num_setter(int i) { x.n = i;        } // Okay
  void num_mangler(void) { x.n ^= 0x0101; } // Illegal
};
```

Note how we used the full name for **num_setter()** in the friend declaration so that the member function would be made a friend and not some standalone function named **num_setter()**:

```
friend void num_mgr::num_setter(num &x, int i);
```

Since we made **num_setter()** a friend, it can access the private member n. However, **num_mangler()** cannot, since it's not a friend.

An example of how we can conveniently make all of the functions of **num_mgr** friends of the **num** class is:

```
class num_mgr;

class num {
private:
  int n;
public:
  num(int i) { n = i; }
  friend num_mgr; // All functions of num_mgr are friends
};
```

The functions **num()**, **num_setter()**, and **num_mangler()** are now all friends of the **num** class. Thus, **num_mangler()** is now legal, since it can access the private member n.

When all of the functions in one class are a friend of another class, the first class is said to be a friend of the second. Thus, the **num_mgr** class is a friend of the **num** class.

Using Friend Classes

A good example of using friend classes is also a solution to our encapsulation problem with the **point** sorting program of the prior section. We want to hide the functions **compare()** and **print_points()** so that their unsafe details are hidden. We can do this by hiding them in another class. Such a class is the following **pt_array** class:

```
class pt_array {
private:
  point *pts;
  int npts;
  static int compare(const void *a, const void *b);
public:
  pt_array(int np) { pts = new point[npts = np]; }
  ~pt_array(void)  { delete[npts] pts; }
  void set(int n, int x, int y);
  void sort(void);
  void print(void);
};
```

The **pt_array** class manages the **point** array **pts**. The constructor and destructor of **pt_array** allocate and deallocate memory for **pts**, and the member functions of **pt_array** provide high-level access to the array.

The **pt_array** class has a static **compare()** function and the function **print()** which takes the place of **print_points()**. We made **compare()** a static function so that it doesn't have the hidden **this** argument and can thus be used in **qsort()**. We didn't make **compare()** a friend function, since we want to make it private (for reasons to be explained shortly), and friends can't be made private.

Although we made **compare()** private, it isn't totally hidden. We can still call it outside the class, but only in one way:

```
pt_array::compare(pa, pb);
```

It turns out that this is the way **compare()** will be called by **qsort()** as well.

Even though we can call **compare()** as just mentioned, we've effectively hidden it. The reasons are as follows: First, we can't call **compare()** through an object, since it is private, so that eliminates one abuse. Also, the **sort()** function (which you'll see in a little bit), hides the call to **qsort()** so that the user of the class doesn't even need to know that **compare()** exists.

The **print()** function also effectively employs encapsulation. The **print()** function isn't private, but the array pointer **pts** and its size **npts** are. Thus, we've successfully encapsulated these array details.

However, how do we get the **pt_array** class to work with the **point** class? The secret is in making **pt_array** a friend of **point**. Listing 8.2, which is a modified version of our point sorting program, shows the complete implementation of **pt_array**.

Tip || Friend classes are useful whenever you have a class of objects that is managed in some way by another class.

Listing 8.2. Another Program Sorting Points

```cpp
// ptsort2.cpp: Another example of sorting an array of points

#include <stdio.h>
#include <stdlib.h>

class pt_array; // Forward declaration

class point {
private:
  int x, y;
public:
  point(int xi, int yi)    { x = xi; y = yi;    }
  point(void)              { x = 0; y = 0;      }
  friend pt_array;         // Whole pt_array class is a friend
};

class pt_array {
private:
  point *pts;
  int npts;
  static int compare(const void *a, const void *b);
public:
  void num_mgr::num_setter(int i);
  pt_array(int np) { pts = new point[npts = np]; }
  ~pt_array(void)  { delete[npts] pts; }
  void set(int n, int x, int y);
  void sort(void);
  void print(void);
};

int pt_array::compare(const void *a, const void *b)
{
  point *pa = (point *)a;
  point *pb = (point *)b;
  return pa->x * pa->x + pa->y * pa->y -
         pb->x * pb->x - pb->y * pb->y;
}

void pt_array::set(int n, int x, int y)
{
  pts[n].x = x; pts[n].y = y;
```

```
}

void pt_array::sort(void)
// Hides the call to qsort()
{
   qsort(pts, npts, sizeof(point), pt_array::compare);
}

void pt_array::print(void)
{
   printf("The sorted points are:\n\n");
   for(int i = 0; i<npts; i++) {
     printf("%d: (%02d, %02d)\n", i, pts[i].x, pts[i].y);
   }
}

main()
{
   pt_array pa(3); // Declare array having 3 points
   pa.set(0, 3, 5); pa.set(1, 17, 12), pa.set(2, 42, 15);
   pa.sort();
   pa.print();
}
```

One of the more interesting functions in this program is **sort()**, which hides the call to **qsort()**. Note how the address of the **compare()** function is passed:

```
qsort(pts, npts, sizeof(point), pt_array::compare);
```

When passing the address of **compare()** to **qsort()**, we had to qualify **compare()** with the name of the class it belongs to. In other words, we're passing a pointer to a member function. However, this is a special case, since **compare()** is a static member function. In general, passing pointers to members of classes is trickier than this. The methods for doing so are beyond the scope of this book.

Using Cooperating Classes

Making one class a friend of another class is useful when you have two cooperating classes. The **point** and **pt_array** classes of the previous section are such an example. In this section we'll look at another example involving a linked-list stack.

Suppose you want to create a stack of characters, and use a linked list to implement the stack. One way to do this is to use two classes: a class for the nodes on the list, and a class for the stack itself. For example, we might have the two classes **cnode** and **cstack**, as illustrated in Figure 8.7, and given as follows:

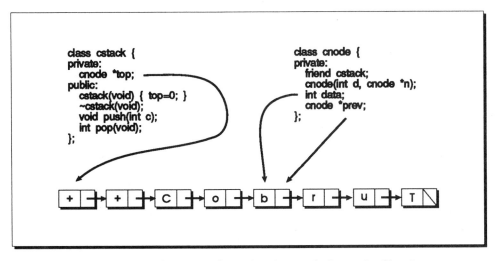

Figure 8.7. Two-Class Implementation of a Stack

```
class cstack;              // Forward declaration

class cnode {              // Private character node class
private:                   // All members are private
  friend cstack;           // Only cstack can create cnodes
  cnode(int d, cnode *n); // Because constructor is private
  int data;
  cnode *prev;
};

class cstack { // Character stack class
private:
  cnode *top;  // Top of stack
public:
  cstack(void) { top = 0; }
  ~cstack(void);
  void push(int c);
  int pop(void);
};
```

Just as the **pt_array** class manages the **point** class, the **cstack** class manages the **cnode** class. This suggests that **cstack** should be a friend of **cnode**. However, we've gone even further than that. We've made all of the members of **cnode** private, including its constructor. Recall that classes having private constructors are called private classes. Such classes can be used only by their friends. Thus, **cnode** is a private class that can be used only by the **cstack** class. In a sense, we've hidden the entire **cnode** class!

The program **reverse.cpp**, given in Listing 8.3, defines our two classes and shows them in action. The program reads characters from the keyboard and pushes them on the stack. When a carriage return is found, the stack is then printed out, causing the characters input to be output in reverse order.

Listing 8.3. A Character Stack Example

```
// reverse.cpp: Example of using friends to implement a stack

#include <conio.h>

class cstack;

class cnode {           // Private character node class
private:                // All members are private
  friend cstack;        // Only cstack can create cnodes
  cnode(int d, cnode *n); // Because constructor is private
  int data;
  cnode *prev;
};

class cstack { // Character stack class
private:
  cnode *top;   // Top of stack
public:
  cstack(void) { top = 0; }
  ~cstack(void);
  void push(int c);
  int pop(void);
};

// Implementation of cnode class

cnode::cnode(int d, cnode *n)
// Constructor to initialize data and previous node pointer
{
  data = d; prev = n;
}


// Implementation of the cstack class

cstack::~cstack(void)
// Delete all remaining nodes
{
  while(pop() != -1) { ; }
}

void cstack::push(int i)
// Create cnode, make it the top
{
  cnode *n = new cnode(i, top);
  top = n;
}
```

```
int cstack::pop(void)
// Pop top of stack, return character
// If stack is empty, return -1
{
  cnode *t - top;      // Save top
  if (top) {           // Stack not empty
    top - top->prev;   // Previous top is now the new top
    int c - t->data;   // Retrieve node data
    delete t;          // Delete the node
    return c;
  }
  else return -1;      // Return stack empty flag
}

main()
{
  int c;
  cstack cs; // Create a character stack

  // Push characters on the stack until newline received
  while((c - getche()) != '\r') { cs.push(c); }
  putch('\n');

  // Print characters out in reverse order
  while((c - cs.pop()) != -1) { putch(c); }
  putch('\r\n');
}
```

Iterator Objects

One use of cooperating classes—and friend functions—is in creating *iterator objects*. Iterator objects are a way to abstract the process of moving through collections of objects, such as arrays, linked lists, and trees. For instance, to move through a linked list, you would normally use a **next** pointer:

```
p - p->next;
```

To move through an array, you would keep incrementing an index:

```
a - b[i++];
```

What we would like to do is hide how this sequencing is implemented. Iterator objects are one solution.

As an example, suppose we created a binary tree class, called **btree**, that holds integer data:

```
class btree { // Binary tree node
private:
  int data;                  // Each node holds integer data
```

```
  btree *left, *right;     // Branches of the tree
public:
  btree(int d=0, btree *l=0, btree *r=0);
  int val(void) { return data; } // Public access function
};
```

Suppose that we want to walk a binary tree in preorder. That is, we'll visit the root, then the left branch, and then the right branch, in a recursive manner. Figure 8.8 shows a sample binary tree and how it is walked in preorder.

We'll create another class, called **preorder_walker**, that works in tandem with **btree**. The **preorder_walker** class has a member function that allows us to walk a binary tree in preorder. At each call of the function, a node in the tree is returned. Such functions are often called *iterator functions*. Each **preorder_walker** object points to a **btree**, and keeps track of where we are in the tree. Since walking trees is recursive in nature, we'll need some kind of stack to keep track of where we are in the tree.

The stack, which we'll call **bstack**, is a list of nodes pointing to **btree** objects. We could implement the stack similar to the way we implemented the character stack in the last section: as a linked list built from two cooperating classes. The following is such a setup:

```
class bstack;      // Forward declaration

class snode {      // Node of bstack
private:           // All members private
  friend bstack;   // Only bstack can use snode
  btree *bn;       // Each snode holds a btree
  snode *prev;     // Previous snode
  snode(btree *b, snode *s) { bn = b; next = s; }
};
```

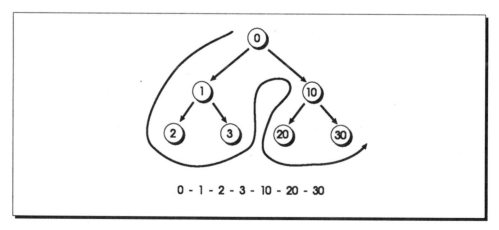

0 - 1 - 2 - 3 - 10 - 20 - 30

Figure 8.8. Preorder Traversal of a Binary Tree

```
class bstack { // Stack of snodes
private:
  snode *top;  // Stack top
public:
  bstack(void) { top = 0; }
  void push(btree *b);
  btree *pop(void);
};
```

Now, our **preorder_walker** class will contain a **bstack** object as a member. The following is the definition for the **preorder_walker** class:

```
class preorder_walker {
private:
  bstack node_stack; // Stack to keep track of where we are
public:
  preorder_walker(btree *root) { reset(root); }
  void reset(btree *root)      { node_stack.push(root); }
  btree *next(void);
};
```

The **preorder_walker** class contains three functions: **preorder_walker()**, **reset()**, and **next()**. The **preorder_walker()** constructor sets up the iteration by calling **reset()**, which pushes the root of the tree we'd like to traverse on the stack. Note that because **bstack** has a default constructor, the top of the stack is initialized by an implicit call to the default **bstack** constructor before **reset()** is called.

All the magic in **preorder_walker** is contained in the **bstack** object, and in the iterator function **next()**. Let's look at this latter function:

```
btree *preorder_walker::next(void)
{
  btree *b = node_stack.pop();
  if (b) {
    if (b->right) node_stack.push(b->right);
    if (b->left)  node_stack.push(b->left);
  }
  return b;
}
```

The iterator function **next()** works by first popping off the current node in the tree, saving it, pushing on the right- and left-child nodes, and returning the current node. When **next()** is called again, the node that gets popped off is the left node. The left node's children are then pushed on the stack. When the left side of the tree has been completely traversed, then the top of the stack will be the right node, and its children will be pushed on the stack.

It's time to see our iterator object in action. Listings 8.4 through 8.6 give a complete program that creates a binary tree and then prints out the nodes in preorder. The program consists of three files: **bstack.h, bstack.cpp,** and **prewalk.cpp**. The first two files define and implement the binary tree and its corresponding stack. Listing 8.6, **prewalk.cpp,** contains the main program. The program builds a binary tree like that shown in Figure 8.7, and produces the following output:

```
0 - 1 - 2 - 3 - 10 - 20 - 30
```

Listing 8.4. The Header File for the Binary Tree and Stack

```
// bstack.h: Definition of binary tree and cooperating stack

#ifndef H_BSTACK
#define H_BSTACK

class preorder_walker;
class inorder_walker;

class btree { // Binary tree node
private:
  friend preorder_walker;  // Iterator is a friend of btree
  int data;                // Each node holds integer data
  btree *left, *right;     // Branches of the tree
public:
  btree(int d=0, btree *l=0, btree *r=0);
  int val(void) { return data; } // Public access function
};

class bstack;

class snode {       // Node of bstack
private:            // All members private
  friend bstack;    // Only bstack can use snodes
  btree *bn;        // Node holds btrees
  snode *prev;      // Previous snode
  snode(btree *b, snode *s) { bn = b; prev = s; }
};

class bstack { // Stack of snodes
private:
  snode *top; // Stack top
public:
  bstack(void) { top = 0; }
  void push(btree *b);
  btree *pop(void);
};

#endif
```

Listing 8.5. Implementation File for Binary Tree and Stack

```
// bstack.cpp: Implementation of binary tree and cooperating stack

#include "bstack.h"

// Implementation of btree class

btree::btree(int d, btree *l, btree *r)
// Constructor
{
  data = d; left = l; right = r;
}


// Implementation of bstack class

void bstack::push(btree *b)
// Push a btree on the stack, make it the new top
{
  snode *n = new snode(b, top);
  top = n;
}

btree *bstack::pop(void)
// Pop top of bstack, return btree
// If bstack is empty, return 0
{
  snode *t = top;         // Save top
  if (top) {              // Stack not empty
    top = top->prev;      // Previous top becomes new top
    btree *b = t->bn;     // Retrieve node data
    delete t;             // Delete the node
    return b;
  }
  else return 0;          // Return bstack empty flag
}
```

Listing 8.6. Sample Program that Walks a Binary Tree in Preorder

```
// prewalk.cpp: A preorder walker of binary trees

#include <stdio.h>
#include "bstack.h"

class preorder_walker { // An iterator class
private:
  bstack node_stack;     // Stack to keep track of where we are
```

```
public:
  preorder_walker(btree *root) { node_stack.push(root); }
  btree *next(void);
};

btree *preorder_walker::next(void)
{
  btree *b = node_stack.pop();
  if (b) {
    if (b->right) node_stack.push(b->right);
    if (b->left)  node_stack.push(b->left);
  }
  return b;
}

main()
{
  // Construct a sample binary tree

  btree b(2, 0, 0);
  btree c(3, 0, 0);
  btree a(1, &b, &c);

  btree bb(20, 0, 0);
  btree cc(30, 0, 0);
  btree aa(10, &bb, &cc);

  btree z(0, &a, &aa);

  preorder_walker w(&z);  // Setup iterator

  while(1) {
    btree *b = w.next();  // Print nodes in sequence
    if (b == 0) break;
    printf("%d - ", b->val());
  }
}
```

Summary

In this chapter, some special types of class members that help fill out the assortment of tools that you can use were discussed. Static class members give you a way to have variables global to class objects, yet still be accessible only to those objects. Constant member functions allow you to fine tune your objects so they can be safely used as constants.

The most important type of function discussed isn't a member function at all. Friend functions allow you to access private class members, without having to declare the functions as member functions. This has an advantage in the following case: Sometimes you have functions that require a specific set of arguments. The hidden argument that member functions have can sometimes get in the way, as you saw with the **compare()** function for **point** objects. With friend functions, you can get around this problem, yet still access private members.

However, a more important advantage of friend functions is that they allow you to have two or more classes working together in tandem, with the ability to have the private variables of one class directly accessible by the other class. This allows you to split up your abstract data types into smaller chunks, and still have those chunks work together smoothly. The binary tree and stack classes were examples of this.

Exercises

1. State which of the functions in the following code are legal, and give the reasons why.

```
class info  {
private:
  int private_data;
public:
  int public_data;
  void insider(int p);
  friend int buddy(my_class *a);
};

void info::insider(int p) {
  private_data = p;
}

int buddy(info *a) {
  return a->private_data;
}

int outsider(info *a) {
  return a->private_data;
}
```

2. In the following code, which of the statements labeled a, b, c, d, and e are legal:

```
class string {
private:
  static char eos;            // Private static member
  char *buff;
  int size;
public:
  string(int sz);
  void copy(string &s);
};
```

```
char string::eos = 0x1a;      // a. Legal?

void string::copy(string &s)
{
  delete buff; // Reallocate buffer
  buff = new char[s.size];
  char *p = buff;
  char *q = s.buff;
  while(*q != eos)              // b. Legal?
    *p++ = *q++;
  *p = eos;                     // c. Legal?
}

main()
{
  string s(80);

  string::eos = 0;       // d. Legal?
  s.eos = '$';           // e. Legal?
}
```

3. Friend functions and static member functions are alike in that neither have a hidden **this** argument. Explain the difference between the two. When are each appropriate?

Answers

1. *The functions* **insider()** *and* **buddy()**, *which are a class member and a class friend, respectively, can access the private member* **private_data**, *but* **outsider()**, *which is not a class member or friend, cannot. All the functions can access* **public_data**, *however.*

2. *Statements a through d are legal. However, statement e, which accesses the private static member* **eos** *through an object, is illegal. Note that statements b and c access* **eos** *through an object, but they are inside a member function. Statement d is legal because it's accessing the private static data member through the class itself, not through an object.*

3. *Since a friend function isn't a member of a class, its name isn't hidden inside any class. Thus, the friend function name may contribute to "global name-space pollution." In contrast, a static member function name is hidden by the class it belongs to.*

   Friend functions are also different from static member functions in that they can actually be members of other classes, just not the class they are friends with.

   In general, you should use friend functions whenever you have cooperating classes that need access to the other's private data. Use static member functions whenever you have some static class data to operate on.

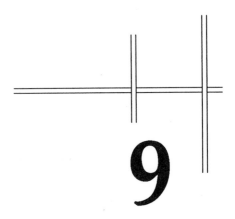

9

Inheritance and Derived Classes

Using classes to provide encapsulation, a Turbo C++ program can be more maintainable than a Turbo C program. Even so, if that's all there were to classes, then programming in Turbo C++ wouldn't be that much different than programming in Turbo C. All that would change is the use of classes as opposed to simple structures to better encapsulate the data structures and functions in your programs.

However, there's one other property of classes that will allow your programs to be more reusable as well as more maintainable. That property is *inheritance*. With inheritance, you can take existing classes and extend them to support new functionality. These new classes, *derived classes*, still retain the data and functions of the original classes. The focus of this chapter, then, is inheritance and how it is accomplished using derived classes.

After completing this chapter, you'll have learned:

- What inheritance is
- How to derive classes
- How to reuse existing classes and override their functionality
- What virtual functions are and how they relate to inheritance
- What polymorphism is and how it relates to virtual functions
- How to work with constructors and destructors in derived classes
- How to work with data hiding in derived classes
- What abstract classes are and how to define them

What Is Inheritance?

Inheritance is a relationship between entities, and has the following key ingredients:

- Traits which are shared among a set of entities
- Slight differences between the entities
- A hierarchical organization

Inheritance is all around you. Just look at yourself and the members of your family. You each inherit the same basic traits from your parents: their overall physical makeup, appearance, and mannerisms. Yet you and your siblings are all different. Your sister may sport lush blonde locks of hair, while your hair might be black as coal.

One characteristic that a family has is a hierarchical organization, with the parents at the top of hierarchy, and children at the bottom. Figure 9.1 illustrates a typical family hierarchy.

In terms of programming, inheritance is similar to the relationship between family members, except it involves the relationship between classes.

For example, take three classes representing points, circles, and rectangles. A point has a location, which we can represent by an (x,y) coordinate pair. A circle also has a location (the coordinates of its center), and it has a radius. Likewise, a rectangle has a location (which we could interpret to be at the upper-left-hand corner), and a width and height. Thus the traits shared among these classes is a location, as illustrated in Figure 9.2.

In any inheritance hierarchy, those entities with the most shared traits will be at the top of the hierarchy. With families, it's the parental traits that are shared among the family members, thus, the parents are at the top of the hierarchy. With the geometric classes, the class representing points is at the top, as shown in Figure 9.3.

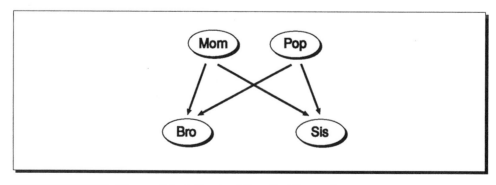

Figure 9.1. A Typical Family Hierarchy

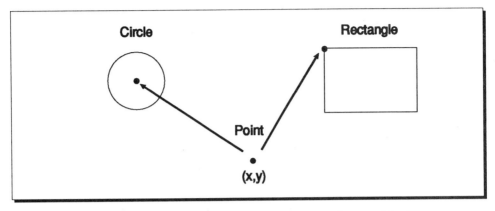

Figure 9.2. Common Traits Among Geometric Classes

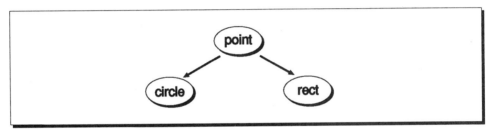

Figure 9.3. A Geometric Class Hierarchy

Some Terminology

The technique of one class inheriting attributes from another class is called *deriving a class*. The first class is called a *base class*, and the second is called a *derived class*. A system of classes created using inheritance is called a *class hierarchy*.

You'll sometimes see other terminology being used for base and derived classes, as shown in Figure 9.4.

Creating Elaborate Hierarchies

The class derivation process can continue indefinitely. That is, a derived class can become a base class for other derived classes. For instance, in the class hierarchy shown in Figure 9.5, a window class is derived from the rectangle class. Then, using the window class as a base class, a text window class and a graphics window class are derived. From these, a text editor class and a icon editor class are derived.

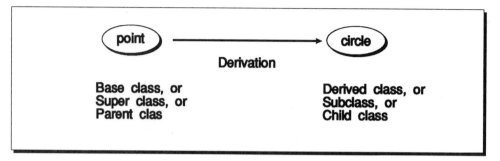

Figure 9.4. Terminology Used with Inheritance

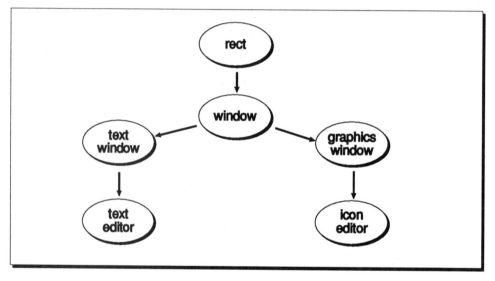

Figure 9.5. A Window Hierarchy

Types of Inheritance

There are two types of inheritance: *single inheritance* and *multiple inheritance*. With single inheritance, a derived class has only one immediate base class. With multiple inheritance, a derived class has more than one immediate base class. The difference between single and multiple inheritance is illustrated in Figure 9.6.

It's possible to use both single and multiple inheritance in Turbo C++ programs. However, we're only going to cover single inheritance in this book. To use multiple inheritance is much trickier.

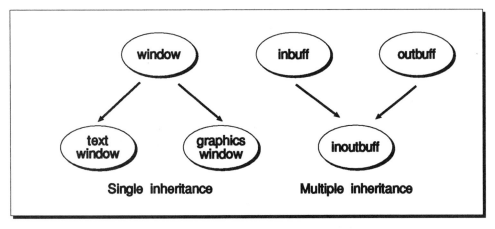

Single inheritance   Multiple inheritance

Figure 9.6. Single versus Multiple Inheritance

1. Suppose you have a class that implements windows with scroll bars, and one that implements windows with simple borders. Suggest how you might use inheritance to represent these two types of windows.
2. Given a file buffer class and a mouse driver class, would it make sense to have these classes in the same hierarchy?

1. *A scroll window has all the properties of a simple window, such as size, location, color, and functions to move it around on the screen. However, it adds scroll bars to these windows and the associated functions to handle the scrolling. Thus, you could make the simple window class a base class and derive the scroll window class from it.*
2. *Probably not. Unless two classes have something in common, it doesn't do much good to have them in the same hierarchy, since they have nothing to share.*

Advantages to Inheritance

There are several advantages that inheritance brings to the Turbo C++ programmer:

- Code can be shared among many classes
- Classes can be extended, and in many cases, this can be done without recompiling the original classes
- Function using base class objects can automatically use objects created from classes derived from the base classes

In the sections that follow, you'll see how these advantages can come about using inheritance. All of these advantages are really aspects of the same thing: reusing code, which is the subject we're going to discuss next.

Reusing Code

Being able to reuse code is every programmer's dream. No one likes to keep "reinventing the wheel." With classes as the prominent component in most Turbo C++ programs, reusing code becomes an issue of reusing classes. There are two basic ways to reuse classes in Turbo C++:

Method	Description
Composition	Include one class object inside another
Inheritance	Derive one class from another

Let's investigate both of these ways. You'll see in the following discussion that the second way, which uses inheritance, is the more powerful way.

Reusing Classes with Composition

One way to reuse a class is to include an object from that class inside another object. That is, you can *compose* one object from another. In doing so, the *composite object* is reusing all of the data and functions of the first class. You have probably used a similar technique in your C programs. Think about all the times you've included a structure variable as a member of another structure.

Let's look at an example in Turbo C++. We'll take a **point** object and use it to create a **circle** class. Figure 9.7 illustrates the composition, and the following code shows how it's implemented:

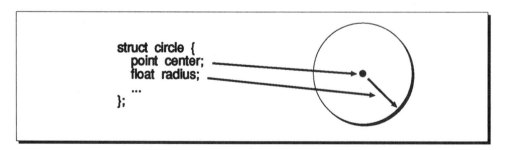

Figure 9.7. Composing a Circle from a Point

```
struct point {
  float x, y; // Location
  void setlocn(float xi, float yi) { x = xi; y = yi; }
};

struct circle {
  point center; // Include a point object
  float radius; // Add a radius
  void setsize(float r) { r = radius; }
};
```

Now, when using the **circle** class, we can use the members **x,y**, and **setlocn()** from the **point** class, as well as the new members **radius** and **setsize()**:

```
circle spotlight;

spotlight.setsize(40.0);
spotlight.radius = 40.0;

spotlight.center.setlocn(320.0, 240.0);
spotlight.center.x = 320.0;
spotlight.center.y = 240.0;
```

Although we can access the members **setsize()** and **radius** directly, we must access the members **x**, **y**, and **setlocn()** through the **center** object. Thus, although we can make use of the **point** class members, it's a little unwieldy. Using inheritance will enable us to get around this problem.

Reusing Classes with Inheritance

A more powerful way to reuse an existing class is to derive a new class from it. For instance, we can derive the **circle** class from the **point** class. In this manner, the **circle** class inherits the members of the **point** class.

To derive a class from a base class, you indicate the name of the base class immediately after the name of the derived class, separated by a semicolon. The basic syntax is:

```
<class_specifier> <derived_class_name> : <base_class_name> {
  <Additional members>
};
```

where **<class_specifier>** is one of the keywords **class** or **struct**.

Note ‖ You can't derive new classes from unions.

Using this syntax, here's how to derive **circle** from **point**:

```
struct point {
  float x, y;
  void setlocn(float xi, float yi) { x = xi; y = yi; }
};

struct circle : point { // Circle inherits point
  // Additional members
  float radius;
  void setsize(float r) { radius = r; }
};
```

Figure 9.8 illustrates the basic components of the derived **circle** class.

In a derived class declaration, you only list the members to be added in the derivation. You don't list the members that are being inherited. For instance, in the **circle** class, only the additional **radius** and **setsize()** members are listed.

You can think of the **circle** class as having a hidden **point** object as a member; and you can access the **x**, **y**, and **setlocn()** members of this object directly, without doing two levels of member accessing. The following code illustrates this:

```
circle spotlight;                  // Declare a circle object

spotlight.setsize(40.0);           // Accessing new members
spotlight.radius = 40.0;           // of the derived class

spotlight.setlocn(320.0, 240.0);   // Accessing point
spotlight.x = 320.0;               // members directly
spotlight.y = 240.0;
```

Contrast this with our class composition technique, where, to access any **point** members, we had to go through the **center** object, as in:

```
spotlight.center.x = 320.0;
```

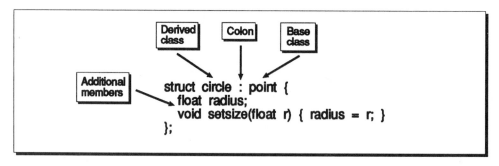

Figure 9.8. The Components of a Derived Class

Using the derived **circle** class, as opposed to the composite **circle** class, is less cumbersome, and a little more natural.

Tip ‖ Whenever you have a class composed of an object from another class, try deriving the first class from the second class. It may prove to be beneficial.

Can you tell what's wrong with the following class hierarchy? (Hint: look at what members are listed in the derived class.)

```
struct point {
  float x, y;
  void setlocn(float xi, float yi);
};

struct rect : point {
  float x, y, wd, ht;
  void setlocn(int xi, int yi);
  void setsize(int w, int h);
};
```

*The derived **rect** class declaration lists all the inherited **point** members again. If you were to compile this code, you would get duplicate definition errors for the instance variables x and y. However, the duplicate setlocn() function would compile just fine. What has happened is that **setlocn()** is overloaded.*

Assignment Compatibility Rule

The naturalness of using derived classes over composite classes goes beyond easier access to inherited members. It turns out that a derived class is treated as a subtype of its base class. One consequence of this is that a derived class object is *assignment compatible* with a base class object.

For instance, you can assign a **circle** object to a **point** object, without any typecasting:

```
point p;
circle c;

p = c; // Assign a circle to a point
```

In such an assignment, only the members in the base class are copied, as illustrated in Figure 9.9. For example, our **circle**-to-**point** assignment translates to:

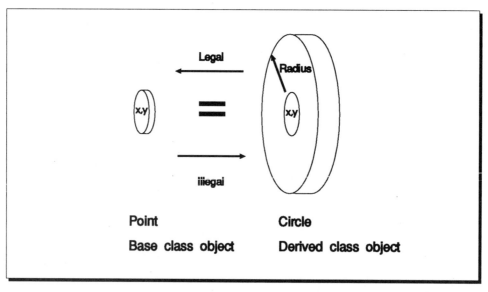

Figure 9.9. Assignment Compatible Objects

```
p.x = c.x;
p.y = c.y;
```

Here, only the **x** and **y** members are copied. The **radius** member is unused in the assignment, because it is not in the **point** base class.

This type of assignment is not possible between two objects that aren't related by inheritance. For instance, if we tried to use the **circle** class that was created by composition from the **point** class, we couldn't assign a **circle** object to a **point** object. The compiler would complain that we were mixing types.

The assignment compatibility rule extends to pointers and references to objects. For instance, we can assign a **circle** pointer to a **point** pointer:

```
point *p_ptr;
circle *c_ptr;

p_ptr = c_ptr; // Assign circle pointer to point pointer
```

and a **circle** reference to a **point** reference:

```
point p;
point &p_ref = p;

circle c;
circle &c_ref = c;

p_ref = c_ref; // Assign circle reference to point reference
```

The assignments can only work in one direction, though. You can assign a derived class object to a base class object, but not the other way around. For instance, you can't assign a **point** object to a **circle** object. Statements like the following are illegal:

```
c = p;        // Can't assign a point to a circle
c_ptr = p_ptr; // Can't assign point pointer to circle pointer
c_ref = p_ref; // Can't do this assignment for references either
```

There's a good reason for the one-way assignment restriction. Suppose we try circumventing it using typecasts. Consider this sequence of statements:

```
point *p_ptr;
circle *c_ptr;

c_ptr = (circle *)p_ptr; // Force illegal assignment
printf("Radius of circle is: %f\n", c_ptr->radius);
```

The **printf()** statement would print out a random value. We're accessing the **radius** of the object pointed to by **c_ptr**. Unfortunately, that object is a **point**, not a **circle**, and a **point** doesn't have a radius.

Being able to assign a derived class object to a base class object turns out to be very helpful in reusing code. In the next section, you'll see how this capability allows us to reuse functions that manipulate base class objects.

Reusing Functions for Derived Class Objects

Because of the assignment compatibility rule, objects created from a derived class can be used anywhere that objects from the base class can be used. For example, any function using a **point** object would work equally well with a **circle** object. That's because **circle** objects include everything that **point** objects do. Thus, there's no possibility that a function using **point** will be accessing any member of **point** that's not also a part of **circle**.

For example, consider a function that determines the distance between two points:

```
float distance(point &a, point &b)
{
  float dx = a.x - b.x;
  float dy = a.y - b.y;
  return sqrt(dx*dx + dy*dy);
}

point mugu, lomas;
float dp = distance(mugu, lomas);
```

Using the assignment compatibility rule, we can pass **circle** objects to the **distance()** function just as well as we can **point** objects:

```
circle k_ranch, r_ranch;
float dc = distance(k_ranch, r_ranch);
```

The **circle** object **k_ranch** is assigned to the formal argument **a**, which is a **point** object. Similarly, **circle** object **r_ranch** is assigned to **point** object **b**. In a sense, we're passing the center of each **circle** to the **distance()** function, which then finds the distance between the two centers. Figure 9.10 illustrates this process.

In the function call, we're taking the **distance()** function, which was written for **point** objects, and reusing it for **circle** objects. There's a lot of power in this type of programming. Not only does deriving classes allow us to reuse the code in a base class, it allows us to reuse any functions that use objects from the base class.

This technique is more powerful than it may first appear, for the function being reused could have been designed and coded long before the derived class was even defined.

For example, consider the **distance()** function. Since it refers to **point** objects, we would include the header file for the **point** class in the file that implements **distance()**. In this respect, the **distance()** function knows only about **point** objects. It knows nothing about **circle** objects. Yet we can still call the function with **circle** objects as parameters. This arrangement is illustrated in Figure 9.11.

Note that we don't have to recompile the **distance()** function to make it work for **circle** objects. This fact has important ramifications. It means that you can compile a class and place it in an object library, yet anyone can take this library, and, armed with only the header file for the class, extend the class and modify it to suit their own purposes. You don't have to give out the complete source code to the class.

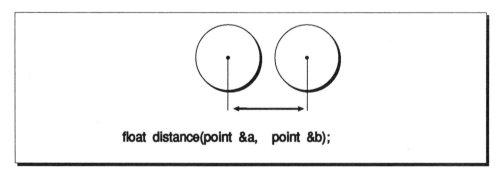

float distance(point &a,   point &b);

Figure 9.10. Reusing the distance() Function

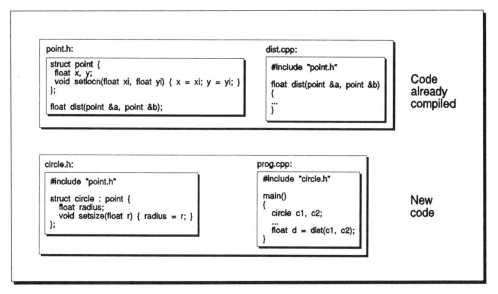

Figure 9.11. Extending Already Compiled Code

1. Given the following class declarations and assignments labeled a, b, c, and d, which of the assignments are legal? Of the legal ones, which would you not recommend?

```
struct simple_num { int num; };
struct bounded_num : simple_num { int upper, lower; };

simple_num s;
simple_num *sp = &s;
bounded_num b;
bounded_num *bp = &b;

sp = bp;                    // a.
sp = (simple_num *)bp;      // b.
bp = sp;                    // c.
bp = (bounded_num *)sp;     // d.
```

2. Given the **point** and **circle** classes discussed earlier, do you think the following statement is legal?

```
point *p = new circle;
```

3. While using inheritance can enable you to extend code that's already been compiled, what does the technique imply about the design process in creating the compiled code?

1. *Assignments a, b, and d are legal, c is not. Assignment b illustrates that you can do an explicit typecast from a derived class pointer to a base class pointer, but as assignment a shows, you don't have to.*

    Assignment d shows that you can use an explicit typecast the other way around, from a base class pointer to a derived class pointer, but it isn't recommended. That's because the derived class pointer assumes all of the additional members of the derived class are present in the object being pointed to, which isn't the case.
2. *Sure. The call to new results in a pointer to a circle, which is then assigned to the pointer p using the assignment compatibility rule. Such shorthand syntax is quite handy.*
3. *It implies that the classes being compiled have been well thought out in their construction. Using inheritance requires more up-front design than more conventional programming methods.*

Polymorphism: Overriding Class Behavior

Often the reason for deriving a class is not to add other instance variables and functions, but rather, to redefine or override the functions of the base class.

When the functions of a base class are overridden in a derived class, the resulting objects are said to be *polymorphic*. This term means to "take on many shapes." We will now see how polymorphic objects look.

Suppose we were to add **draw()** functions to our **point** and **circle** classes. The **draw()** function for **point** would merely plot a single point on the screen, whereas the **draw()** function for **circle** would draw a series of dots in the form of a circle. Figure 9.12 illustrates this scenario.

Since the **circle** class is a subtype of the **point** class, **circle** and **point** objects come from the same "stock." Yet they take on different shapes if you draw them. That's the reason such objects are called polymorphic.

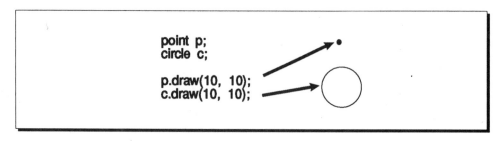

Figure 9.12. Polymorphic Objects

To get polymorphic objects, you must create a class hierarchy, and then redefine the base class functions in the derived classes. You can do this two ways:

- By using overloaded functions
- By using virtual functions

You've seen overloaded functions before; they were discussed in Chapter 5. However, virtual functions are probably new to you. They are similar to overloaded functions, but they are implemented quite differently. That difference has to do with *static* and *dynamic binding*, which are different techniques for calling functions.

In the next few sections, we'll explore how to achieve polymorphism using overloaded and virtual functions. We'll also discuss static and dynamic binding and how they relate to polymorphism.

Using Overloaded Functions in Derived Classes

As an example of overriding the functions in a class, the program in Listing 9.1 adds an **area()** function to the **point** class, which is then overloaded in the **circle** class. For **points**, the area is always zero. For **circles**, the area is computed by the pi-r-squared formula.

Listing 9.1. The overld.cpp Program

```
// overld.cpp: Example of using overloaded functions to
// override class behavior

#include <stdio.h>

struct point {
  float x, y;
  void setlocn(float xi, float yi) { x = xi; y = yi; }
  float area(void) { return 0.0; } // Define area function
};

const float pi = 3.14159;

struct circle : point {
  float radius;
  void setsize(float r) { radius = r; }
  // Overload area function
  float area(void) { return pi * radius * radius; }
};
```

```
main()
{
  point of_no_return;
  float a = of_no_return.area();
  printf("The area of the point of no return is: %5.2f\n", a);

  circle universe;
  universe.setsize(3.65637);
  a = universe.area();
  printf("The area of the universe is: %5.2f\n", a);
}
```

The program prints out the following:

```
The area of the point of no return is: 0.00
The area of the universe is: 42.00
```

It looks as though we've successfully overridden the **area()** function in the derived class. We have, as long as we're using objects directly, and not pointers to objects.

Recall that we could define a pointer to a **point** and have it reference a **circle** object, as the following code fragment shows:

```
point *p;                   // Define point pointer
circle universe;            // Define circle object
universe.setsize(3.65637);  // Initialize circle radius

p = &universe;              // Point to circle
float my_area = p->area();  // Call area() function
```

What happens in the call to **area()** from the pointer **p**? Which **area()** function is called, the one for **point** or the one for **circle**?

The answer is that the **point::area()** function is called, which is incorrect. The problem is that the compiler determines statically, at compile time, which function to call. The compiler can't know for sure what type of object **p** points to, so it assumes **p** points to a **point** object, since that is **p**'s type.

What we need is a way to determine which **area()** function to call, dynamically, at run time. Virtual functions will do this for us, but to understand how they work, you must better understand static versus dynamic function calling. The next section will discuss this.

You learned in Chapter 5 that when overloading functions, you must use different argument types for each of the overloaded functions. Why didn't we have to do this when we overloaded the **area()** function for the **point** and **circle** classes?

*Because the **area()** functions are class members, they have the hidden **this** argument. For each class, **this** is typed differently. Thus, taking **this** into account, we did have different argument types in the **area()** functions.*

Static versus Dynamic Function Binding

When a function call is linked up to the code comprising the body of the appropriate function, the process is called *function binding*. Figure 9.13 shows some examples of function binding.

There are two types of function binding available in a Turbo C++ program:

- Static binding
- Dynamic binding

Static binding is what takes place in normal function calls. The compiler takes the name of the function, the arguments, and if a member function is involved, the class name of the object, and determines which function to call. Figure 9.14 shows an example of this.

In dynamic binding, the function to call isn't determined until run time. How can this be done? One way is to use function pointers. That way, it isn't until run time, when the pointer is traversed that the actual function being called is known.

We could use function pointers to solve our problem with the **point** and **circle** area functions. The trick is to define a function pointer inside the **point** class that points to an appropriate **area()** function. Keep in mind that this function pointer would be inherited by the **circle** class. After creating a **point** or **circle** object, we merely initialize the function pointer to reference the correct **area()** function. Figure 9.15 provides a sketch of this process.

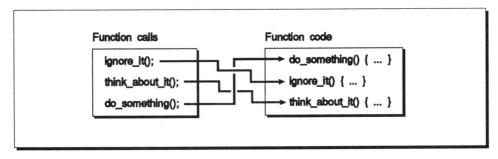

Figure 9.13. Function Binding

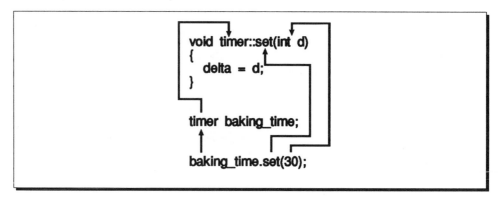

Figure 9.14. Static Function Binding

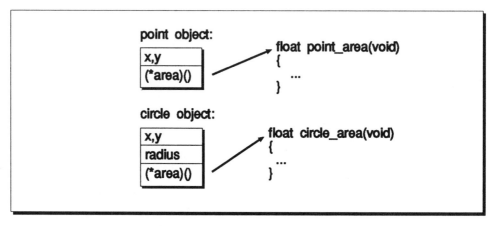

Figure 9.15. Dynamic Function Binding

While we could go ahead and code up this function pointer technique, there's no reason to. Turbo C++ provides a better solution through the use of virtual functions. It turns out that virtual functions use a similar function pointer technique, but it's all behind the scenes. Let's see how to declare and use virtual functions.

Using Virtual Functions

Virtual functions are used to override a base class member function, but in such a way that the overriding works in both static and dynamic situations. You make a member function virtual by placing the **virtual** keyword before its prototype. For example:

```
struct point {
  float x, y;
  void setlocn(float xi, float yi);
  // Declare virtual function:
  virtual float area(void) { return 0.0; }
};
```

Once you've declared a function virtual in a base class, it will be virtual for all subsequent derived classes. You don't need to specify the **virtual** keyword in the derived classes, but they'll still be virtual nonetheless.

Here's how to override the virtual **area()** function in the **circle** class:

```
const float pi - 3.14159;

struct circle : point {
  float radius;
  void setsize(float r);
  // Override virtual function
  float area(void) { return pi * radius * radius; }
};
```

Figure 9.16 emphasizes the fact that the **virtual** keyword is optional in the derived class.

Note || When overriding a virtual function, make sure the new function has the same type and number of arguments that the original function has.

Let's see virtual functions in action. The **vfunc.cpp** program given in Listing 9.2 shows how virtual **area()** functions are used to assure the proper function is called when using a **point** pointer. The output from the program is:

```
First area is :  0.00
Second area is: 42.00
```

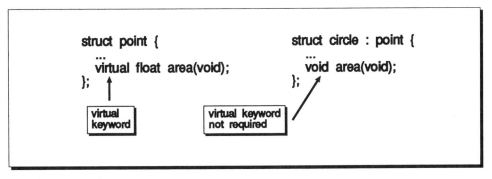

Figure 9.16. Declaring a Virtual Function

Listing 9.2. The vfunc.cpp Program

```
// vfunc.cpp: Example of dynamic binding using virtual functions
#include <stdio.h>

struct point { // Point class
  float x, y;
  void setlocn(float xi, float yi) { x = xi; y = yi; }
  virtual float area(void) { return 0.0; }
};

const float pi = 3.14159;

struct circle : point { // Derived circle class
  float radius;
  void setsize(float r) { radius = r; }
  float area(void) { return pi * radius * radius; }
};

main()
{
  point of_no_return;       // Declare point object

  circle universe;          // Declare circle object
  universe.setsize(3.65637); // Initialize radius

  point *p_ptr;             // Declare point pointer
  p_ptr = &of_no_return;    // Address a point with it
  float ap = p_ptr->area(); // Call virtual area function

  p_ptr = &universe;        // Now address a circle
  float ac = p_ptr->area(); // Call virtual area function

  printf("First area is : %5.2f\n", ap);
  printf("Second area is: %5.2f\n", ac);
}
```

1. Given a base window class and a derived scroll window class, where scroll windows have scroll bars on their border, suggest a possible function common to both classes that would make a good candidate as a virtual function.
2. What's the problem with the virtual functions in the following class declarations?

```
struct shape {
  virtual draw(void);
};

struct jigsaw : shape {
  void draw(void);
};
```

3. In the following class declarations, we forgot the **virtual** keyword in the **shape::draw()** function declaration, but we used the keyword in the **jigsaw::draw()** function. What do you suppose happens?

```
struct shape {
  void draw(void);          // No virtual keyword used
};
struct jigsaw : shape {
  virtual void draw(void); // Virtual keyword used
};
```

---

1. *The function used to draw the window border should be virtual, since each window has a different type of border to draw.*
2. *We forgot to give a **void** return type in the first **draw()** function, so its return type defaults to **int**. Therefore, even though we made the first **draw()** virtual, the second **draw()** function isn't virtual. It still uses static binding.*

   This type of subtle error is easy to make. Fortunately, Turbo C++ traps such errors and gives you a "virtual function conflict" error message.
3. *For **shape** objects, **draw()** is not virtual, but for **jigsaw** objects, and all objects created from classes derived from **jigsaw**, **draw()** is virtual.*

Passing Polymorphic Objects to Functions

Earlier you saw where we could reuse the **distance()** function by passing it both **point** and **circle** objects. There's another way we can reuse a function that has objects as arguments: Inside the function we can have the objects call some of their virtual functions. By doing so, we've in a sense made the original function virtual as well.

For example, the following **paint_cost()** function computes the cost to paint a **point** or **circle** object, given a cost-per-unit-area amount:

```
float paint_cost(point *p, float cost_per_unit_area)
{
  return p->area() * cost_per_unit_area;
}
```

The function works by calling the virtual **area()** function through the base pointer **p**, which points to either a **point** or a **circle** object. The function will work for any object that comes from a derived class of **point**. For instance, we could derive a **cylinder** class from **circle**, and pass **cylinder** objects to the **paint_cost()** function:

```
struct cylinder : circle {
  float ht; // Add a height
  float area(void); // Override area function
};

cylinder beer_can;
...
float amt = paint_cost(&beer_can, 0.17);
```

1. Suppose we changed the **paint_cost()** function to use pass-by-value instead of pass-by-reference for the **point** object:

   ```
   float paint_cost(point p, float cost_per_unit_area)
   // Use pass by value
   {
     return p.area() * cost_per_unit_area;
   }
   ```

   What would be the results of the following calls?

   ```
   point p;
   circle c;
   c.setsize(55.0);

   float p_amt = paint_cost(p, 0.17);
   float c_amt = paint_cost(c, 0.17);
   ```

2. Suppose we changed the **paint_cost()** function to take a **point** reference argument, as in the following prototype. Would the cost function work properly now?

   ```
   float paint_cost(point &p, float cost_per_unit_area);
   ```

3. Suppose we changed the **paint_cost()** function to take a pointer to a **circle** instead of a pointer to a **point**. Could we use the function for **points**?

---

1. *Both **p_amt** and **c_amt** would get set to zero. For **point p**, the area is zero, so the cost would be too. However, why is the cost for the **circle c** zero? Since we used pass-by-value for the **point** object in the function call, a temporary **point** object is created which is initialized from the **circle c**. That object has the **point::area()** function, not the **circle::area()** function, so the cost would always come out zero. Therefore, to get the full benefits of virtual functions, always use pointers or references to objects.*
2. *Yes, the function would work correctly. As far as virtual functions go, using a pointer or reference is the same.*

3. *No. In trying to pass a **point** object pointer, you would be going from a base class pointer to a derived class pointer. That's not allowed. Therefore, to get the full benefits of virtual functions, always use base class pointers or references.*

Calling Inherited Functions

While sometimes you'll have a derived class function completely override the base class version, it's often useful to let the base class version do as much of the work as possible. For example, let's finish the **cylinder** class derivation we sketched out in the last section, and define the **area()** function for cylinders:

```
const float pi = 3.14159;

struct cylinder : circle {
  float ht; // Add a height
  void set_height(int h) { ht = h; }
  float area(void);
};

float cylinder::area(void)
// Cylinder area function calls circle area
// function for some of the calculations
{
   return 4 * pi * radius * ht + 2 * circle::area();
}
```

Part of the formula for computing the area of a cylinder (which we interpret to mean surface area) includes adding the circular areas of the ends of the cylinder. We can compute the areas of the cylinder ends by calling the inherited **circle::area()** function, and that's exactly what we do in the expression:

```
2 * circle::area() // Calls inherited function
```

Figure 9.17 illustrates the process of calling an inherited function.

```
float cylinder::area(void)
{
   return 4*pi*radius*ht + 2 * circle::area();
}
```
Base class name — Inherited function

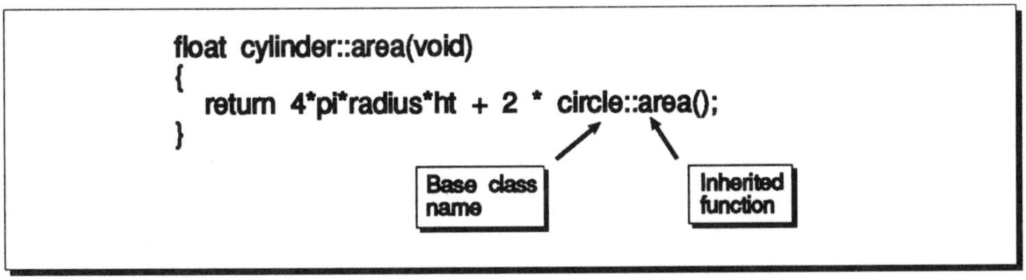

Figure 9.17. Calling an Inherited Function

Tip Calling an inherited function is actually another form of reusing code. When you start creating class hierarchies, try to make the inherited functions do most of the work. The derived class functions should only have to do an incremental amount of work.

Skipping Levels

When calling the inherited **circle::area()** function in the **cylinder** class, we're going back one level in the class hierarchy. We could go back another level and call the **point** version of **area()**. All we need to do is qualify the function call with the class name **point**. For instance, we could write the **cylinder::area()** function as follows:

```
float cylinder::area(void)
{
  return 4 * pi * radius * ht +
         2 * circle::area() + // Go back one level
         point::area();       // Go back two levels
}
```

Since **point::area()** always returns zero, this doesn't change the result of the **cylinder** area formula.

Note You can skip back as many levels in a class hierarchy as you like when calling inherited functions.

What does the following program print out?

```
#include <stdio.h>

struct grandpa {
  virtual void advice(void) { printf("Enjoy life!\n"); }
};

struct pa : grandpa {
  void advice(void) { printf("Do your homework!\n"); }
};

struct son : pa {
  void advice(void) { grandpa::advice(); }
};

main()
{
  son frankie;
  frankie.advice();
}
```

---

*The **son::advice()** function skips back two levels and calls the **grandpa::advice()** function. Thus, the program prints out "Enjoy life!"*

Virtual Functions versus Overloaded Functions

When dealing with derived classes, it's easy to make a mistake and turn what's supposed to be a virtual function into an overloaded function. Although virtual functions seem similar to overloaded member functions, the two are actually quite different. In particular:

- Overloaded member functions use static binding; virtual functions use dynamic binding.
- Overloaded member functions may or may not have different explicit argument types. Virtual functions must have the same explicit argument types. (Remember that both types of functions have the hidden **this** argument.)

The following is an example of what can go wrong when declaring virtual functions:

```
#include <stdio.h>

struct doit_less {
   virtual int doit(unsigned char c) { return --c; }
};

struct doit_more : doit_less {
   int doit(char c) { return ++c; }
};

main()
{
   doit_less *p = new doit_more;
   int k = p->doit(43);
   printf("k = %d\n", k);
}
```

What do you think this program prints out? If you guessed 44, you've been fooled.

Look carefully at the **doit()** function declarations. The **doit_less** version takes an **unsigned char** argument, but the **doit_more** version takes a **char** argument. Because the types don't match, the second **doit()** function is not virtual, it's overloaded. Thus, even though we point to a **doit_more** object with **p,** when calling **doit()** from **p**, it's the **doit_less** version that is used. Therefore, the program prints out 42.

Tip ‖ If a class hierarchy isn't working the way you think it should, check all your virtual function declarations to ensure you've used consistent argument types.

Virtual and Nonvirtual Function Interaction

Once you start using virtual functions, you'll begin to have questions about how they interact with other types of functions. For instance, what happens when a virtual function calls a nonvirtual function? What about overloaded functions? Can they be called from virtual functions? Can virtual functions call overloaded functions?

In order to help you sort all this out, the program **twotales.cpp**, Listing 9.3, shows examples of the possible interactions between the different kinds of functions. The program declares two classes, a base **fairy_tale** class and a derived **unhappy_tale** class. The **fairly_tale** class consists of five functions that represent the acts in a play. Except for the last act, each act calls the function for the next act. All of the different types of member functions—virtual, nonvirtual, and overloaded—are represented. The **unhappy_tale** class overrides the last three acts to change the outcome of the story.

There are two possible outcomes to the story which you can select at runtime. The following output shows the **fairy_tale** outcome:

```
Which tale would you like to hear (f/u)? f
Princess meets Frog
Princess kisses Frog
Frog turns into Prince
They live happily ever after
The end
```

And here is the **unhappy_tale** outcome:

```
Which tale would you like to hear (f/u)? u
Princess meets Frog
Princess kisses Frog
Frog stays a frog
Princess runs away in disgust
The not-so-happy end
```

Each of the five acts illustrates one of the possible interactions between the different types of functions. (Not all of the combinations are covered.) The acts will now be explained one at a time.

Note ‖ In the following discussion, the term "originating object" means the object through which **act1()** is invoked.

Act 1
Virtual functions don't have to be overridden. Class **fairy_tale** declares **act1()** virtual, but class **unhappy_tale** doesn't override it. Nevertheless, **act1()** is still callable from **unhappy_tale** objects.

Act 2
Virtual functions can call nonvirtual functions. The virtual **act1()** function calls the nonvirtual **act2()** function. Even if the originating object is an **unhappy_tale** object, the **fairy_tale act2()** function is called here.

Act 3
Nonvirtual functions can call virtual functions. The nonvirtual **act2()** function calls the virtual **act3()** function. Note that **act3()** is overridden in the **unhappy_tale** class. If the originating object is an **unhappy_tale** object, then the **unhappy_tale act3()** function will be called. Otherwise, **fairy_tale act3()** will be called.

Act 4
Virtual functions can call other virtual functions. The virtual **act3()** function calls the virtual **act4()** function. The version of **act4()** used depends on the type of the originating object.

Act 5
Virtual functions can call overloaded functions. Note that **act5()** is overloaded, not virtual. The virtual **act4()** function calls this overloaded function. The version of **act5()** used depends on the originating object.

Listing 9.3. The twotales.cpp Program

```
// twotales.cpp: Two fairy tales in one

#include <stdio.h>

struct fairy_tale {
  virtual void act1() { printf("Princess meets Frog\n"); act2(); }
  void act2()         { printf("Princess kisses Frog\n"); act3(); }
  virtual void act3() { printf("Frog turns into Prince\n"); act4(); }
  virtual void act4() { printf("They live happily ever after\n");
                        act5(); }
  void act5()         { printf("The end\n"); }
};
```

```
struct unhappy_tale : fairy_tale {
  void act3() { printf("Frog stays a frog\n"); act4(); }
  void act4() { printf("Princess runs away in disgust\n"); act5(); }
  void act5() { printf("The not-so-happy end\n"); }
};

main()
{
  char c;
  fairy_tale *tale;
  printf("Which tale would you like to hear (f/u)? ");
  scanf("%c", &c);
  if (c == 'f')
     tale = new fairy_tale; else tale = new unhappy_tale;
  tale->act1();
  delete tale;
}
```

Inside Virtual Functions

To understand how to use virtual functions, it's instructive to see how they are implemented. While function pointers are used, as we hinted earlier, it's not quite as simple as that. What's actually used is a *table* of function pointers. These tables are called *virtual function tables*.

Each class having at least one virtual function has a virtual function table associated with it. The table has an entry for each virtual function in the class, including those that had been inherited from a base class. Each table entry is a pointer to the actual function to call for the corresponding virtual function.

An object created from a class having virtual functions has an extra pointer stored in it that points to the virtual table for the class. Whenever a virtual function is called from that object, this pointer is traversed to locate the virtual function table, and then the appropriate function pointer is dereferenced from this table.

Figure 9.18 shows the virtual function tables used for the **fairy_tale** and **unhappy_tale** classes of the last section. Note how both tables point to the same **act1()** function. That's because that function wasn't overridden in the derived class. Note how the nonvirtual functions, **act2()** and **act5()**, don't appear in the tables at all.

Using Constructors and Destructors in Derived Classes

In this chapter's examples, we haven't used any constructors or destructors. In this section, we're going to show you how they work with derived classes.

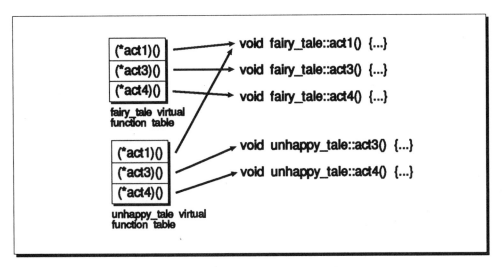

Figure 9.18. Virtual Function Tables

We'll start by adding constructors to the **point** and **circle** classes:

```
struct point {
  float x, y;
  point(float xi, float yi) { setlocn(xi, yi); } // Constructor
  void setlocn(float xi, float yi) { x = xi; y = yi; }
};

struct circle : point {
  float radius;
  circle(float xi, float yi, float r);
  setsize(float r) { radius = r; }
};

circle::circle(float xi, float yi, float r)
: point(xi, yi) // Call base class constructor
{
  setsize(r); // Initialize additional data
}
```

There's nothing special in the way you declare constructors for base classes, but there is for derived classes. Take a close look at the **circle** constructor. Note how it calls the constructor from the base class using the same syntax we used to initialize member objects:

```
: point(xi, yi) // Call base class constructor
```

This line initializes the inherited portion of a **circle** object, that is, the members **x** and **y** from the **point** class. Figure 9.19 illustrates the process of calling a base class constructor.

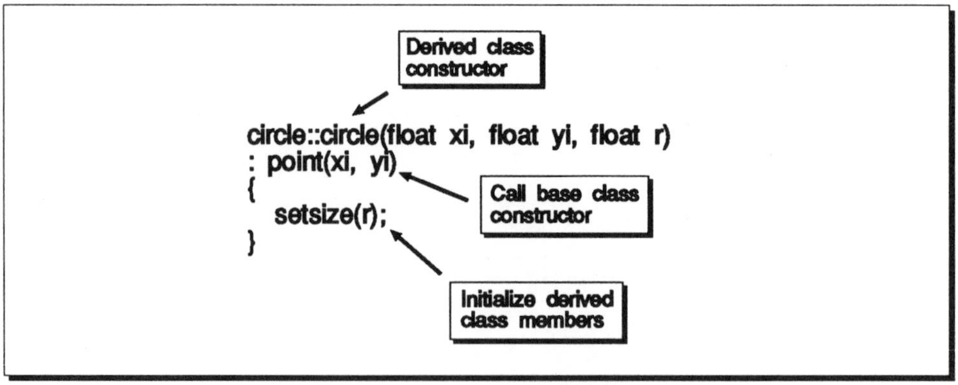

Figure 9.19. Calling a Base Class Constructor

As we've suggested before, you can think of the inherited part of a class as a hidden member. For instance, you can treat the **circle** class to have a hidden **point** member. We initialize this member with a constructor call. The trouble is, our hidden **point** member doesn't have a name, so we use the name of its class in the constructor call.

After calling the base class constructor, our **circle** constructor then initializes **radius** in the body of the derived class constructor. A base class constructor is always called before the body of the derived class constructor. It's also always called before any member constructors are. This ensures that the base portion of an object is completely initialized before the derived portion is.

Even though the base portion is initialized first, you don't always have to call a constructor to have that portion initialized. If the base class has a constructor requiring no arguments, or if all the arguments have defaults, then you don't need to make a call to a base class constructor. The compiler will do it for you, and supply the default arguments, if necessary.

For instance, let's add another constructor to the **point** class taking no arguments:

```
struct point {
  ...
  point(void) { set(0, 0); }
};
```

We could also add another constructor to the **circle** class that calls this new **point** constructor implicitly:

```
struct circle : point {
  ...
  circle(float r);
};
```

```
circle::circle(float r)
// Call to base class constructor is implicit
{
   setsize(r);
};
```

Here, the inherited members **x** and **y** are implicitly initialized to zero, and then **radius** is initialized in the derived class constructor body.

There's another rule about constructors and derived classes: If all the constructors in the base class require parameters, then the derived class must have a constructor, and it must call one of the base class constructors. Thus, in the original **point** and **circle** classes that had constructors, the **circle** constructor was not optional, and it had to call the **point** class constructor.

Destructors work the opposite way constructors do. Since destructors take no arguments, destructor calls are implicitly made for you by the compiler. When an object from a derived class goes out of scope, the destructor for the derived class is called first. This is followed by calls to any destructors for the additional members of the derived class, which is then followed by a call to the base class destructor. Finally, calls are made to any destructors for the members of the base class.

To see these rules about constructors and destructors in action, the program in Listing 9.4 shows a **computer** class that knows how to add, but has no memory, and a derived **smart_computer** class that has memory. Both classes have default constructors, and both classes have destructors. Thus, calls to the constructors and destructors are made implicitly.

The program produces the following output (which we've annotated to show you the order of function calling). Note the reverse order in which the constructors and destructors are called with respect to each other:

```
Booting up ...              // Base class constructor
Resetting memory            // Derived class constructor
Total so far is: 42.000000
Clearing contents of memory // Derived class destructor
Powering down ...           // Base class destructor
```

Listing 9.4. The compadd.cpp Program

```
// compadd.cpp: Example of calling constructors and destructors
// implicitly in base and derived classes.

#include <stdio.h>

struct computer {
  computer(void)  { printf("Booting up ...\n"); }
```

```
  ~computer(void) { printf("Powering down ...\n"); }
  float add(float a, float b) { return a + b; }
};

struct smart_computer : computer {
  float memory;
  smart_computer(void);
  ~smart_computer(void);
  void memorize(float m)      { memory = m;        }
  float add_to_memory(float f) { return memory += f; }
  float recall(void)          { return memory;     }
};

smart_computer::smart_computer(void)
// This constructor implicitly calls the computer
// constructor before executing the body
{
  printf("Resetting memory\n");
  memory = 0;
}

smart_computer::~smart_computer(void)
// This destructor implicitly calls the computer
// destructor after executing the body
{
  printf("Clearing contents of memory\n");
  memory = 0;
}

main()
{
  smart_computer i786;
  i786.memorize(20.0);
  i786.add_to_memory(5.0);
  i786.add_to_memory(17.0);
  printf("Total so far is: %f\n", i786.recall());
}
```

Virtual Constructors and Destructors

Sooner or later you are going to encounter situations where you would like to make a constructor or destructor virtual. The following are some rules relevant to these situations.

- *Constructors are not inherited*. This means you can't use a base class constructor to initialize a derived class object. The derived class must have a constructor of its own, although it can call the base class constructor.
- *Constructors can't be virtual*. Since constructors aren't inherited, there's not much point in making them virtual.

- *Destructors can and probably should be virtual.* If you override a destructor, then you should make it virtual to guarantee that the correct version will be called even when a base class pointer is used.

You might be tempted to get around the restriction that a constructor can't be virtual. One possible scenario for doing this would be to have the constructor call a virtual function. Can this be done? The answer is that it can, but it won't produce the right results. The problem is that when a virtual function is called from a base class constructor, the base class version of that function is always called. The constructor doesn't know about any overridden versions of that same function.

1. What does the following program output, and why?

```
#include <stdio.h>

struct silent_man {
  silent_man(void) { talk(); }
  virtual void talk(void) { return; } // Don't say anything
};

struct gabby_man : silent_man {
  int some_var;
  gabby_man(int v)     { some_var = v; }
  void talk(void) { printf("Gab gab gab\n"); }
};

main()
{
  gabby_man neighbor(17);
}
```

2. Type in and run the following program. What does it output?

```
#include <stdio.h>

struct sun {
  virtual ~sun(void) { printf(" It's bright!\n"); }
};

struct fun : sun {
  ~fun(void) { printf("Wow!"); }
};

main()
{
  sun *s = new fun;
  delete s;
};
```

3. In the program given in Question 2, what happens if you remove the **virtual** keyword from the **sun** destructor declaration?

---

1. *Even though **neighbor** is a **gabby_man** object, nothing is output. The **gabby_man** constructor calls the **silent_man** constructor which in turn calls the virtual **talk()** function. However, **silent_man::talk()** is called instead of **gabby_man::talk()** in the **silent_man** constructor.*

   *You should avoid calling a virtual function from a constructor. The fix for the program here is to take out the **talk()** function, and have the **gabby_man** constructor handle the talking directly:*

```
struct silent_man {
  silent_man(void) { return; } // Constructor no longer needed
};

struct gabby_man : silent_man {
  int some_var;
  gabby_man(int v) { some_var = v; printf("Gab gab gab\n"); }
};
```

2. *The program uses a **sun** base class pointer to point to a **fun** derived class object that was allocated dynamically. When the **delete** statement executes, the destructor for the **fun** object is called, which prints out "Wow!" Then, the destructor for the **sun** base class is called, which prints out "It's bright!" Thus the total output is "Wow! It's bright!"*

3. *If we remove the **virtual** keyword from the **sun** destructor, then the destructor won't be virtual. Thus, when the **delete** statement is executed, only the **sun** destructor is called, not the **fun** destructor. The program prints out only "It's bright!" In this case, the skipped destructor call is relatively harmless. However, what if the **fun** destructor was supposed to deallocate some dynamic memory created by a **fun** object? The memory wouldn't be deallocated.*

Inheritance and Data Hiding

Thus far in this chapter, we haven't considered the interaction between inheritance and data hiding. All of the members of the classes we've shown have been public. We haven't had any private members to contend with. In this section, we'll study how to control the access of inherited members in a derived class.

There are several rules that govern the access rights of an inherited member:

- If a member is private in the base class, then it's not accessible in the derived class. However, public base class members can be accessed in the derived class.
- If a derived class is declared using the **struct** keyword, then by default, the public base class members are public in the derived class.
- If a derived class is declared using the **class** keyword, then by default, the public base class members are private in the derived class.

The first rule may surprise you a little. Let's look at an example. Consider the following base class **spy** and derived class **informant**:

```
struct spy {
private:
  char *secret_document; // Private secret information
public:
  char *alias;            // Spy's public alias name
};

struct informant : spy {
  char *leak_to_press(void) {
    return secret_document;    // Illegal
  }
  char *source(void) {
    return alias;              // Legal
  }
};
```

Here, **secret_document** is private to **spy**, and cannot be used outside the **spy** class, not even in the derived class **informant**. However, since **alias** is public in **spy**, it can be accessed in **informant**.

Even though a public base class member is accessible to a derived class, that doesn't necessarily mean it's accessible to users of the derived class. That is, the member might be private to all functions outside the class. The third rule indicates this fact.

The third rule mentions that a derived class can be declared using the **class** keyword. We haven't done that yet in this chapter, so let's look at an example. In the following code, we derive the class **secret_code** from the class **code_data**, using the **class** keyword.

```
struct code_data {
  int code; // Public data
};

class secret_code : code_data {
public:
  int another_code;
  void set_code(void) { another_code = code; }
};
```

```
code_data cd;
secret_code sc;

cd.code = 42;          // Ok, public to base class
sc.code = 42;          // Illegal, private to derived class
sc.another_code = 42;  // Ok, public to derived class
```

Because the **class** keyword was used when declaring **secret_code**, the inherited member **code** is private to the **secret_code** class, and can thus not be accessed through a **secret_code** object. The member **code** can still be accessed through a **code_data** object, though. And it can also be accessed inside the **secret_code** class, as we've done in the function **set_code()**.

The last two rules we gave are only default rules. You can override these defaults by using the **public** or **private** keyword before the base class name in a derived class declaration. For instance:

```
class secret_code : public code_data { // Note public keyword
public:
  int another_code;
  void set_code(void) { another_code = code; }
};

secret_code sc;

sc.code = 42;     // Now this is legal
```

Using the **public** keyword before the base class name makes that base class a *public base class*. That is, all public members of the base class are public in the derived class. Thus, in this example, **code** is public in the **secret_code** class, rather than private as it would have been by default.

Likewise, using the **private** keyword before the base class name makes the base class a *private base class*. That is, all public members of the base class are now private in the derived class. For instance, in the following code, the public **financial_data** members **income** and **expenses** become private in the **corporation** class:

```
struct financial_data {
  float income;
  float expenses;
};

struct corporation : private financial_data {
  float stock;
  void set_stock_price(void) {
    stock = (income-expenses)/42.0; // Legal accesses
  }
};
```

```
financial_data fd;
corporation c;

fd.income = 0.0;         // Legal, member is public
fd.expenses = 10000.00;  // Legal, member is public
c.income = 1000000.00;   // Illegal, member is private
c.expenses = 0.00;       // Illegal, member is private
c.stock = 3000.0;        // Legal, member is public
```

Using Protected Members

In some situations, you want to have members that are accessible to both a base class and a derived class, but that are otherwise private. The **protected** keyword is provided for this purpose.

For example, suppose you have the following **editor_buffer** class:

```
class editor_buffer {
private:
  char *text;     // Text buffer for edited data
  int dirty_bit;  // Flag indicating buffer was modified
public:
  void replace(int start, int len, char *newtext);
};
```

The **editor_buffer** class manages a text buffer and "dirty bit" flag which indicates when the buffer has been modified. We made these members private, since they are details best left hidden. However, suppose we derive a **file_editor** class that allows us to edit a file:

```
class file_editor : public editor_buffer {
public:
  int open(char *fname);
  void close(void);
  int read_text(void);
  int edit_text(void);
  int write_text(void);
};
```

In order to be efficient, **file_editor** will most likely have to access the members **text** and **dirty_bit** of **editor_buffer** directly. However, **file_editor** can't access them at all, since they are private members of the base class. What do we do?

The solution is to make **text** and **dirty_bit** *protected members*. A protected member in a base class is in between a public and private member. It is accessible to members of a derived class, almost as if it were public in the base class. However, it is private to users of the derived class.

Here's a modified version of **editor_buffer**, using the **protected** keyword:

```
class editor_buffer {
protected:         // Note new keyword
  char *text;      // Text buffer for edited data
  int dirty_bit;   // Flag indicating buffer was modified
public:
  void replace(int start, int len, char *newtext);
};
```

Now **text** and **dirty_bit** can be used inside the derived class **file_editor** without making them public.

There's one more thing you should know about protected members: If a public base class has protected members, then those members stay protected in the derived class. If a private base class has protected members, then those members become private in the derived class.

Tip ‖ It's typical to make base classes public. This provides the greatest flexibility for the derived classes. Figure 9.20 shows an example, using our edit buffer and file editor classes.

Abstract Classes

In most situations, the base class of a hierarchy should be very general. It should contain very little code at all. Instead, it should leave all of the specifics to the derived classes. In fact, in some cases, it makes sense for the base class to be so general that it shouldn't even be used to directly create objects. Turbo

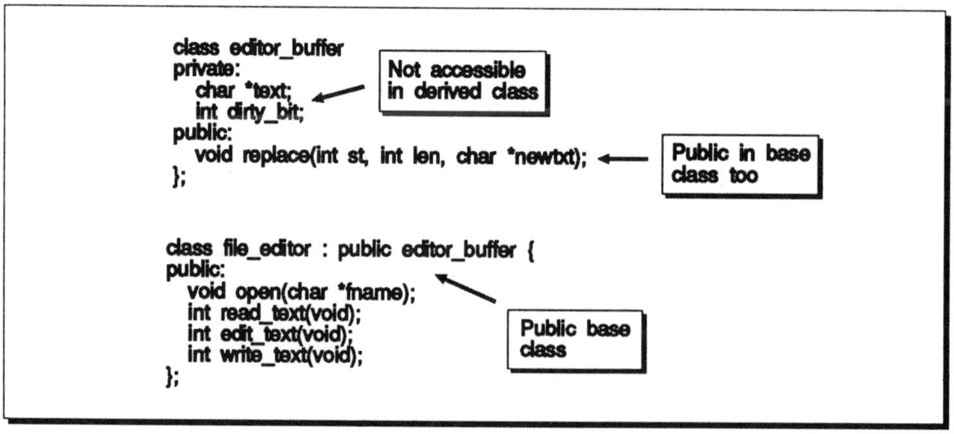

Figure 9.20. Access Control in a Class Hierarchy

C++ supports such classes, which are called *abstract classes*. Abstract classes use special types of functions called *pure virtual functions*.

To see how to declare abstract classes, consider an abstract stack class. This class should contain functions that define at a high level the operations that stacks have, such as push and pop. We don't want to actually define these functions in the abstract class. Thus what we do is make them *pure virtual functions*. Such functions don't have definitions. That is, they don't have function bodies.

To make a virtual function pure, you use syntax such as the following:

```
virtual int push(int) = 0;
```

This syntax may look a little strange at first. It looks as though you're setting the function to zero. In a sense, you are. You're setting the body to "nothing."

Any class that has at least one pure virtual function is called an *abstract class*. This type of class is truly abstract. The compiler won't let you create objects from such a class. You can only create objects from classes derived from the abstract class, and then only as long as the derived classes provide bodies for the pure virtual functions.

Tip Although you can't create an object from an abstract class, nothing stops you from declaring an abstract class pointer or reference. In fact, it's typical to do so. Such pointers and references can only point to derived class objects, though.

Using pure virtual functions, the following code shows how to declare an abstract stack class:

```
class abstk {
public:
  abstk(void)           { return; }
  virtual ~abstk(void) { return; }
  // Pure virtual functions
  virtual int push(int)   = 0;
  virtual int pop(int &) = 0;
  virtual int top_of()    = 0;
  virtual int isempty()   = 0;
  virtual int isfull()    = 0;
};
```

Note Constructors and destructors can't be declared as pure virtual functions.

When defining an abstract class, what you're doing is setting up a common protocol for all the derived classes. That is, you're determining what common set of functions the derived classes will have, and what the arguments to those functions look like.

Along these lines, you might wonder what the return values on the functions **push()**, **pop()**, and **top_of()** are for. The return values indicate the success or failure of the particular operation. A zero means the operation failed, a one means it succeeded. The **push()** function fails when the stack is full, and the **pop()** and **top_of()** functions fail when the stack is empty.

Now that we have our abstract class defined, let's put it to use in creating a hierarchy of stack classes. In particular, we'll derive two stack classes from the **abstk** class. One will implement a stack using an array. The other will use a linked list.

The code for our stack classes is given in Listings 9.5 to 9.9. There are three header files involved, **abstk.h**, **astk.h**, and **lstk.h**, which declare the three stack classes. And there are two implementation files, **astk.cpp** and **lstk.cpp**, that implement the array-based and list-based stack classes, respectively. No implementation file is needed for the abstract stack class, since it doesn't have any noninline functions that have bodies.

Listing 9.10, **stkrev.cpp**, is the program that uses the stack class hierarchy. It uses a stack to print out in reverse order a string of characters input from the keyboard. In the program, a pointer to an abstract stack object is used in the stack operations. The pointer is initialized to point to either an array-based stack or a list-based stack. Note that the code using the abstract pointer has no idea what kind of stack is actually being used.

A sample output from the program is:

```
Turbo C++
++C obruT
```

Listing 9.5. The abstk.h Header File

```
// abstk.h: Header file for abstract integer stack class

#ifndef H_ABSTK
#define H_ABSTK

class abstk { // Abstract stack
public:
  abstk(void) { return; } // Shown for completeness. Not needed.
  virtual ~abstk(void) { return; } // Can't make this pure virtual!
  virtual int push(int)    = 0;
  virtual int pop(int &)   = 0;
  virtual int top_of(int &) = 0;
  virtual int isempty(void) = 0;
```

```
    virtual int isfull(void)  = 0;
  };

  #endif
```

Listing 9.6. The astk.h Header File

```
// astk.h: Header file for array-based integer stack

#ifndef H_ASTK
#define H_ASTK
#include "abstk.h"

class astk : public abstk { // array-based stack
private:
  int *memory;
  int size, top_elem;
public:
  astk(int sz);
 ~astk(void) { delete[size] memory; }
  virtual int push(int v);
  virtual int pop(int &v);
  virtual int top_of(int &t);
  virtual int isempty(void) { return top_elem == -1; }
  virtual int isfull(void)  { return top_elem == size-1; }
};

#endif
```

Listing 9.7. The astk.cpp Implementation File

```
// astk.cpp: Implementation file for astk class

#include "astk.h"

astk::astk(int sz)
// Allocate room for sz integers. Initialize
// top of stack.
{
  memory = new int[size = sz];
  top_elem = -1;
}

int astk::push(int v)
// Pushes v onto the stack. Returns 1 if successful,
// returns 0 if stack is full
{
  if (top_elem < size-1) {
```

```
      memory[++top_elem] = v;
      return 1;
   }
   else return 0;
}

int astk::pop(int &v)
// Pops the number off the stack and stores in v.
// Returns 1 if successful, 0 if stack empty
{
   if (top_elem != -1) {
      v = memory[top_elem--];
      return 1;
   }
   else return 0;
}

int astk::top_of(int &t)
// Place the top of the stack in t. Returns
// 1 if successful, 0 if stack is empty
{
   if (top_elem != -1) {
      t = memory[top_elem];
      return 1;
   }
   else return 0;
}
```

Listing 9.8. The lstk.h Header File

```
// lstk.h: Header file for list-based integer stack

#ifndef H_LSTK
#define H_LSTK
#include "abstk.h"

class lstk;

class snode {    // Private stack node class
private:
   friend lstk;  // Only list stack class can use
   int val;      // Node value
   snode *prev;  // Pointer to node below this one
   snode(int v, snode *p) { val = v; prev = p; }
};

class lstk : public abstk { // List-based stack
private:
   snode *top_node; // Pointer to top of stack
   int allocerr;    // Private flag indicating no more room
```

```
public:
  lstk(void) { top_node = 0; allocerr = 0; }
  ~lstk(void);
  virtual int push(int v);
  virtual int pop(int &v);
  virtual int top_of(int &t);
  virtual int isempty(void) { return top_node == 0; }
  virtual int isfull(void)  { return allocerr; }
};

#endif
```

Listing 9.9. The lstk.cpp Implementation File

```
// lstk.cpp: Implementation file for the list-based stack

#include "lstk.h"

lstk::~lstk(void)
// Delete all nodes on the stack
{
  while(top_node) {
    snode *s = top_node->prev;
    delete top_node;
    top_node = s;
  }
}

int lstk::push(int v)
// Push v on the stack by creating a new node for it
// Returns 1 if successful, 0 if out of memory
// Sets allocerr flag too if out of memory
{
  snode *t = new snode(v, top_node);
  if (t) top_node = t;
  if (!t) allocerr = 1;
  return !allocerr;
}

int lstk::pop(int &v)
// Pops the top of the stack into v. Returns 1 if
// successful, 0 if stack is empty
{
  if (top_node) {
    snode *t = top_node;
    v = t->val;
    top_node = top_node->prev;
    delete t;
    return 1;
  }
```

```
  else return 0; // Stack empty
}

int lstk::top_of(int &t)
// Puts top of stack into t. Returns 1 if
// successful, 0 if stack is empty
{
  if (top_node) {
     t = top_node->val; return 1;
  }
  else return 0;
}
```

Listing 9.10. The stkrev.cpp Program

```
// stkrev.cpp: String reversal program using a stack class hierarchy

#include <conio.h>
#include "astk.h"  // Uncomment this to use array stack
// #include "lstk.h"  // Uncomment this to use list stack

main()
{
  int c;
  abstk *cs = new astk(255); // Uncomment this to use array stack
  //abstk *cs = new lstk;  // Uncomment this to use list stack

  // The code that follows doesn't know what kind of stack is
  // really being used

  // Push characters on the stack until newline received
  while((c = getche()) != '\r') { cs->push(c); }
  putch('\n');

  // Print characters out in reverse order
  while(cs->pop(c)) { putch(c); }
  putch('\r\n');

  delete cs;
}
```

Summary

Classes are the most important aspect of Turbo C++ programming, and you could argue that inheritance is the most important aspect of classes. Even though the class features of data hiding and encapsulation are very important, it's inheritance that really makes a C++ program different from a C program.

The two key components needed to achieve inheritance are derived classes and virtual functions. The magic behind derived classes is that derived class objects can be substituted for base class objects in existing code. This makes the original code, even if it's already compiled, instantly reusable for new applications. However, couple derived classes with virtual functions, and suddenly, you have the ability to override the way the original code works. If you're lucky (i.e., if the original programmer designed the classes right), you can do this all without touching the original source code.

Exercises

1. Write a class with a function that accepts an floating point argument to be added to a running total. Also, provide a function to retrieve that total. Then, derive a class that adds the ability to keep an average of the numbers input, along with a function to retrieve the average. Include a constructor in each class, and use appropriate data hiding.
2. Name the two ways that polymorphism can be achieved in Turbo C++. Which uses static binding, and which uses dynamic binding?
3. Name two ways to achieve dynamic binding in Turbo C++.
4. Find four mistakes in the following class hierarchy:

```
class one_num {
private:
  int n;
  one_num(int v) { n = v; }
public:
  virtual void inc(void) { n++; }
  int get(void) { return n; }
};

class two_num : one_num {
private:
  int m;
public:
  two_num(int v1, int v2) { m = v2; }
  void inc(void) { n++; m++; }
  int get_second(void) { return m; }
};
```

5. If you type in and run the following program, you'll get a null pointer assignment. Can you discover what is wrong? (Hint: Look at the way the constructors are coded.)

```
// smartcmp.cpp: This sample program has a problem with the
// way the constructors are coded.
```

```
#include <stdio.h>

struct computer {
  computer(void);
  virtual ~computer(void)  { printf("~computer() body called\n"); }
  virtual void setup(void) { printf("computer::setup() called\n"); }
  int add(int a, int b)    { return a + b; }
};

computer::computer(void)
{
  printf("computer() body called\n");
  setup(); // Call virtual function here
}

struct smart_computer : computer { // Computer with memory
  int *ram;                        // Here's the memory
  smart_computer(void);
  ~smart_computer(void);
  void setup(void); // Override the setup function
  void store(int mem_loc, int num) { ram[mem_loc] = num;  }
  int recall(int mem_loc)          { return ram[mem_loc]; }
};

smart_computer::smart_computer(void)
// Calls the computer() constructor implicitly, hoping that
// it will in turn call smart_computer::setup() and allocate
// the ram.
{
  printf("smart_computer() body called\n");
}

smart_computer::~smart_computer(void)
// Deallocate 128 ram locations
{
  printf("~smart_computer() body called\n");
  delete[128] ram;
}

void smart_computer::setup(void)
// Allocate 128 ram locations
{
  printf("smart_computer::setup() called\n");
  ram = new int[128];
}

main()
{
  smart_computer deep_thought;
  deep_thought.store(0, 42); // Probable system crash!!
}
```

Answers

1. *Here's one way:*

```
class sigma {
protected:
   float total; // The total so far
public:
   sigma(void) { total = 0; }
   virtual void accumulate(int v) { total += v; }
   float running_total(void)     { return total; }
};

class mu : public sigma {
protected:
   int n; // Keeps track of how many numbers have been counted
public:
   mu(void) { n = 0; } // Remember, sigma() called implicitly
   void accumulate(int v);
   float average(void) { return n ? total/n : 0.0; }
};

void mu::accumulate(int v)
// Count the input, and then add to the total
{
   n++; sigma::accumulate(v);
}
```

2. *Polymorphism can be achieved by using overloaded functions (static binding) and virtual functions (dynamic binding).*
3. *You can use function pointers or virtual functions.*
4. *First, the **two_num()** constructor doesn't call the **one_num()** constructor, even though it's supposed to. Second, the **one_num()** constructor is private, so there's no way for **two_num()** to call **one_num()** even if it wanted to. Third, since **one_num** was declared as a private base class (by default), the function **one_num::get()** is private in the derived class, although it probably shouldn't be. Finally, **two_num::inc()** tries to access **n**, even though **n** is private in the base class, and is thus not accessible in the derived class.*
5. *In the base class constructor **computer()**, we try to pull a trick and have the virtual **setup()** function called, in the hopes that it will allocate the memory needed for **smart_computer()** objects. The problem is that it won't. The base class version of **setup()** will always be used, so the memory would never be allocated. The result is a probable system crash if you should run the program.*

   Here's what the output of the program would be (which we've annotated with comments):

```
computer() body called    // Correct
computer::setup() called   // Wrong setup() called
```

```
smart_computer() body called    // Correct
~smart_computer() body called   // Correct
~computer() body called         // Correct
Null pointer assignment         // Oops!
```

*You might think this is a serious flaw in Turbo C++. This is not true. The problem with our program is that it is organized incorrectly. We should throw out the **setup()** function altogether, and have the derived class constructor handle the memory allocation. The two constructors should be coded as follows:*

```
computer::computer(void)
// Don't call setup()
{
  printf("computer() body called\n");
}

smart_computer::smart_computer(void)
// Allocate memory right here
{
  printf("smart_computer() body called\n");
  ram = new int[128];
}
```

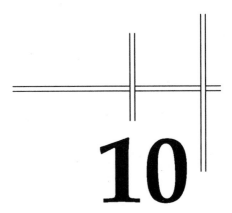

Using Operator Functions

In previous chapters we've seen the rich set of features that Turbo C++ provides for writing high-level programs. We've seen classes, inline functions, constructors, destructors, and overloaded and virtual functions. These features make Turbo C++ much more expressible than C at creating user-defined types. However, there's still one more feature to add to your arsenal: *operator functions*.

Operator functions are special types of functions which you can use to redefine the basic operators available in Turbo C++. For instance, you can redefine the + operator to not only add numbers, but to concatenate strings as well. Two of the operators (which you may not have known were operators at all) are particularly important: the assignment operator =, and the subscript operator []. You'll see how these operators can be redefined to create robust user-defined arrays.

There are also special types of operator functions, *conversion operator functions*, which aren't tied to any of the usual operators, but rather, are used to create user-defined type casts. You'll see these kind of functions in action too.

After completing this chapter, the following will have been discussed:

- How to define and call operator functions
- How to overload operator functions
- How to declare member operator functions
- When and how to use friend operator functions
- How to overload the assignment and subscript operators

- How to overload arithmetic operators
- How to create conversion operator functions

An Operator Overloading Example

Before we begin an in-depth discussion of operator functions, let's plunge right in and create an operator function. Consider the += operator. It's normally used to add a value to a number, be it a **char, int, float,** or **double.** However, we can redefine += to work with, let's say, **circular_num** objects as well. Recall the **circular_num** class of previous chapters:

```
class circular_num {
private:
  int num;
  int upper, lower, range;
public:
  circular_num(int v, int 1, int u);
  int set_val(int v);
  int get_val(void) { return num; }
};
```

To overload the binary += operator for our **circular_num** class, we must declare a function whose name is **operator+=().** This function must take two arguments corresponding to the two operands for +=:

```
void operator+=(circular_num &c, int v)
{
  c.set_val(c.get_val() + v); // Add v to value of c
}
```

We've made the first argument a reference to a **circular_num** object, and the second an integer. These two arguments map to the left and right operands of the operation. Figure 10.1 shows this mapping.

The following code is a call to the newly redefined += operator:

```
circular_num c(0, 0, 9);

c += 5; // Adds 5 to c
```

It's also possible to call the operator function with a normal function call:

```
operator+=(c, 5);
```

You can also declare operator functions to be class members. For instance, we could change **operator+=()** to be part of the **circular_num** class:

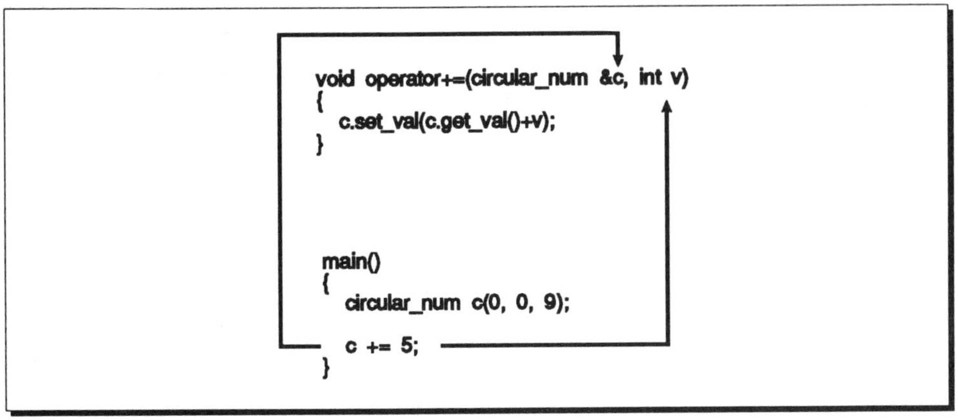

Figure 10.1. Operator Function Calling

```
class circular_num {
  ...
  void operator+=(int v); // Member operator function
};

void circular_num::operator+=(int v)
// Implement operator function
{
  set_val(num+v);
}
```

Member operator functions take one less visible argument than do nonmember operator functions. Although += is a binary operator, our member operator function has only one visible argument, which is the right-hand integer operand. The left-hand operand comes from the hidden **this** argument.

We could call the member operator function two ways: either using operator syntax or using function call syntax:

```
c += 5;
c.operator+=(5);
```

Figure 10.2 illustrates the mapping between operator expressions and member operator function calls.

Declaring Operator Functions

Now that you've seen firsthand what operator functions are and what they can do for you, let's take a closer look at how they are declared. The syntax for an operator function, shown for both members and nonmembers, is as follows:

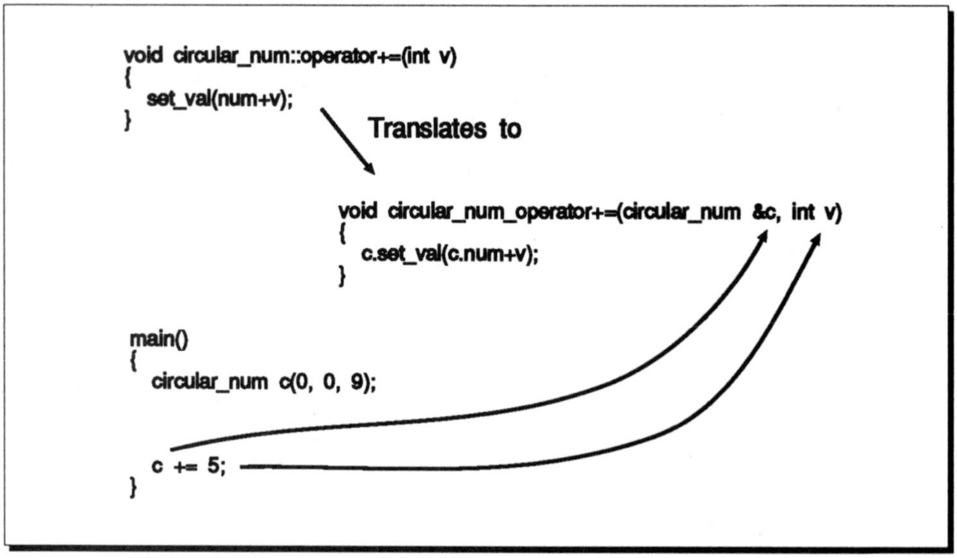

```
void circular_num::operator+=(int v)
{
    set_val(num+v);
}                        Translates to


                    void circular_num_operator+=(circular_num &c, int v)
                    {
                        c.set_val(c.num+v);
                    }

main()
{
    circular_num c(0, 0, 9);


    c += 5;
}
```

Figure 10.2. Member Operator Function Calling

Class Member:

```
<Return_Type> <Class>::operator<Op>(Arg, ...)
{
  <Body>
}
```

Non-Member:

```
<Return_Type> operator<Op>(Arg, ...)
{
  <Body>
}
```

As you can see, an operator function has the same components that any function has, including a name, return type, arguments, body, and possible class scope. What sets an operator function apart from other functions is its name: **operator<Op>**, where **<Op>** is one of the C++ operators. Table 10.1 shows which operators can be used in an operator function.

There are two basic issues involved when you wish to declare an operator function:

- Whether the operator itself is unary or binary
- Whether the operator function is a class member or not

======== Table 10.1. Overloadable Operators

+	-	*	/	%	^	&	|
~	!	,	=	<	>	<=	>=
++	--	<<	>>	==	!=	&&	||
+=	-=	/=	%=	^=	&=	|=	<<=
>>=	[]	()	->	->*	new	delete	

These two issues work in conjunction, and determine the number and type of arguments the operator functions take. All together, there are four ways to declare operator functions. Figure 10.3 shows examples of each using the **circular_num** class.

Understanding Operator Function Calling

The key to understanding how to design and create operator functions is in understanding how operator expressions are translated into function calls. This translation depends on whether the operator is unary or binary, and on the member status of the operator function. Tables 10.2 and 10.3 show how the translation works for unary and binary operators, respectively.

Unary Operators

Member

```
void circular_num::operator++(void)
{
    set_val(num+1);
}
```

Nonmember

```
void operator++(circular_num &c)
{
    c.set_val(c.get_val()+1);
}
```

Binary Operators

Member

```
void circular_num::operator+=(int v)
{
    set_val(num+v);
}
```

Nonmember

```
void operator+=(circular_num &c, int v)
{
    c.set_val(c.get_val()+v);
}
```

======== Figure 10.3. Examples of Declaring Operator Functions

Table 10.2. Calling Binary Operator Functions

Member Function	Syntax	Actual Call
Yes	X Op Y	X.operatorOp(Y)
No	X Op Y	operatorOp(X,Y)

Table 10.3. Calling Unary Operator Functions

Member Function	Syntax	Actual Call
Yes	Op X	X.operatorOp()
Yes	X Op	X.operatorOp()
No	Op X	operatorOp(X)
No	X Op	operatorOp(X)

You can see how for member operator functions, the first operand of an operator expression always translates into the object through which the operator function is called.

Table 10.3 points out an unfortunate fact. It's not possible to differentiate between prefix and postfix uses of overloaded unary operators. For example, suppose we define a unary ++ operator function for our **circular_num** class:

```
class circular_num {
  ...
  int operator++(void) { return set_val(num + 1); }
};

main()
{
  circular_num c(0, 0, 359);

  c++;  // Calls x.operator++()
  ++c;  // Also calls x.operator++()
}
```

This can get you into trouble if you're not aware of when the increment actually takes place. Note that as we've defined **operator++()**, it works as a prefix operator. The value of the **circular_num** is incremented, and then the value is returned. Thus, in the following statements, the first works as expected, but the second does not:

```
int k - ++c; // Increment c, then set k to the value
int k - c++; // Same order, but misleading
```

Suppose we did want to define our **operator++()** function to work for postincrement cases. The following is how we could do it:

```
int circular_num::operator++(void)
{
  int v - num;     // Save value
  set_val(num+1);  // Increment value
  return v;        // Return old value
}
```

1. If we overloaded the + operator for the **circular_num** class, and made the operator function a member, how many explicit arguments should it have?
2. Write a member operator function for the **circular_num** class to overload the equality operator ==. Is there more than one way to write the function?

1. *It depends which version of + we're trying to overload. The + operator has both unary and binary forms. For unary plus, the function should take no arguments. For binary plus, it should take one argument.*
2. *Here are two possible solutions:*

```
int circular_num::operator--(circular_num &other)
// The objects are equal if their values are the same
{
  return num -- other.num;
}
```

```
circular_num::operator--(circular_num &other)
// The objects are equal if the values are the same
// AND their ranges are the same
{
  if (num !- other.num) return 0;
  if (lower !- other.lower) return 0;
  return upper -- other.upper;
}
```

Overloading Operator Functions

In the first operator overloading example we gave, we defined the **operator+=()** function so that we could add integers to **circular_num** objects. We could also define another **operator+=()** function so that we could add one **circular_num** object to another. That is, we can overload the operator function itself. Here's how:

```
class circular_num {
  ...
  void operator+=(int v);          // First version
  void operator+=(circular_num &x); // Another version
};

void circular_num::operator+=(int v)
// Add integer to circular_num
{
  set_val(num + v);
}

void circular_num::operator+=(circular_num &x)
// Add value of one circular_num to another
{
  set_val(num + x.num);
}

circular_num a(0, 0, 9), b(17, 1, 360);

a += 2; // Add 2 to value of a
a += b; // Add b's value of 17 to a
```

Using Reference Arguments in Operator Functions

Note that we used a reference argument in the second version of **operator+=()** in the previous section:

```
void circular_num::operator+=(circular_num &x);
```

This was no accident. One of the reasons that reference variables were added to C++ was to make operator functions work more naturally. For example, suppose we didn't have reference variables. Then the source operand to **operator+=()** would either have to be passed by value, which means an extra copy of the source would be made, or we would have to use a pointer.

Suppose we changed our **operator+=()** function to use a pointer:

```
void circular_num::operator+=(circular_num *x);
```

The following code shows what assignments to **circular_num** objects would then look like:

```
circular_num a(0, 0, 9), b(17, 1, 360);
a += &b; // Take address of b first
```

We had to take the address of **b** in order for the call to be correct. This is clumsy and error prone. Using a reference argument is much cleaner.

Tip ‖ It's often useful to declare arguments to operator functions as reference arguments, since it makes the resulting operator syntax cleaner. It also makes the operator function more efficient, as no copying has to be done.

Restrictions on Operator Functions

While operator functions can add versatility to your C++ programs, there are some restrictions you should be aware of:

- *You can't define new operators.* For example, the two-character symbol $ is not an operator in C++, so you can't define an operator function named **operator$^()**.
- *You can't change the arity or precedence of an operator.* For example, the = operator is binary, so you can't declare a unary operator function using that symbol. Also, = binds looser than +. Thus, the expression **x = a + b** always means **x = (a+b)** not **(x=a) + b**. You can't change the way these two operators group together.
- *At least one argument of an operator function must be a class object, or the operator function must be a class member.* For instance, you can't redefine the + operator to concatenate character strings:

```
char *operator+(char *a, char *b);  // Illegal
```

This restriction means you can't change the way the operators work with any of the built-in types.
- *Operators can't be combined to create new operators.* For example, you can't take an operator function named **operator+()** and combine it with a function named **operator=()** and expect to be able to use it in expressions like **a += b**. Of course, nothing stops you from defining an operator function named **operator+=()**, as you saw earlier. It's just that you can't split the task into two operator functions.
- *The operators =, [], (), and -> must be nonstatic member functions.* In a later section when we study the assignment operator, you'll learn why this restriction exists.

While these rules might seem complicated and arbitrary, they have two common purposes:

1. To keep the compiler from having to change its parsing rules for each

program compiled. We don't want it to have to accommodate additional operators or changes to the precedence or arity of existing operators

2. To ensure that the use of the operators with built-in types cannot be modified. Imagine the chaos that would ensue if, for instance, you were able to make the addition of two integers cause a multiplication instead.

Now that you know about the restrictions for using operator functions, in the next sections we'll take a look at overloading some of the more common operators, such as =, [], and +.

Which of the following operator functions are legal?

a. `complex operator+(complex a, complex b);`
b. `void clock::operator++(void);`
c. `char *operator+(char *a, char *b);`
d. `void operator@(menu bar1, menu bar2);`
e. `menu operator++(menu a, menu b);`
f. `void string::operator+=(char *s);`

The answers and reasons why are:

a. Legal, since the function takes the proper number of arguments for the binary + operator, and at least one of the arguments is an object.

b. Legal, because ++ is a unary operator, and for member unary functions, no arguments are specified.

c. Illegal, because the function has no arguments that are objects, and it is not a member function.

d. Illegal, since @ is not a built-in C++ operator.

e. Illegal, because ++ is a unary operator, so the function should only have one argument.

f. Legal, because binary operator functions that are members take only one argument, and that argument does not have to be an object.

Overloading the Assignment Operator

Perhaps the most important operator that you can overload is the assignment operator. This allows you to take control over what happens when one object is assigned to another. This is particularly important when your object points to dynamic memory, for you can ensure that the dynamic memory is handled properly. However, before we show how that's done, we'll first look at some simpler examples.

The easiest way to do assignments between objects is to let Turbo C++ do the work for you. Unless you specify otherwise, whenever you assign one object to another of the same type, Turbo C++ performs what is known as a *memberwise copy*. This means that each instance variable of the source object is copied into the corresponding instance variable of the destination object. The copy takes place in the order the members were declared. For example, given the following assignment between two **circular_num** objects:

```
circular_num a(0, 0, 9), b(17, 1, 360);
a = b;
```

code such as the following will be generated:

```
a.num = b.num;        // Copy member by member
a.upper = b.upper;
a.lower = b.lower;
a.range = b.range;
```

Note that the default memberwise assignment is not performed if you're assigning objects of a class that has constant members, reference members, or members that have private **operator=()** functions of their own. You cannot assign to these types of objects unless you overload the assignment operator for them.

The default memberwise copy that takes place for **circular_num** objects is probably not what we want. That's because the limits and range are copied in the assignment. These variables are properties of the target object, and should probably be preserved.

To see why, assume we have a **circular_num** object that represents geometric angles ranging from 0 to 359 degrees. Suppose we assign to it another **circular_num** object that ranges from 0 to 179 degrees:

```
circular_num angle(0, 0, 359), half_angle(0, 0, 179);

angle = half_angle;
```

What happens in this seemingly innocuous assignment is that **angle** no longer ranges from 0 to 359 degrees, but rather from 0 to 179 degrees.

What we really want to do is to use only the value of the source object (i.e., its **num** member) in the assignment. This can be accomplished by taking over the assignment, and allowing only the value of the destination to be modified. To this end, let's add an **operator=()** function to the **circular_num** class:

```
class circular_num {
  ...
  void operator=(circular_num &src);
};

void operator=(circular_num &src)
// Sets the value of the destination (this) using
// the value of the source object.
{
  set_val(src.num);
}
```

Now, the following assignment:

```
angle = half_angle;
```

is translated into

```
angle.operator=(half_angle);
```

and the range and limits of **angle** won't be modified by the assignment.

Assignments Involving Dynamic Memory

Many times, using the default memberwise assignment is satisfactory. However, there are other cases besides the one shown for **circular_num** objects where it's not. Those cases involve objects that allocate dynamic memory. A typical example is with the following **ch_array** class, which dynamically sizes a character array:

```
class ch_array {
private:
  char *text;     // Storage for array
  unsigned size;  // Size of the array
public:
  ch_array(int sz) { text = new char[size = sz]; }
  ~ch_array(void)  { delete[size] text; }
  char &elem(unsigned i);
};

char &ch_array::elem(unsigned i)
// Return reference to the i'th element
// If i out of range, return last element
{
  if (i > size-1) i = size-1;
  return text[i];
}
```

Given two **ch_array** objects **a** and **b**, let's see what happens if we allow C++ to perform default memberwise copying during an assignment:

```
ch_array a(40), b(80);
...
a = b;   --->    a.text = b.text; // Copy pointers
                 a.size = b.size; // Copy size
```

Although **size** is copied correctly, all that happens for **text** is that the pointer is copied, rather than the character data to which it points. In some cases, that may be what you want to do, but most likely it isn't.

The reason is this: By copying the **text** pointers, the address in **a.text** is replaced by the address in **b.text**. As shown in Figure 10.4, the data pointed to by **a.text** is no longer accessible, and will never be freed. Even worse, when the destructor is called for **a** and **b**, **delete** is used twice for the same memory: that pointed to by **b.text**. The result is a corrupted heap.

The way to correct this problem is to define an **operator=()** function for **ch_array** objects. This function will correctly handle the assignment by ensuring that the data **text** points to is copied, rather than the pointer itself:

```
class ch_array {
  ...
  void operator=(ch_array &src);
};
```

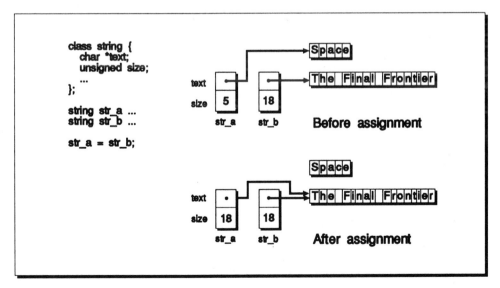

Figure 10.4. Copying Objects with Embedded Pointers

```
void ch_array::operator=(ch_array &src)
// Copies one character array object into another
// Reallocates the space of the destination array
{
  delete[size] text; // Free up old space
  text = new char[size = src.size]; // Allocate new space
  memcpy(text, src.text, src.size); // Copy the data
}
```

Note how the assignment operator function not only copies the data of the source array, it deallocates the old space of the target, and allocates new space to match the size of the source array.

We didn't have to do the assignment in this manner. We could have merely copied as much data as possible into the destination, truncating if necessary, and leaving **size** alone. There is no "right" way. It all depends on what you want to do. However, you do want to ensure that all your dynamic memory is accounted for, and that you don't accidentally free up memory twice in a row, as our first **ch_array** example did.

Assignment versus Initialization

One thing you should be aware of when overloading the assignment operator is the difference between assignment and initialization. These two operations often look similar, but they are really quite different.

For example, in the following code,

```
ch_array s(80);
ch_array t = s; // Initialization
```

the second statement is an initialization. That is, we're declaring the **ch_array** object **t**, and initializing it with the **ch_array** object **s**. Recall that initializations are done using constructors. If **ch_array** had a copy constructor, then that constructor would be called for **t**. Otherwise, a default memberwise copy would take place.

In contrast, the following code shows an assignment:

```
ch_array s(80), t(80);
s = t; // Assignment
```

In this case, since **ch_array** has an **operator=()** function, then that function is called. Otherwise, a default memberwise assignment would have taken place.

You can always tell the difference between an assignment and an initialization by the following rule: Initializations declare the type of object whose value is being set, assignments don't. Figure 10.5 illustrates this point.

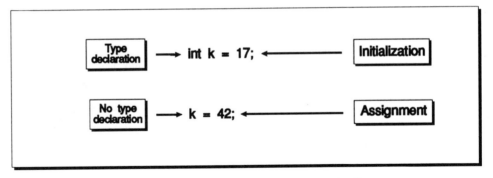

Figure 10.5. Assignment Versus Initialization

Besides the obvious situations of variable declarations and assignment statements, there are other cases where you must know whether an initialization or an assignment is taking place. In Chapter 7, you learned that these other situations are when an object is passed to a function by value, and when an object is returned by value from a function. In these cases, an initialization is taking place, and the copy constructor for each object is called. If an object has no copy constructor, a default one is created that does a memberwise copy.

Comparing operator=() to a Copy Constructor

As defined, the **ch_array** class discussed in the last section has another mistake in it. Since there is no copy constructor defined for **ch_array**, a memberwise copy takes place if you initialize one **ch_array** object with another. Of course, this memberwise copy has the same problem that a memberwise assignment does: It only copies the **text** pointers, and not what they point to. Thus, the **ch_array** class should really have a copy constructor:

```
class ch_array {
  ...
  ch_array(ch_array &src); // Copy constructor
};

ch_array::ch_array(ch_array &src)
// Copy constructor
{
  text - new char[size - src.size];
  memcpy(text, src.text, size);
}
```

If you compare this copy constructor with the **operator=()** function, you'll notice that they are very similar:

```
void ch_array::operator=(ch_array &src)
{
  delete[size] text; // Free up old space
  text = new char[size = src.size]; // Allocate new space
  memcpy(text, src.text, size);     // Copy the data
}
```

The difference is that the copy constructor does not have to deallocate the original array before allocating a new one. That's because we're just now creating the array.

Chaining Assignments Together

There's one improvement we could make to the way we've defined **operator=()** for our **ch_array**, and that involves changing the return type from **void** to **ch_array&**. The reason for this change has to with allowing assignments to be chained together, as you'll now see.

Recall that you can make assignments such as the following:

```
a = b = c;
```

This multiple assignment is actually interpreted as:

```
a = (b = c);
```

That is, the assignment to **b** is made, and then the result of that assignment is used as the source in the assignment to **a**.

However, what happens if we try assignments like this for **ch_array** objects? We would get an error:

```
ch_array sa(80), sb(80), sc(80)
sa = sb = sc; // Error here
```

The result of the first assignment, **sb = sc**, is **void**, since that's what is returned by the **operator=()** function. This void result is then used as the source to the assignment to **sa**, which clearly doesn't make sense.

The solution is to modify the **operator=()** function to return a reference to the target **ch_array** object:

```
ch_array &ch_array::operator=(ch_array &src)
{
  delete[size] text;              // Free up old space
  text = new char[size = src.size]; // Allocate new space
  memcpy(text, src.text, size);   // Copy the data
  return *this; // Return reference to target
}
```

The trickiest part of this function is the return statement. We want to return a reference to the target, which happens to be pointed to by **this**. We dereference **this** to get an actual **ch_array** object, and then a reference of this object is made to be returned.

Now we can chain together assignments to **ch_array** objects. Each assignment returns a reference to the target of the assignment, which can then be used as the source to the next assignment. Figure 10.6 illustrates the process.

Note | When designing an operator function such as **operator=()**, you may want to consider having the function return the target of the operation. This allows the operations to be chained together.

Special Rules for the Assignment Operator

There are some restrictions to overloading the **operator=()** function that don't apply to most of the other operator functions:

- The **operator=()** function must be a nonstatic class member.
- The **operator=()** function cannot be inherited.

Let's investigate the first restriction. Recall how binary member operator functions work. The first operand is actually the object itself. For example, **a = b** is translated as follows:

```
a = b;   ---> a.operator=(b);
```

Given this fact, forcing **operator=()** to be a member function guarantees that the target operand of an assignment controlled by an overloaded

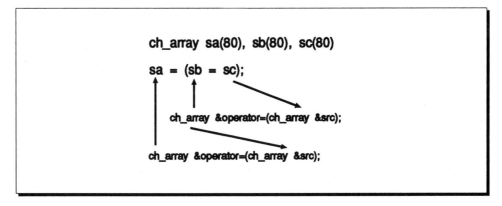

Figure 10.6. Chaining Assignments Together

operator=() function is always an object. It's not possible to have **operator=()** functions such as:

```
void operator-(int &i, circular_num &c);
```

This means that you can't change the way assignment works for the built-in types, which is a very reasonable restriction. Imagine the confusion that would be caused if you were reading C++ code where assignments to integers worked differently from what you were used to!

By the way, there are other operator functions that also must be member functions. They are **operator()()** (for the function call operator), **operator[]()** (for the subscript operator), and **operator->()** (for the member access operator.) These operator functions are probably the strangest in the bunch. You'll be seeing how to overload the subscript operator later in this chapter, and overloading the function call operator will be one of the exercises. Overloading the member access operator is more of an advanced technique that will not be discussed in this book.

Using a Base Class operator=() Function

The second restriction about **operator=()** functions is that, like constructors, they cannot be inherited. This means you can't use the base class version of **operator=()** to do assignments to derived class objects.

For example, suppose we derive a new class from **ch_array** that adds an integer **id** field:

```
class array_with_id : public ch_array {
public:
  int id;
  array_with_id(int sz, int n) : id(n), ch_array(sz) { ; }
};
```

We couldn't use the **ch_array::operator=()** function for **array_with_id** objects. We wouldn't want to anyway. The **ch_array** version doesn't know about copying the **id** member, since that member isn't a part of the **ch_array** class.

If you don't define a new **operator=()** function in a derived class, then assignments to derived class objects are made by doing memberwise copying on all additional members in the derived class. The base class members are copied using the base class **operator=()** function.

For example, if we make assignments such as:

```
array_with_id a(80, 1), b(80, 2);
a - b;
```

then **id** is copied by the default memberwise copy, and the rest of the members, **size** and **text**, are handled by the **ch_array::operator=()** function.

If you wish to overload the assignment operator for derived class objects, you must define a new **operator=()** function in the derived class. Let's see how to do this for the **array_with_id** class.

The trick is to define the **operator=()** function in such a way that it copies **id**, and then chains back and calls the base class version to handle the copying of the dynamic data. Figure 10.7 and the following code illustrate how this can be done:

```
class array_with_id : public ch_array {
public:
  int id;
  array_with_id(int sz, int n) : id(n), ch_array(sz) { ; }
  array_with_id &operator=(array_with_id &x);
};

array_with_id &array_with_id::operator=(array_with_id &x)
{
  id = x.id;               // Copy additional errcode member
  ch_array::operator=(x); // Copy the base part
  return *this;
}
```

This code shows a case where it's useful to call an operator function explicitly. Note that we had to qualify the call to the base class **operator=()** function with the name **ch_array**. If we hadn't done this, a recursive call to **array_with_id::operator=** would have resulted.

Note how we're passing an **array_with_id** object to **ch_array::operator=()** where a **ch_array** object is expected. Recall that such argument passing is legal, and as this case shows, quite useful. Keep in mind that only the base portion of the object is used in the call.

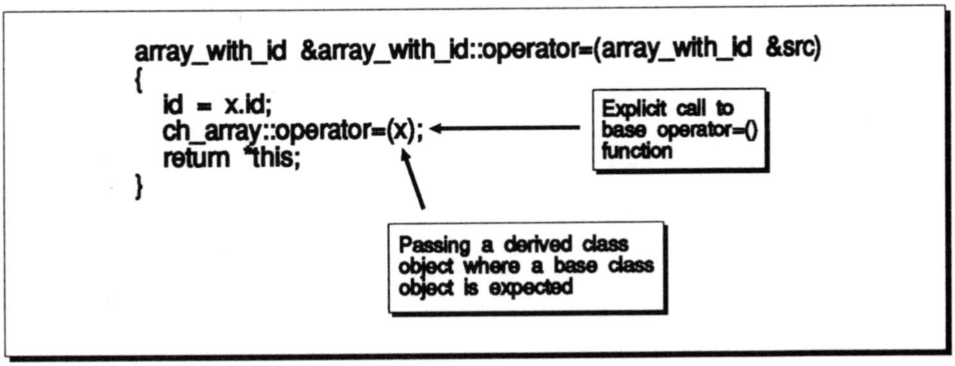

Figure 10.7. Calling a Base Class operator=() Function

Overloading the Subscript Operator

Overloading the assignment operator makes working with user-defined objects safer and more expressive. Another operator that you can overload to achieve these goals is the subscript operator **[]**. Recall how subscripts are used to access array elements:

```
char name[80];   // Declare array
ch = name[42];   // Access element 42
```

The latter statement shows the use of the subscript operator. (The first statement doesn't. There, the brackets are used merely to denote the size of the array.)

You may not have known that the subscript operator was an operator at all. Most operators are either prefix, postfix, or infix. The subscript operator is none of these. It is a binary operator, but it doesn't sit between its operands like most binary operators do. Thus, what are the operands to the subscript operator? The left operand is the array being subscripted, and the right operand is the subscript itself. Therefore, in the expression **name[42], name** is the left operand, 42 is the right operand.

Like the assignment operator, a function overloading the subscript operator must be a class member. As with all binary member operator functions, the first operand is the object itself, the second operand is the single explicit argument to the function. Figure 10.8 shows the translation from a subscripting operation to the corresponding operator function call.

An example of overloading the subscript operator is with our **ch_array** class. Recall that it has a function, **elem()**, which returns a reference to an element in the array. It's a perfect function to turn into an operator function. The following code shows how:

```
class string {
    ...
    char &operator[](unsigned i);
};

string name(80);

name[42] = 'A';    ────►    name.operator[](42) = 'A';
```

Figure 10.8. Calling a Subscript Operator Function

```
class ch_array {
private:
  char *text;     // Storage for array
  unsigned size;  // Size of the array
public:
  ch_array(int sz) { text = new char[size = sz]; }
  ~ch_array(void)  { delete[size] text; }
  void operator=(ch_array &src);
  char &operator[](unsigned i); // Overload the subscript operator
};

char &ch_array::operator[](unsigned i)
// Return reference to the i'th element
// If i out of range, return last element
{
  if (i > size-1) i = size-1;
  return text[i]; // Normal subscript operation used here
}
```

Note the return statement of the subscript operator function:

```
return text[i];
```

Doesn't this look like a recursive call? That is, aren't we causing the **operator[]()** function to be called again? The answer is no. The reason is that **text** is typed to be a character array. Thus, the compiler is smart enough to know that a normal subscripting operation is to be performed here. That is, **text[i]** is translated as follows:

```
text[i]  --->  *(text + i);
```

Incidentally, we couldn't ever change the way that subscripting works on character arrays. Why not? Because character arrays are built-in types, not classes. Since the **operator[]()** function can only be a class member, there's no way to declare such a function for character arrays. We can, however, wrap a class around a character array, and overload the subscript operator for this class, as we've done with **ch_array**.

It's also worth noting that we're passing back a reference to the array element, and not merely just a copy. That way, we can use a subscript on both sides of an assignment statement. For example, we can now write code such as:

```
ch_array a(10);

a[2] = 17;    // Calls a.operator[](2)
a[5] = a[2];  // Calls a.operator[](2) and a.operator[](5)
a[10] = 42;   // Calls a.operator[](10), subscript out of range
```

The third statement passes an out-of-range subscript to the **operator[]()** function. Here's where overloading the subscript operator pays off. We can check for subscripts being out of range and force them to be in range. Thus, code that subscripts a **ch_array** object is perfectly safe, and we're guaranteed never to access out-of-bounds array elements.

Although overloading the subscript operator lets you trap for errors, what to do with those errors is another matter. Error handling is a complex subject. There is no easy way to accomplish it.

Our **operator[]()** simply forces the subscript to be in range. You might want an error message to be printed and the program aborted instead:

```
char &ch_array::operator[](unsigned i)
// Aborts program on an illegal subscript
{
  if (i > size-1) {
    printf("Subscript error\n");
    exit(1);
  }
  return text[i];
}
```

1. Is the subscript operator used in the following statement?

   ```
   char title[80];
   ```

2. Write a character array class that uses an offset on all subscript operations. Have the offset specified in the constructor. For simplicity, use an internal fixed-length array of 80 bytes, and don't worry about range errors.

---

1. *No. The square brackets aren't being used as a subscript here. Instead, they're being used to denote the size of the array.*
2. *Here's one solution:*

   ```
   class array {
   private:
     char text[80];
     int offset;      // Subscript offset
   public:
     array(int ofs) { offset = ofs; }
     char &operator[](int i) { return text[i-offset]; }
   };

   array my_arr(1); // So you can start indexing from 1

   my_arr[1] = 17;  // Causes zero'th element to be set
   my_arr[80] = 55; // Causes 79'th element to be set
   ```

Overloading the + Operator

Next, we'll show you how to overload the + operator. The issues involved in overloading the + operator are typical of those in overloading any binary arithmetic operator.

To see an example, let's revisit our **circular_num** class. We'll include functions for operators = and +=, like we did before, and then add one for the + operator. We'll also include a copy constructor for the class. (You'll see why shortly.)

```
class circular_num {
private:
  int num;
  int upper, lower, range;
public:
  circular_num(int v, int l, int u);
  circular_num(circular_num &src);
  int set_val(int v);
  int get_val(void) { return num; }
  circular_num &operator-(circular_num &src);
  circular_num &operator+=(int v);
  circular_num &operator+=(circular_num &src);
  circular_num operator+(circular_num &other);
};
```

Let's take a close look at the **operator+()** function. Here is its implementation:

```
circular_num circular_num::operator+(circular_num &other)
{
  circular_num temp(*this);        // Create a temporary object
  temp.set_val(temp.num + other.num); // Add to it
  return temp;                     // Return copy of it
}
```

The **operator+()** function creates a temporary object, **temp**, that will hold the result of the addition. The **temp** object is initialized to hold the value of the left operand of the addition—the object pointed to by **this**. Note how the call to the copy constructor for **temp** is made. We must dereference **this**, so that the argument type matches the type required by the copy constructor.

After initializing our **temp** object, we add the value of the right operand to it. Now look closely at the return value for **operator+()** function. Unlike the others we've defined for the class, this operator function doesn't return a reference to the target **circular_num** object, but rather it returns a copy of the temporary result. (This copy of **temp** is made by calling the copy constructor implicitly.)

There are two questions you might be asking here: First, why do we need to create a temporary object? Second, why can't we return a reference?

The answer to the first question is this: We need to create a temporary object to hold the result of the addition. We can't use either the left- or right-operand object to hold the result, because then we would be changing the value of one of the operands, violating the semantics of addition.

For example, suppose we allowed the left operand to be modified. We could then write **operator+()** as:

```
circular_num &circular_num::operator+(circular_num &other)
{
  set_val(num + other.num);
  return *this; // Return reference to this object
}
```

Compare this to the second **operator+=()** function:

```
circular_num &circular_num::operator+=(circular_num &src)
{
  set_val(num + src.num);
  return *this; // Return reference to this object
}
```

You'll see that these two functions do the same thing. In other words, we unintentionally made **operator+()** work like **operator+=()**.

Tip When overloading the operators, it's best to preserve their meanings. For example, don't make the + operator do what += does. You'll just confuse yourself and the readers of your code.

The answer to the second question—why we can't return a reference—is: The temporary object we use in the function is created on the stack. As you learned in earlier chapters, you should avoid returning a reference to something created on the stack. Thus, our only choice is to make a copy of the object.

Using Friend Operator Functions

With the exception of overloading the operators =, [], (), and ->, you have a choice whether to make operator functions class members or not. How do you make the choice? In this section, some tips are provided. A good case study is with the **operator+()** function.

In the last section, we made **operator+()** a member function. While this works, there are places where it can cause problems. To see why, suppose we wanted to be able to mix types in the addition, and allow integers to be added with **circular_num** objects as well:

```
circular_num a(0, 0, 9), b(5, 0, 9);

a - 35 + b; // Addition involving mixed types
```

Can we do this with our **operator+()** function? The answer is no. The left operand to the addition must always be a **circular_num** object, since the **operator+()** is a member function.

Our only choice is to declare another **operator+()** function that's not a member. Since this function will access the private members of **circular_num**, it must be a friend function. Here's how to declare it:

```
class circular_num {
  ...
  friend circular_num operator+(int i, circular_num &x);
};

circular_num operator+(int i, circular_num &x)
{
  circular_num temp(x); // Create copy of x
  x.set_val(num.x + i); // Add to it
  return temp;          // Return copy of temp
}
```

Note | Nonmember operator functions do not have to be declared as friends, but they typically are, since they usually access private class members.

Now our assignment will work:

```
circular_num a(0, 0, 9), b(5, 0, 9);

a - 35 + b; // Addition involving mixed types
```

The problem is, it only works if the left operand is an integer. What if we want the right operand to be an integer instead? We'd have to declare yet another **operator+()** function, with the arguments switched around:

```
circular_num operator+(circular_num &x, int i);
```

Thus, declaring operator functions this way involves defining a function for each combination of argument types. This is not very satisfactory, but fortunately, there is a solution to this problem, using *conversion operator functions*, as you'll discover next.

1. In the preceding discussion, why didn't we mention the combination of argument types shown in the following function prototype?

```
circular_num operator+(int i, int j);
```

2. Given the following operator function prototype and assignment statement, what does the statement translate to? Does the translation make sense?

```
circular_num circular_num::operator+(circular_num &src);
```

```
circular_num a(0, 0, 9), b(0, 0, 9);
b - 12 + a;
```

---

1. *Because it's not possible to have both arguments be nonclass types.*
2. *It translates into*

```
b - 12.operator+(a);
```

We're trying to use 12 as a circular_num object and call operator+() from it, which clearly doesn't make sense.

Conversion Operator Functions

There's another set of functions that are close cousins to the operator functions we've been discussing. These are called *conversion operator functions*. Recall that C++ allows two forms of syntax for doing type conversions:

```
(new_type)(var_of_old_type); // C and C++ typecast
```

```
new_type(var_of_old_type);   // C++ only typecast
```

The latter form suggests that the type cast is actually a function call. For example, suppose we cast a **double** as an **int**:

```
double d - 3.14159;
int i;
```

```
i - int(d);
```

It looks as though we're calling the function int(). When converting some types to **int**, that's exactly what can happen. For example, we can create a function that converts a **circular_num** to an integer. This function will have the name **operator int()**. Such a function is called a conversion operator function. In general, you can define a conversion operator function to convert from any class type to any other type.

The following is how we can define **operator int()** for our **circular_num** class:

```
class circular_num {
  ...
  operator int(void);
};

circular_num::operator int(void)
// Converts from a circular_num object to an integer
{
  return num;
}
```

Conversion operator functions must be member functions, and they take no explicit arguments. The hidden **this** argument is passed, however. If you think of a conversion operator as being a unary operator, then **this** is the single operand for the operator. It points to the object we're trying to convert to another type. Figure 10.9 illustrates the components of a conversion operator function, and how to call such a function.

Note that you can't specify a return type for a conversion operator function. Actually, the return type happens to be the name of the function itself. For instance, the return type for **operator int()** is **int**.

An example of calling our **operator int()** function is:

```
circular_num c(0, 0, 9);
int k;

c.set_val(11);
k = int(c); // Convert c to an integer
```

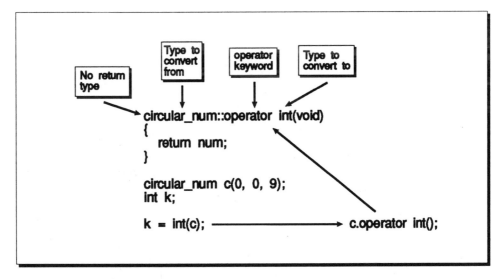

Figure 10.9. Declaring and Using a Conversion Operator Function

The last statement translates to:

```
k = c.int();
```

In this case, **k** takes on the value of 1, since that's what the value of **c** is after the call to **set_val()**. The value of 11 is wrapped around to 1 by the call to **set_val()**.

Type Conversions in Both Directions

Conversion operator functions allow us to convert a class object into an object of another type, or into a variable of one of the built-in types. However, if you remember what you learned in Chapter 7, there's also another kind of function that you can define to do conversions: type conversion constructors. For example, a type conversion constructor for our **circular_num** class is:

```
class circular_num {
   circular_num(int v, int l = 0, int u = 32767);
};
```

Recall that the first argument of a type conversion constructor is of a different type than the class itself, and if it has other arguments, they are all default arguments. The **circular_num()** constructor allows us to convert an integer into a **circular_num** object—just the opposite of what the **operator int()** function does. We've let the limits of this new object default to (0, 32767) for lack of anything better to set them to.

By using both type conversion constructors and conversion operator functions, you can define type conversions two ways, both to and from a class type. The following code illustrates both methods:

```
circular_num c(0, 0, 9);
int k;

k = int(c);         // Use conversion operator function int()
c = circular_num(k); // Use type conversion constructor
```

The last statement actually causes an unnamed temporary **circular_num** object to be created, which is initialized with the value of **k**. This temporary object is then assigned to **c**.

---

1. Could we define a user-defined conversion to go from a **double** to an **int**?
2. Given two classes **bignum** and **smallnum**, write the prototypes for both a

type conversion constructor and a conversion operator function that will convert **bignum** objects to **smallnum** objects. Could both conversion functions be declared and used in the same program?

3. Suppose you have a BCD class (for Binary Code Decimal numbers) that's already compiled with the source no longer available, and you want to be able to convert **circular_num** objects into BCD objects. Which type of conversion function can you use to do this?

---

1. *No. Both **double** and **int** are built-in types, they are not class types. Thus, we can't define a type conversion constructor because a constructor can only be defined for class types. And we can't define a conversion operator function because it too must be a class member.*

2. *The prototypes would look like:*

```
smallnum::smallnum(bignum &); // Type conversion constructor
bignum::operator smallnum();  // Conversion operator function
```

   You couldn't declare and use both conversion functions in a program because it would be ambiguous. How would the compiler know which one to call?

3. *Since you don't have the source code to the BCD class, you can't add a type conversion constructor to it to convert from **circular_num** objects to BCD objects. You could, however, add a conversion operator function to the **circular_num** class, assuming that the source to it is available. The prototype would look something like:*

```
circular_num::operator BCD(void);
```

Implicit Type Conversions

In the previous section, we showed type conversions that were specified using an explicit typecast. It's also possible to have conversions happen implicitly. For instance:

```
circular_num c(0, 0, 9);
int k;

k = c; // Calls c.operator int()
c = k; // Calls circular_num(k);
```

In such assignments, the compiler sees that the types don't match and looks for a conversion operator function or type conversion constructor that can do the conversion.

With such implicit conversions, seemingly simple statements can in fact cause a lot of action to take place. In the assignment

```
c - k;
```

a temporary **circular_num** object is created, and **k** is used as the argument to the type conversion constructor for that temporary object. Then, this temporary object is assigned to **c** using the **operator=()** function. Figure 10.10 illustrates the process.

As you can imagine, when you have type conversion constructors, conversion operator functions, and operator functions defined for a class, the interactions between them can get complex. However, this complexity notwithstanding, such implicit conversions can come in handy.

For instance, recall the problem of having to define different operator functions for each combination of argument types. For the **operator+()** function of the **circular_num** class, we had to define three separate versions:

```
friend circular_num &operator+(circular_num &x, circular_num &y);
friend circular_num &operator+(int v, circular_num &x);
friend circular_num &operator+(circular_num &x, int v);
```

If we define a type conversion constructor for our **circular_num** class that converts from **int** to **circular_num**, we can get rid of the last two **operator+()** functions. Should we use an integer as one of the operands, it will be converted to a **circular_num** for us. Note, however, that a temporary **circular_num** object is created in the process. For example, in a call such as

```
a - 42 + b;
```

where **a** and **b** are **circular_num** objects, the following code is generated:

```
circular_num temp(42);
a - operator+(temp, b);
```

```
circular_num(0, 0, 9);
int k;

k = c;    ⟶    k = int(c);    ⟶    k = c.operator int();

c = k;         c = circular_num(k);    circular_num temp(k);
                                        c.operator=(temp);
```

Figure 10.10. Implicit Type Conversions

Of course, calling a constructor to convert from an integer to a **circular_num** object is somewhat inefficient. You may want to go back and use the versions of **operator+()** that pass integers directly. These versions are more efficient since no temporary objects are created.

Consider the two **operator+=()** functions we declared for **circular_num** objects:

```
circular_num &circular_num::operator+=(int v);
circular_num &circular_num::operator+=(circular_num &src);
```

Given that we have two conversions that go between integers and **circular_num** objects, we can get rid of one of the **operator+=()** functions. In terms of efficiency, which should we keep? The two conversion functions are:

```
circular_num::circular_num(int v, int 1, int u)
// Type conversion constructor
{
  lower = 1; upper = u;
  range = upper - lower + 1;
  set_val(v); // Must do range check
}

circular_num::operator int(void) { return num; }
```

We should keep the operator=() function that takes an integer argument. The conversion from circular_num to int is very efficient, since all the operator conversion function has to do is return the internal num member. In contrast, the type conversion constructor, going from int to circular_num, is much more costly, since it involves several more operations.

Revisiting the circular_num Class

Now that you've learned about the different types of operator functions, let's take our **circular_num** class and overload all of the arithmetic and comparison operators for it. This will give you a good working example of how to create a user-defined type that can be used in arithmetic calculations just as easily as the built-in types can.

Listings 10.1 and 10.2 give the header and implementation file for our complete circular number class. In order to make the listings a little more readable, we've shortened the name of the class from **circular_num** to **cnum**.

As you can see from the listings, we've defined all the arithmetic operators for **cnum**, including all those that do addition, subtraction, multiplication, and division. We also defined operator functions for all the comparison operators, such as <, ==, and !=. We've made many of the functions inline to make the class as efficient as possible.

Notice how each arithmetic operator function returns the target object of the operation, allowing such operations to be chained together. Thus, we can write code such as:

```
cnum a(45, 0, 359), b(6, 0, 60), c(0, 0, 359);

c = a*b + a/b;
```

This translates into the following operator function calls:

```
c.operator=(operator+(operator*(a,b),operator/(a,b)));
```

Note from the listings that the functions handling the binary arithmetic operators are declared as friend functions, and that they return a copy of the result, rather than a reference. This is the setup that was suggested earlier for binary arithmetic operators.

We also defined two functions to handle conversions between **cnum** objects and integers:

```
cnum::cnum(int v, int l = 0, int u = 32767); // From int
cnum::operator int(void) { return num; }     // To int
```

As the last checkpoint explained, these conversion functions allow us to eliminate some of the operator functions we would have otherwise needed. For example, we only have one **operator+=()** function:

```
circular_num &circular_num::operator+=(int v);
```

If we need to pass in a **circular_num** object to this function, it is efficiently converted to an integer using the conversion function.

One other design issue that our sample class illustrates is what to do with the unary operators ++ and --. Recall that when we overload such operators, we can't distinguish between prefix and postfix usage. Thus, we have to choose which to support in the operator functions. We chose the prefix usage. That is, **operator++()** does the increment before returning the result, and **operator--()** does the decrement before returning the result.

Listing 10.3 presents a program that illustrates the use of the unary ++ and -- operators with the **cnum** class. The program is a modified version of an example we gave in Chapter 6 that used a circular number as an index for a character string. In the following example, we've simplified the input by fixing the string to

"Say old man, can you play the fiddle?"

and we then scan forward and backward through the "fiddle" portion of the string using the operator ++ and operator -- functions on the index. The output of the program is:

fiddlefiddlefiddlefiddlefiddlefiddle
elddifelddifelddifelddifelddifelddif

Listing 10.1. The cnum.h Header File

```
// cnum.h: Header file for cnum class

#ifndef H_CNUM
#define H_CNUM

class cnum {
private:
  int num;
  int upper, lower, range;
public:
  cnum(int v, int l = 0, int u = 32767);
  cnum(cnum &src);
  operator int(void) { return num; }
  int set_val(int v);
  int get_val(void) { return num; }
  cnum &operator=(int v);
  cnum &operator+=(int v);
  cnum &operator-=(int v);
  cnum &operator*=(int v);
  cnum &operator/=(int v);
  cnum &operator++(void);
  cnum &operator--(void);
  friend cnum operator+(cnum &a, cnum &b);
  friend cnum operator-(cnum &a, cnum &b);
  friend cnum operator*(cnum &a, cnum &b);
  friend cnum operator/(cnum &a, cnum &b);
  friend int operator>(cnum &a, cnum &b) {
     return a.num > b.num;
  }
  friend int operator<(cnum &a, cnum &b) {
     return a.num < b.num;
  }
  friend int operator==(cnum &a, cnum &b) {
     return a.num == b.num;
  }
```

```
   friend int operator!=(cnum &a, cnum &b) {
      return a.num != b.num;
   }
   friend int operator>=(cnum &a, cnum &b) {
      return a.num >= b.num;
   }
   friend int operator<=(cnum &a, cnum &b) {
      return a.num <= b.num;
   }
};

#endif
```

Listing 10.2. The cnum.cpp Implementation File

```
// cnum.cpp: Implementation file for cnum class

#include "cnum.h"

cnum::cnum(int v, int l, int u)
// Type conversion constructor
{
   lower = l; upper = u;
   range = upper - lower + 1;
   set_val(v);
}

cnum::cnum(cnum &src)
// Copy constructor
{
   lower = src.lower; upper = src.upper;
   range = src.range; num = src.num;
}

int cnum::set_val(int v)
// Set the value, wrapping to keep it in range
{
   while(v > upper) v -= range;
   while(v < lower) v += range;
   return num = v; // Record and return result
}


cnum &cnum::operator=(int v)
{
   set_val(v);
   return *this;
}

cnum &cnum::operator+=(int v)
{
```

```
  set_val(num + v);
  return *this;
}

cnum &cnum::operator-=(int v)
{
  set_val(num - v);
  return *this;
}

cnum &cnum::operator*=(int v)
{
  set_val(num * v);
  return *this;
}

cnum &cnum::operator/=(int v)
{
  set_val(num / v);
  return *this;
}

cnum &cnum::operator++(void)
// Use prefix semantics
{
  set_val(num + 1);
  return *this;
}

cnum &cnum::operator--(void)
// Use prefix semantics
{
  set_val(num - 1);
  return *this;
}

// These are friend functions, not member functions.
// They all return a copy of the resulting operation.

cnum operator+(cnum &a, cnum &b)
{
  cnum temp(a);
  temp.set_val(temp.num + b.num);
  return temp;
}

cnum operator-(cnum &a, cnum &b)
{
  cnum temp(a);
  temp.set_val(temp.num - b.num);
  return temp;
}
```

```
cnum operator*(cnum &a, cnum &b)
{
  cnum temp(a);
  temp.set_val(temp.num * b.num);
  return temp;
}

cnum operator/(cnum &a, cnum &b)
{
  cnum temp(a);
  temp.set_val(temp.num / b.num);
  return temp;
}
```

Listing 10.3. The cnumex.cpp Sample Program

```
// cnumex.cpp: Sample program for cnum class

#include <stdio.h>
#include "cnum.h"

char phrase[] - "Say old man, can you play the fiddle?";

main()
{
  int i;
  // Set up number poised to be incremented to the value 0
  cnum index(35, 30, 35);

  // Go round in circles forward
  for (i - 0; i<36; i++) putchar(phrase[++index]);
  putchar('\n');

  // Go round in circles backward

  for (i - 0; i<36; i++) putchar(phrase[--index]);
}
```

Summary

In this chapter, we discussed how to make user-defined types use the same operator syntax that the built-in types do. This is another example of how you can work with user-defined types in C++ almost as though these types were part of the language.

You've seen that using operator functions allows your programs to be safer when assigning objects that utilize dynamic memory. By overloading the assignment operator, you can ensure that dynamic data isn't inadvertently made inaccessible or that it isn't freed too many times. You can also ensure that during assignments, the data is actually copied, instead of just the pointers to the data.

You've also seen where overloading the subscript operator allows you to perform range checking on arrays. If a subscript is found to be out of range, you can choose to ignore it, print out an error message and abort the program, or do whatever you want.

Finally, through the use of conversion functions, you've seen how you can easily handle conversions to and from your user-defined types.

All of these features allow you to create user-defined types that almost appear to be part of the C++ language itself.

Exercises

1. Comment on the advisability of writing operator functions such as:

```
my_num::operator+(my_num &a, my_num &b)
{
    return a.val * b.val;
}
```

2. Write a two-dimensional matrix class that allows you to specify the dimensions of the matrix at run time. Try overloading the () operator to perform subscripting into this matrix. That is, you should be able to write statements such as:

```
matrix m(3, 5); // Declare 3x5 matrix

m(3, 2) = 17.5; // Calls m.operator()(3, 2)

print("m(3,2) = %f\n", m(3,2));
```

Hint: The operator()() function can have as many arguments as you like, in contrast to most operator functions.

3. Given the following class:

```
struct mynum {
    int n;
    mynum(int i)    { n = i; }
    mynum(mynum &x) { n = x.n; }
    mynum &operator++(void);
};
```

Try implementing the **operator++()** function to have postincrement usage. That is, the value of the **mynum** object being returned should be the value before the increment takes place. The function should return a reference to the **mynum** being incremented. What problem do you encounter? Can it be fixed?

Answers:

1. *The operator function does multiplication instead of addition as the + operator would suggest. Needless to say, this would be very confusing to anybody reading your code.*
2. *Here's one solution:*

```
#include <stdio.h>

// Class declaration

class matrix {
private:
  float *elements;
  int nrow, ncol;
public:
  matrix(int nr, int nc);
  ~matrix(void) { delete[nrow*ncol] elements; }
  float &operator()(int r, int c);
  int width(void)  { return ncol; }
  int height(void) { return nrow; }
};

// Class implementation

matrix::matrix(int nr, int nc)
// Constructor
{
  elements = new float[nr * nc];
  nrow = nr; ncol = nc;
}

float &matrix::operator()(int r, int c)
{
  return elements[r*ncol + c];
}

main()
{
  matrix m(3, 5);

  m(3, 2) = 17.5;
  printf("m(3,2) = %f\n", m(3, 2));
}
```

3. *You could try to make a copy of the* **mynum** *object before the increment takes place, and return that copy:*

```
mynum &mynum::operator++(void)
{
  mynum temp(*this); // Make temp copy
  n++;               // Increment value
  return temp;       // Return reference to temp
}
```

However, this won't work, because we're returning a reference to a temporary variable on the stack. Not a good idea!

You could try changing the prototype and just returning a copy of the temporary object:

```
mynum mynum::operator++(void)
// Note: not returned by reference here!
{
  mynum temp(*this); // Make temp copy
  n++;
  return temp;       // Return copy of temp
}
```

However, this can lead to some strange results. A program that shows what happens is:

```
#include <stdio.h>

struct mynum {
  int n;
  mynum(int i) { n = i; }
  mynum(mynum &x) { n = x.n; }
  mynum operator++(void);
};

mynum mynum::operator++(void)
{
  mynum temp(*this);
  n++;
  return temp;
}

main()
{
  mynum myn(5);

  (myn++)++;
  printf("%d\n", myn.n); // Does it print 6 or 7
}
```

Here, **myn** *is supposedly incremented twice, so you would think that 7 would be printed. Instead, the first increment returns a copy of* **myn** *before the increment,* and it's this copy that gets incremented again. Thus, **myn** only gets incremented once, and a 6 is printed.

There's no easy way to correct the problem.

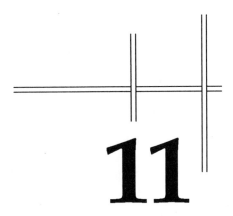

The C++ Stream I/O Library

Turbo C++ provides a new library of routines for performing I/O operations: the **iostream** library. This library is meant to replace the **stdio** library of C. The new **iostream** library is object oriented, providing full control over the input and output of objects.

Thus far, you've seen little of this new way of doing I/O. The reason is that the **iostream** library uses many of the advanced features of C++, such as operator overloading and inheritance. However, now that you know how these features work, it's time to see how they are used in creating a more flexible I/O system. In fact, a study of the **iostream** library is also a good study of how to put C++ to work in a real application.

Earlier versions of C++ had a different stream I/O library, of which the **iostream** library is largely a superset. Turbo C++ still provides the old stream library, but we won't be using it in this book. If you've been using the old library, you should switch to the new one.

After completing this chapter, we'll have discussed:

- The concept of stream I/O
- The system of classes in the **iostream** library
- How the stream input and output operators work
- How to do character-level I/O
- How to test the state of a stream
- How to do formatted I/O
- How to overload the input and output operators
- How to attach streams to files

The Stream Model

Like the C **stdio** library, the C++ **iostream** library is based on the concept of *streams*. At an abstract level, a stream is a way of describing the flow of data from some source to some destination. For instance, when inputting characters from the keyboard, you can think of the characters as flowing or streaming from the keyboard into the data structures of your program. Likewise, when writing to a file, you can think of bytes streaming from your program onto your disk.

Even though the **stdio** library provides for stream-oriented I/O, the **iostream** library takes advantage of the powerful object-oriented features of C++, and implements the stream I/O in a manner closer to the conceptual stream model.

For example, consider the following call to the **stdio printf()** routine, which inserts some data into the **stdin** stream:

```
int x = 42;
printf("The answer is: %d", x);
```

With calls like this to **printf()**, you still think in terms of procedural programming. It's hard to conceptualize the stream model here. There are really two pieces of data being written, a character string "The answer is: ," and the number 42. Yet the output of these pieces is lumped together into one function call.

In contrast, with the **iostream** library, you think in terms of stream objects, and operators acting on those objects. You read and write to stream objects piece by piece. For instance, the following code shows how to generate the equivalent output for our example, using the **iostream** library:

```
int x = 42;
cout << "The answer is: " << x;
```

In this statement, **cout** is a stream object that's analogous to **stdout**. The left-shift operator << has been overloaded, and is used to insert data into the stream. The direction of the arrow suggests the direction of data flow into the stream object: first the character string is inserted, and then the number 42. Figure 11.1 illustrates this process.

Meet the Stream Operators

The **iostream** library overloads both the left- and right-shift operators, << and >>. When used in conjunction with stream objects, the << operator is known as

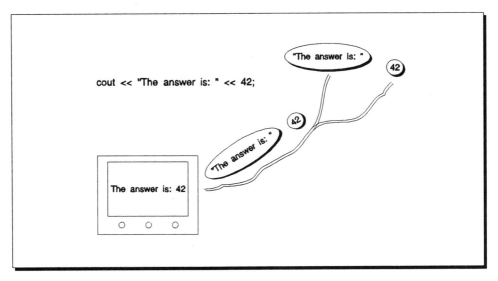

Figure 11.1. The Stream Model

the *output operator,* and is used to write data into a stream. Likewise, the >>
operator is known as the *input operator,* and is used to read data from a stream
object. Collectively, the two operators are known as the *stream operators.*

The following program shows an example of using the stream operators:

```
// mpg.cpp: Example of using the stream operators

#include <iostream.h>  // You must include this header

main()
{
  float miles, gallons, mpg;
  cout << "Welcome to the MPG computer\n";
  cout << "--------------------------\n";
  cout << "Enter miles traveled: ";
  cin  >> miles;
  cout << "Enter gallons used: ";
  cin  >> gallons;
  mpg = miles/gallons;
  cout << "You got " << mpg << " miles per gallon.\n";
}
```

A sample output from the program is:

```
Welcome to the MPG computer
--------------------------
Enter miles traveled: 45
Enter gallons used: 2.5
You got 18 miles per gallon
```

As the program shows, to access the **iostream** library, you must include the header **iostream.h**. This header defines many of the classes that make up the **iostream** library. It also defines the predefined stream objects **cin** and **cout**, which we've used in our program. These objects correspond roughly to the **stdin** and **stdout** streams of C.

Note ‖ Earlier versions of the C++ stream library used the header **stream.h**. If you have code using the old stream library, you should change any **stream.h** references to **iostream.h**.

The stream operators are "smart." They know about the types of their operands, and can do formatting accordingly. For example, in the preceding program, both character strings and floating point numbers were input and output.

How did the stream operators come to be so smart? They got that way by being overloaded for each of the built-in types. You can even overload the stream operators yourself, and have them work with your own types of objects.

What's In the iostream Library?

The **iostream** library is actually a complex system of classes. In fact, there are 18 classes making up the library. The classes are organized into two parallel hierarchies with the classes **ios** and **streambuf** at the top of these hierarchies. Figure 11.2 shows a portion of the **ios** hierarchy, and Figure 11.3 shows the **streambuf** hierarchy.

Figure 11.2 doesn't show all of the **ios** class hierarchy, due to its complexity. However, don't worry. Most of the time, you'll only be dealing with the following classes:

Class	Purpose
ios	Manages the overall I/O operations
istream	For input streams
ostream	For output streams

Note ‖ Any object created from the **ios** class or any of its derived classes is generically referred to as a *stream object*.

The **ios** class hierarchy manages all of the I/O operations, and provides the high-level interface to the programmer. There are many constants and flags that the **ios** class defines that you'll be seeing in this chapter.

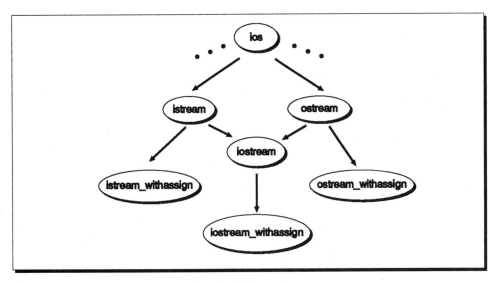

Figure 11.2. The ios Hierarchy

Note that the **ios** class hierarchy uses multiple inheritance. The class **iostream** is derived from both **istream** and **ostream**, and can thus do both input and output. While we won't be covering multiple inheritance in this book, you might spend some time studying the header file **iostream.h**, for it shows a good example of how to set up multiple inheritance.

Just as the **stdio** library provides for buffering, so does the **iostream** library. The classes in the **streambuf** hierarchy handle that task. The general **streambuf** class does most of the chores, while **filebuf** handles file-specific buffer operations, and **strstreambuf** manages the task of performing in-memory I/O buffering.

A pointer to one of the buffer class objects is included in each class from the **ios** hierarchy. That's how buffering is added to the streams. Also, the type of buffer used determines what kind of stream it is. For instance, by using a **filebuf** object, you can attach a stream to a file. You'll see how to do this later in the chapter.

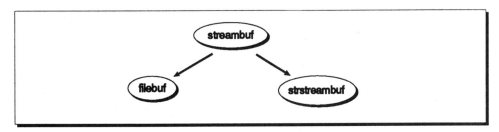

Figure 11.3. The streambuf Hierarchy

Predefined Stream Objects

The **iostream** library provides some predefined stream objects that closely parallel those in the **stdio** library. There are four predefined stream objects, as shown in Table 11.1. The first three stream objects, **cin**, **cout**, and **cerr**, correspond to the **stdio** streams **stdin**, **stdout**, and **stderr**. The fourth stream object, **clog**, is like **cerr**, except it uses a different buffering strategy.

The **cin** object, which is used for the standard input file, is created from the **istream_withassign** class. The other objects come from the **ostream_withassign** class.

For much of this chapter, we'll be using only **cin** and **cout** in our examples. However, keep in mind that the examples will work for any appropriate stream objects.

Table 11.1. The Predefined Stream Objects of Turbo C++

Object	Description
cin	Used for input.
cout	Used for output.
cerr	Used for error message output. The buffer is flushed after each output.
clog	Like cerr, but the buffer is flushed only when full.

Using the Character-Level Stream Functions

Though you'll often be using the high-level stream operators, there are some low-level routines that you can use in conjunction with the stream operators. In particular, the **iostream** library provides a set of routines for doing unformatted character-level I/O. We'll study these routines before discussing the stream operators in detail.

Tables 11.2 lists the character-level routines available. Most of the routines belong to the **istream** class, and are associated with input. The only output routine, **put()** belongs to the **ostream** class.

An example of using two of the functions, **get()** and **put()**, to copy the standard input to the standard output file is:

```
// copy1.cpp: File copy program using cin and cout

#include <iostream.h>
```

Table 11.2. The Character Level I/O Routines

Function	Description
ostream &put(char c);	Inserts a character into the output stream. Returns the output stream.
int get(void);	Extracts the next character from the input stream and returns it. An EOF (-1) is returned upon end of input.
int peek(void);	Returns the next character from the input stream without extracting it. An EOF (-1) is returned upon end of input.
istream &putback(char c);	Pushes back the character onto the input stream. The input stream is returned.
istream &get(signed char &c); istream &get(unsigned char &c);	Extracts the next character from the input stream. Returns the input stream.
istream &get(signed char *s, int n, char t='\n'); istream &get(unsigned char *s, int n, char t='\n');	Extracts up to n characters into s, stopping when the termination character is found. The termination character is not stored in s. Returns the input stream.
istream &getline(signed char *s, int n, char t='\n'); istream &getline(unsigned char *s, int n, char t='\n');	Extracts up to n characters into s, stopping when the termination character is found. The termination character is stored in s. Returns the input stream.
instream &ignore(int n, int t=EOF);	Extracts and discards up to n characters, or until the termination character t is found. The termination character is left on the input stream. The input stream is returned.
int gcount(void);	Returns the number of characters extracted in the last extraction.

```
main()
{
  int c;
  while((c = cin.get()) != EOF) cout.put(c);
  return 0;
}
```

The version of **get()** that we're using here has an **int** return type, allowing it to return both character values and an EOF flag (which is -1). This version of **get()** works like the **fgetc()** function works. In fact, if you examine Table 11.2, you'll notice other routines that are similar to those you might find in the **stdio** library. Table 11.3 shows the correspondence.

Table 11.3. Correspondence between C and C++ I/O Routines

C++ call	C call
c = cin.get();	c = fgetc(stdin);
cin.getline(buff, 80);	fgets(buff, 80, stdin);
cin.putback(c);	ungetc(c, stdin);
cout.put(c);	fputc(c, stdout);

The correspondence isn't exact though. Most of the **stdio** routines return an **int**, whereas most of the **iostream** routines return a reference to a stream object. Let's examine this further.

Concatenating I/O Operations Together

A sketch of the **put()** routine looks like:

```
ostream &ostream::put(char c)
{
  <Insert the character into the stream>
  return *this;
}
```

The **put()** function inserts a character into a stream, and then returns the stream itself. The stream object used is pointed to by the hidden **this** argument, hence the reason for using **this** in the return statement. You'll find that most of the **iostream** functions are coded in this matter. But why?

One reason is so that you can concatenate I/O operations together. For example, suppose you wanted to output the characters 'A,' 'B,' and 'C.' One way to do this would be as follows:

```
cout.put('A'); cout.put('B'); cout.put('C');
```

However, a shorter way would be to code the following:

```
cout.put('A').put('B').put('C');
```

The dot operator groups to the left. Thus the preceding statement could also be written as:

```
((cout.put('A')).put('B')).put('C');
```

What happens is that 'A' is inserted into **cout,** then **cout** is returned to be used in the second call to **put()**, which outputs 'B,' and then **cout** is returned again to be used in outputting 'C.' Figure 11.4 illustrates this process.

An Example of Character Level I/O

The **iostream** library contains a more versatile set of character-level routines than does the **stdio** library. The following program, **cntcom.cpp,** shows an example of using some of these routines. It counts the number of C++ comments found in the standard input file, along with the total number of characters that the comments contain.

```
// cntcom.cpp: Comment counting program

#include <iostream.h>
const int linesize = 1024; // Maximum line size
```

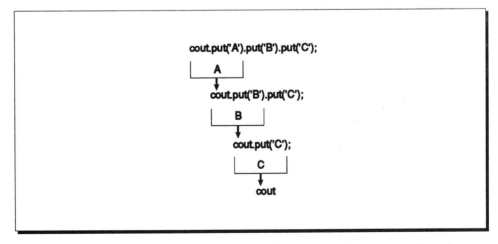

Figure 11.4. Concatenating Stream Operations Together

```
main()
{
   int c, cnt = 0, charcnt = 0;
   while(1) {
     c = cin.get();
     if (c == EOF) break;
     if (c == '/' && cin.peek() == '/') { // Found a comment?
        cnt++;                            // Count it
        cin.ignore(linesize, '\n');       // Then ignore rest of line
        charcnt += cin.gcount();          // Count comment characters
        charcnt++;                        // Include first '/'
     }
   }
   cout << cnt << " comments found, totaling ";
   cout << charcnt << " characters\n";
}
```

Note how the program uses **peek()** to look ahead one character when testing for a '//,' and how it uses **ignore()** to skip to the end of the line if a comment is found. It also uses **gcount()** to count the number of characters extracted during the skip.

You'll also notice that we're using the high-level output operator as well in this program.

Tip || It's perfectly legal to mix the use of the low-level I/O functions and the high-level stream operators.

If you run this program using the following command line:

```
cntcom < cntcom.cpp
```

you'll get the following output:

```
10 comments found, totaling 312 characters
```

The **iostream** library includes the overloaded functions **get()** and **getline()** which can read in a string of characters. Which of these functions is analogous to the **stdio** function **fgets()**?

The getline() functions store the termination character, just like fgets() does. The get() functions don't.

Testing the State of the Stream

Each stream object has an instance variable storing the current state of the stream. The possible states are given in an enumerated type, **io_state**, which is defined in the **ios** class. Here is the definition of **io_state**:

```
enum io_state {
  goodbit  = 0x00, // Normal working order
  eofbit   = 0x01, // At end of stream
  failbit  = 0x02, // Last I/O operation failed. Stream
                   // is still usable if error is cleared
  badbit   = 0x04, // Invalid operation attempted. Stream
                   // may be usable if error is cleared
  hardfail = 0x08  // Unrecoverable error
};
```

Note that the bit patterns are defined for these states so that they can be ORed together. For instance, if you try to read past the end of file, then both **eofbit** and **failbit** might be set.

You can't access the stream state directly. True to the ideals of encapsulation, a set of functions are provided to both set and retrieve the stream state. The prototypes for these functions are given in Table 11.4.

The following program shows an example of using one of these routines, **eof()**. The program is a modification of the first copy program we wrote earlier in the chapter. Note that in this program, we're using a different version of **get()** that returns the input stream object, rather than the character read. The character read is passed back in the argument.

Table 11.4. Functions for Setting and Testing the State of a Stream

Function	Description
int rdstate();	Returns current stream state
int good();	Returns nonzero if in good state
int eof();	Returns nonzero if at end of file
int fail();	Returns nonzero if **failbit**, **badbit**, or **hardfail** is set
int bad();	Returns nonzero if **badbit** or **hardfail** is set
void clear(int v=0);	Sets the state, (default is "good")
operator void *();	Returns 0 if **failbit**, **badbit**, or **hardfail** is set
int operator!();	Returns nonzero if **failbit**, **badbit**, or **hardfail** is set

```
// copy2.cpp: A Copy program using the eof() Function

#include <iostream.h>

main()
{
  // Copy from stream to stream
  while (1) {
    char c;
    cin.get(c);
    if (cin.eof()) break; // End copy
    cout.put(c);          // Else copy character
  }
}
```

Most of the stream status functions given in Table 11.4 are straightforward, except for the last two. Let's take a look at these.

The operator **void *()** function is perhaps the most unusual stream state testing function. It's actually a conversion operator function that converts a stream object into a **void** pointer. Why would we want to do such a conversion? It turns out that we can use the conversion to provide a shorter way to test the state of the stream. To see how, let's look at the definition of **operator void*()**:

```
ios::operator void *(void)
{
  if (fail()) return 0; else return this;
}
```

This function returns either a null pointer or the **this** pointer, depending on what was returned from **fail()**. Note that inside a member function, the **this** pointer can never be null. Thus, the only way for **operator void *()** to return a null pointer is when the stream has failed. Since a null pointer is equivalent to zero, it can be used in boolean tests. Thus we can write code such as:

```
while(cin) {  // While input stream hasn't failed
  cin.get(c); // Get a character
};
```

Figure 11.5 illustrates how the **while** loop test works.

There is another operator function, **operator!()**, that can also test the state of the stream. This function is the opposite of the **operator void *()** function. It returns nonzero if the stream has failed, rather than zero. **operator!()** is defined as:

```
int ios::operator!() { return fail(); }
```

```
while(cin) {                    ios::operator void *(void)
 ...                           {
};                                 if (fail()) return 0; else return this;
          cin.operator void *();   }
```

Figure 11.5. Testing the State of the Stream

An example of using the **operator!()** function is:

```
cin.get(c);
if (!cin) // operator!() called here
   cout << "Input stream failed during read\n";
   else cout << "The line read was: " << buff;
```

What does the following test in the **if** statement do? Translate it into explicit function calls.

```
if (!cin.get(c)) { ... }
```

*Two operations have been concatenated together. First, a character is read into c, and then the stream is tested using the **operator!()** function. The code translates into something like the following:*

```
istream &temp = cin.get(c);
if (temp.operator!()) { ... }
```

Setting the State of the Stream

Normally, the stream state is set automatically for you when you call the stream functions. However, there are times when you might want to set the state yourself. For example, you might want to reset the state after an invalid operation, so that you can continue using the stream. Another example is in writing a custom parsing routine, where you can set the state to indicate that a syntax error has occurred.

You can set the stream state by calling the **clear()** function. This function takes an argument indicating what you'd like the state to become. The default value for this argument is 0x00, which means to clear the state. An example of calling **clear()** to set **badbit** is:

```
cin.clear(ios::badbit | cin.rdstate());
```

There are two things to notice here. First, we had to qualify **badbit** with the class name **ios**. This is because the enumerator is hidden inside **ios**. Second, note how we have ORed this bit with the current state of the stream (which is obtained by calling **rdstate()**). The reason for doing this is to preserve the status of the other bits.

Note || The **clear()** function cannot reset the **hardfail** bit. Getting a hard failure means that the stream is in an irrecoverable state. You should not use the stream after getting such an error.

The program **pname.cpp**, given in Listing 11.1, shows an example of using the **clear()** function. The program prompts you to enter a valid C++ identifier, which is parsed by the function **parse_name()**. If the first character found isn't a letter or underscore, then **badbit** is set to indicate this. If the first character is legal, then more characters are read until either an invalid character is found or 32 characters have been read in. No white space is allowed in front of the identifier.

The stream state is tested in **main()** to see whether or not to accept the input. If an error is indicated, the stream state is first cleared, and then **ignore()** is called to skip the rest of the line.

A sample run of the program is:

```
Enter identifier: @set_locn(40, 12);
Invalid identifier syntax, try again ...
set_locn(40, 12);
The identifier you entered was: 'set_locn'
```

After the identifier **set_locn** is parsed, the input stream position points to the '(' character.

Listing 11.1. The pname.cpp Program

```
// pname.cpp: Sample parsing program using stream state tests.
// This program parses a C++ identifier, up to 32 characters in length.
#include <iostream.h>
#include <ctype.h>
```

```
istream &parse_name(istream &strm, char *name, int n)
// Looks for a C++ identifier, up to n characters long.
// The length includes the null byte, and should be >= 2.
{
  int i = 0;
  char c;
  if (strm.get(c)) { // Get character, continue if stream okay
      // First character must be letter or underscore
      if (isalpha(c) || c == '_') {
          // First character valid, so store it
          // and get the rest of the characters
          name[i++] = c;
          while(i < n-1) {
              if (strm.get(c)) { // Get character
                  if (isalnum(c) || c == '_') {
                      // Valid  character, so store
                      name[i++] = c;
                  }
                  else {            // End of identifier, so
                      cin.putback(c); // restore character to input
                      break;
                  }
              }
              else break; // Stream input failed, so get out
          }
      }
      else {
          cin.putback(c);  // Restore character to input
          strm.clear(ios::badbit | strm.rdstate()); // Set bad bit
      }
  }
  name[i] = 0; // Null terminate string
  return strm;
}

const max_line_size = 1024;
const int max_ident_len = 32;
char ident[max_ident_len+1];

main()
{
  cout << "Enter identifier: ";
  while(cin) { // While stream is okay
    if (parse_name(cin, ident, max_ident_len+1)) break;
    cout << "Invalid identifier syntax, try again ...\n";
    cin.clear(); // Clear stream state
    cin.ignore(max_line_size, '\n'); // Skip to end of line

  }

  cout << "The identifier you entered was: '" << ident << "'\n";
  return 0;
}
```

Assume in the following code that **get_token()** reads a token and sets the **failbit** of **cin** if there is a syntax error. The code should then loop again but stop if the token is okay or if there is some irrecoverable stream error. Is the code correct?

```
while(cin) { // While stream in good state
  token = get_token(cin);
  if (cin) break; // valid token received
}
```

If a syntax error is found and failbit is set, then the loop will erroneously terminate. We should clear the stream state before looping again. (Recall that clear() doesn't reset irrecoverable errors.) The code should be:

```
while(cin) {
  token = get_token(cin);
  if (cin) break;
  cin.clear(); // Clear state to try again
};
```

Using the High-Level Stream Operators

In the following sections, you'll learn how to use the high-level input and output operators. We'll start by showing you how to read and write the built-in types using default formatting. Then we'll show you how to control the formatting, and how to customize the stream operators for your own user-defined objects.

Using the stream operators differs from using the low-level routines like **get()** and **put()** in significant ways. The main difference is that the low-level routines do no formatting, but the stream operators do. Also, the input operator normally causes white space to be skipped, but the low-level input functions like **get()** do not.

Note || By *white space*, we mean the space, tab, and newline characters.

As an example, a short program that reads an integer, and then writes it right back out follows:

```
#include <iostream.h>

main()
```

```
{
  int i;
  cin >> i;  // Like scanf("%d", &i);
  cout << i; // Like printf("%d", i);
}
```

As the comments point out, using the stream operators for integer I/O is equivalent to using the "%d" format code in **scanf()** and **printf()**. When used with **scanf()**, the format "%d" means to skip any white space appearing before the first digit of the number. Also, the scanning stops as soon as a nondigit is found. Likewise, using "%d" for **printf()** means that only as many digits as necessary are used when outputting the number.

The "%d" format is the default format for integers. There's a default format for every built-in type. Table 11.5 shows what those formats are in terms of their equivalent **scanf()** and **printf()** format codes. For the output formats, the basic idea is to output the minimum number of characters.

The secret behind the stream operators is that they are overloaded, with a different operator function for each of the built-in types. The prototypes for the stream operator functions have the following forms:

```
istream &istream::operator>>(type &obj);
ostream &ostream::operator<<(type obj);
```

Note how for **operator>>()**, the argument is passed by reference so it can be modified by the read operation.

An example of what the prototypes for these functions look like for integer I/O is:

<hr/>

Table 11.5. Default Formats for the Built-In Types

Type	Default format	Type	Default format
signed char	"%c"	unsigned char	"%c"
char *s	"%s"	unsigned char *s	"%s"
short	"%hd"	unsigned short	"%hu"
int	"%d"	unsigned int	"%u"
long	"%ld"	unsigned long	"%lu"
float	"%.g"	double	"%.lg"
long double	"%.Lg"	void *	"%p" **

** void* format available only for output

```
istream &istream::operator>>(int &in_data);
ostream &ostream::operator<<(int out_data);
```

As with most of the low-level routines, the stream operator functions return the stream objects being operated on. This allows the stream state to be tested immediately after an output or input. For example, in the following program, an attempt is made to read an integer, and then the stream state is tested to see if the read was successful:

```
// intread.cpp: Program to read in an integer

#include <iostream.h>

main()
{
  int i;
  if (cin >> i) // Read integer, then test the state
     cout << "Integer read successfully\n";
     else cout << "Integer not read successfully\n";
}
```

The **if** statement test translates into the following:

```
istream &temp = cin.operator>>(i); // Attempt the read
if (temp.operator void *())         // Test stream state
```

Concatenating the Stream Operators

Returning stream objects from the stream operator functions also allows you to concatenate the operations together, just as you can for **get()** and **put()**. For instance, consider the following statement:

```
cout << "The answer is: " << 42;
```

Note that the output operator groups to the left, so the preceding statement could be written equivalently as:

```
(cout << "The answer is: ") << 42;
```

This code translates into the following explicit operator function calls:

```
(cout.operator<<("The answer is: ")).operator<<(42);
```

The ordering used by the output operator ensures that the objects are output in the order that they are written in the statement: from left to right.

In a similar manner, the input operator also groups to the left, so the objects are input from left to right. An example of reading a pair of integers which are separated by a non-white space character, such as a comma, is:

```
int x, y;
char sepchar;

cin >> x >> sepchar >> y;
```

Since the output operator allows white space to be skipped, the following data would be valid input to the preceding statement:

```
40 ,    12
```

In this case, 40 would be read into x, a ',' would be read into **sepchar**, and 12 would be read into y.

Because the stream operators group to the left, it allows the input and output operations to be expressed naturally. However, you can get into trouble. For example, in the following statement, parentheses are needed to override the default grouping:

```
cout << (x & y) << "\n"; // Need parentheses here
```

In terms of its **printf()** equivalent, the default format for floating point is "%.g". Explain what that format does.

The floating point number is output using the minimum number of characters. If the decimal point isn't needed, it isn't printed, and neither are any trailing zeros. That is, the number "18.00" prints as "18".

Controlling the Formatting

You've seen where the stream operators use default formats for the built-in types. However, you can also control the formatting yourself. The technique used to control the formatting is consistent with the stream model. During the input and output of objects, you can embed commands to modify the formatting for the objects, before they are read or written.

As a quick example, the following statement outputs an integer in a field of four characters, padded with leading zeros:

```
cout << setfill('0') << setw(4) << 42;
```

The resulting output is

0042

Each stream has an associated formatting state that determines the formatting to be used. This state is stored as a combination of bit flags. Table 11.6 shows the flags available. The flags are defined by an anonymous enumerated type inside the **ios** class. To use the flags, you must qualify them with the name **ios**, as in **ios::skipws**.

Using the I/O Manipulators

The **ios** class provides a series of high-level functions to set and reset the formatting flags. These functions, which are called *manipulators*, allow you to alter the formatting state of the stream while you're reading and writing.

Table 11.7 lists the manipulator functions available. Many of the manipulators are defined for both input and output, as noted in the table. Also, note that some of the manipulators take parameters.

Table 11.6. Formatting Flags

Label	Value	Action
skipws	0x0001	Skip white space on input
left	0x0002	Left justify output
right	0x0004	Right justify output
internal	0x0008	Use padding after sign or base indicator
dec	0x0010	Use decimal conversion
oct	0x0020	Use octal conversion
hex	0x0040	Use hexadecimal conversion
showbase	0x0080	Use base indicator on output
showpoint	0x0100	Always show decimal point and trailing zeros on floating point output
uppercase	0x0200	Use uppercase for hex output
showpos	0x0400	Add '+' to positive integers on output
scientific	0x0800	Use exponential floating notation
fixed	0x1000	Use fixed point floating notation
unitbuf	0x2000	Flush all streams after output
stdio	0x4000	Flush cout, cerr after output

Table 11.7. The I/O Manipulators

Function	Direction	Action
dec	in/out	Sets the base to decimal
oct	in/out	Sets the base to octal
hex	in/out	Sets the base to hexadecimal
ws	in	Extract white space characters
endl	out	Inserts a newline, flushes stream
ends	out	Inserts a null byte
flush	out	Flushes a stream
setbase(int b)	in/out	Sets conversion base (0, 8, 10, 16). Base 0 means use base 10 for output, use C parsing rules for integer literals on input
setiosflags(long f)	in/out	Sets specified bits
resetiosflags(long f)	in/out	Clears specified bits
setfill(char c)	out	Sets the fill character
setprecision(int n)	out	Sets precision to n digits after the decimal point
setw(int w)	in/out	Sets the total field width

Note To use any of the I/O manipulator functions that take parameters, you must include the header file **iomanip.h**. For the other manipulators, including the **iostream.h** header will suffice.

The program **basefmt.cpp**, given in Listing 11.2, shows the use of manipulators to control the conversion base when outputting numbers. A sample run of the program is:

```
Enter integer number: 42
The number in decimal is 42
The number in octal is 52
The number in hex is 2a
```

Note The number base conversions stay set until specified by another base conversion command.

Listing 11.2. The basefmt.cpp Program

```
// basefmt.cpp: Example using manipulators to convert base

#include <iostream.h>

main()
{
  int x;
  cout << "Enter integer number: ";
  cin >> x;
  cout << "The number in decimal is " << x << endl;
  cout << "The number in octal is " << oct << x << endl;
  cout << "The number in hex is " << hex << x << endl;
}
```

1. The following program is supposed to copy the standard input to the standard output. Will it make an exact copy?

```
#include <iostream.h>
main()
{
  char c;
  while(1) {
    cin >> c;
    if (cin.eof()) break;
    cout << c;
  }
}
```

2. Using one of the manipulators, fix the problem with the program in Question 1.

1. *No. Because the input operator skips all white space, the output copy has all white space characters removed.*

2. *You can prevent white space from being skipped by resetting the **ios::skipws** flag, as follows:*

```
#include <iostream.h>
#include <iomanip.h>  // Need this for resetiosflags()
main()
{
  char c;
  cin >> resetiosflags(ios::skipws);
  while(1) {
    cin >> c;
    if (cin.eof()) break;
```

```
        cout << c;
    }
  }
}
```

Formatting Numbers

Three of the most important manipulators shown in Table 11.7 are **setfill()**, **setw()**, and **setprecision()**, which are useful in formatting numbers. The program **fmtnum.cpp**, given in Listing 11.3, shows an example of formatting the number 765.4321. The first time the number is output, a format equivalent to the **printf()** format of "%09.3f" is used. The second time, the format is equivalent to "%.3f". The output to the program is:

```
00765.432
765.432
```

You might wonder why the format changes for the second output, since we didn't give any additional format commands. The reason is as follows: For most of the format states, once you set them, they stay set until you say otherwise. One exception is the field width, which gets reset to zero after every output. Thus, in the second output statement, the width used is the minimum required, so there's no leading zeros on the number. Note, though, that the precision is still set to three digits after the decimal point.

Note || A width of 0 means to use the minimum width necessary to output the value.

Listing 11.3. The fmtnum.cpp Program

```
// fmtnum.cpp: Example of formatting floating point numbers

#include <iostream.h>
#include <iomanip.h>   // Need this for the manipulators with
                       // parameters

main()
{
  // Set up the format to output number with the equivalent
  // printf() format of "%09.3f"

  cout << setfill('0') << setw(9) << setprecision(3);

  float f = 765.4321;

  cout << f << "\n";
  // Note that the width gets reset to 0 after every
```

```
// output, so the number is not padded if we output it again.
cout << f << "\n";
}
```

Write a program that will take the following variables and print them out in the format 12:01:55. The minutes and seconds field should use a '0' fill character. The hours field need not.

```
int hr = 12, min = 1, sec = 55;
```

One solution is:

```
#include <iostream.h>
#include <iomanip.h>
main()
{
  int hr = 12, min = 1, sec = 55;
  // Start '0' fill character after hr is output
  cout << setw(2) << hr << ':' << setfill('0');
  cout << setw(2) << min << ':';
  cout << setw(2) << sec << "\n";
}
```

The trick to this program is to keep setting the width to 2 before outputting each number. That's because the width gets set back to zero after each output.

Using Input Formats

Don't be misled into thinking that the I/O manipulators work only for output; many of them work for input as well. For example, the program given in Listing 11.4 shows how to set up the input to read in hex numbers. A sample run of the program is:

```
Enter integer number in hex:    g10
Invalid hex number, try again
Enter integer number in hex: 10)
The number in decimal is 16
```

When trying to input a hex number, if the first character found (after skipping white space) is not a valid hex digit, then the input stream fails. If the character is valid, then the input is scanned until the first nonhexadecimal character is found.

In our first read attempt, a 'g' was found (after skipping white space), which is not a hex digit. Thus the program asks the user to try again. In the second read attempt, a hexadecimal 10 is read, and the input stops at the closing parenthesis.

Listing 11.4. Using Hex Input

```
// fmt4.cpp: Example using hex base conversion on input

#include <iostream.h>

const int linesize = 1024;

main()
{
  int x;
  while(cin) { // While input stream is okay
    cout << "Enter integer number in hex: ";
    cin >> hex >> x; // Use hex base conversion
    if (cin) { // Did the input work okay?
      cout << "The number in decimal is " << x << endl;
      break;  // Get out of loop
    }
    else {
      cout << "Invalid hex number, try again\n";
      cin.clear(); // Reset input stream
      cin.ignore(linesize, '\n'); // Skip rest line
      cin.get();   // Consume newline too
    }
  }
}
```

Inputting Strings

By passing the input operator a **char***, you can read in strings from the input. The input operator considers a string to be any sequence of non-white space characters. The following program is an example that reads in four strings:

```
// strinput.h: Example of reading in four strings
#include <iostream.h>
main()
{
  char buff[4][80];
  cout << "Enter some strings: ";
  for (int i = 0; i<4; i++) cin >> buff[i];
  for (int j = 0; j<4; j++) {
    cout << "String(" << j << ") = '" << buff[j] << "'\n";
  }
}
```

A sample output from the program is:

```
Enter some strings: dogzilla, he's a killa
String(0) - 'dogzilla,'
String(1) - 'he's'
String(2) - 'a'
String(3) - 'killa'
```

You can use **setw()** to restrict the number of characters read in to a string, as the following program shows:

```
// readsafe.cpp: Safely reads in a string without going
// out of bounds of the string
#include <iostream.h>
#include <iomanip.h>
main()
{
  char tenbuff[10];
  cin >> setw(10); // 10 - 9 characters + 1 null byte
  cout << "Enter a string: ";
  cin >> tenbuff;
  cout << "The string read was '" << tenbuff << "'\n";
}
```

A sample output from the program is:

```
Enter a string: dogdilldahedakilldadogdillda
The string read was 'dogdillda'
```

Write a code fragment that will read in the data

```
022wheelsoffortune
```

into a number and string, and output that same number and string as

```
18 wheels
```

Here's one solution:

```
int k;
char buff[7];
cin >> oct >> k >> setw(7) >> buff;
cout << k << " " << buff;
```

Overloading the Stream Operators

What really sets the **iostream** library apart from the **stdio** library is the ability for you to write custom I/O routines for your own objects. These routines can be integrated smoothly into the existing stream operator syntax. In this section, you'll see how this can be done.

The way to write custom I/O routines is by overloading the stream operator functions. You must define the overloaded functions in a special manner. The basic forms you should use are:

```
// For inputting objects

istream& operator>>(istream &strm, <class_name> &obj)
{
  < Read data into obj >
  return strm;
}

// For outputting objects

ostream& operator<<(ostream &strm, <class_name> obj)
{
  < Write out data from obj >
  return strm;
}
```

For each stream operator function, you must pass a reference to a stream object as the first argument, and the object you wish to input or output as the second argument. For the input operator, the second argument should be passed by reference so that it can be modified during the reading process. For the output operator, you can use either pass-by-value or pass-by-reference. Also, you should make the stream operator functions return a reference to the stream object used. This is so the operators can be concatenated together.

Note ‖ The stream operator functions must have stream objects as their first arguments. This precludes them from being members of any classes except **istream** and **ostream**. Since the functions will typically be accessing private members of the objects being processed, it's typical for them to be friend functions.

Let's see an example of overloading the stream operators. The program **ptio.cpp** given in Listing 11.5 overloads the operators to work with **point** objects. A sample run of the program is:

```
Enter coordinates: 3 6
Wrong syntax, please use: x,y
Enter coordinates: 3, 6
Coordinates you entered were: (3,6)
```

As the sample run shows, the **operator>>()** function we define uses a specific syntax for reading in the coordinates of a **point**: two integers separated by a comma, with white space permitted. The **operator<<()** function uses the same syntax, but with a pair of parenthesis surrounding the coordinates.

If you examine Listing 11.5, you'll notice that the **operator>>()** function is more complicated than the **operator<<()** function because it must handle syntax errors in the input. At first glance, you might think our **operator>>()** function is calling itself recursively, but it's really not. It's calling the predefined **operator>>()** functions to read in the integer coordinates and comma separator. Figure 11.6 highlights these points.

If a syntax error occurs in the input process, the **operator>>()** function sets **badbit** of the stream state. The stream state is tested in **main()** and an error message is issued accordingly.

Notice the simple syntax needed to read in **a point** object:

```
point p;
cin >> p;
```

What we've done is made the stream I/O system work as smoothly for **point** objects as it does for integers.

Listing 11.5. The ptio.cpp Program

```
// ptio.cpp: Example of overloaded input and output for points

#include <iostream.h>

class point {
private:
  int x, y;
public:
  point(void) { set(0, 0); }
  void set(int xi, int yi) { x = xi; y = yi; }
  friend istream &operator>>(istream &strm, point &p);
  friend ostream &operator<<(ostream &strm, point &p);
};

ostream &operator<<(ostream &strm, point &p)
// Display points using (x,y) syntax
{
  return strm << "(" << p.x << "," << p.y << ")";
}

istream &operator>>(istream &strm, point &p)
// Input routine for points. Looks for x,y pattern,
// disregarding white space.
{
  int x, y;
  char c;
```

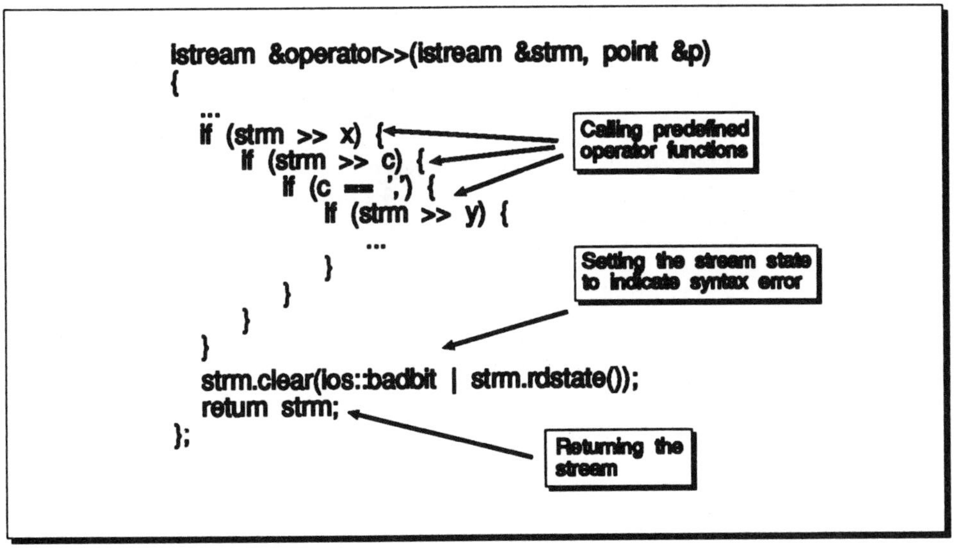

Figure 11.6. Basic Features of a Custom Input Routine

```cpp
  if (strm >> x) {          // Found integer x just fine
    if (strm >> c) {        // Look for comma
      if (c == ',') {       // Yes, we found a comma
        if (strm >> y) {    // Found integer y just fine
          p.set(x,y);       // So set point coordinates
          return strm;      // Return stream as good
        }
      }
    }
  }
  strm.clear(ios::badbit | strm.rdstate()); // Set badbit
  return strm;
}

const int linesize = 1024;

void main()
{
  point p;

  while(1) {                         // Validation loop
    cout << "Enter coordinates: ";
    if (cin >> p) break;             // Point read successfully
    cout << "Wrong syntax, please use: x,y\n";
    cin.clear();                     // Reset stream state
    cin.ignore(linesize, '\n');      // Read to end of line

  }
  cout << "Coordinates you entered were: " << p << "\n";
}
```

Is it possible to redefine the output operator for integers?

*No. The output operator is already overloaded for integers in the **ostream** class, so you can't write your own output operator for integers.*

Creating Virtual I/O Functions

One useful technique is to combine virtual functions with the stream operator functions. What you end up with are *virtual I/O functions*. In this section, you'll learn how to create a virtual output function that works with **clock** objects. The same technique could be used to create virtual input functions.

Although the stream operator functions can be overloaded, they can't be made virtual. Thus how can we create virtual I/O functions? The trick is to have the stream operator functions call virtual functions. For example, we could define an **operator<<()** function for the **clock** class that looks like the following:

```
ostream &operator<<(ostream &strm, clock *c)
// Clock passed using a pointer
{
  c->display(); // Could be virtual
}
```

The strategy is to pass a **clock** pointer to the operator function, and then inside the function, call a virtual function whose purpose is to do the actual output operation. Here, we've named the virtual function **display()**. Note that the **clock** pointer can point not only to **clock** objects, but also to objects of any derived class of **clock**. Each derived **clock** class could override **display()** to change the output format used. The result is that our single operator function can work with many different types of clocks.

The program **virtclock.cpp**, given in Listing 11.6, shows this technique in action. The program defines the base class **clock24** and the derived class **clock12**. The first displays the time in a 24-hour format, the last displays the time using a 12-hour format with an AM/PM indicator. The output from the program is:

```
The time is 17:30:45
No, the time is 5:30:45 PM
```

Listing 11.6. The virtclk.cpp Program

```cpp
// virtclk.cpp: Virtual clock output example
#include <iostream.h>
#include <iomanip.h>

//////////////////////////////////////////////////
// 24 hour clock class
//////////////////////////////////////////////////

class clock24 {
protected:
  int hr, min, sec;
public:
  clock24(int h, int m, int s) { hr = h; min = m; sec = s; }
  virtual ostream &display(ostream &s);
};

ostream &clock24::display(ostream &strm)
// Virtual function to display the time with a 24-hour
// format. The hour field has blank padding, the other
// fields use a '0' fill character.
{
  return strm << setfill(' ') << setw(2) << hr << ":"
              << setfill('0') << setw(2) << min << ":"
              << setw(2) << sec;
}

ostream &operator<<(ostream &strm, clock24 *c)
// This operator function calls a virtual function.
// Note: This function is not a member function.
{
  return c->display(strm);
}


//////////////////////////////////////////////////
// 12 hour clock
//////////////////////////////////////////////////

class clock12 : public clock24 {
public:
  clock12(int h, int m, int s) : clock24(h, m, s) { ; }
  virtual ostream &display(ostream &strm);
};

ostream &clock12::display(ostream &strm)
// Function to override the clock24 display() function
// to include an AMPM indicator
{
  int amflag, hrold = hr; // Save hour setting
```

```
      if (hr < 12) amflag = 1; else { amflag = 0; hr -= 12; }
      clock24::display(strm); // Call base class version
      if (amflag) strm << " AM"; else strm << " PM";

      hr = hrold; // Restore hour setting
      return strm;
    }

void main()
{
    clock24 this_time(17, 30, 45), *some_clock;
    clock12 that_time(17, 30, 45);

    some_clock = &this_time;
    cout << "The time is " << some_clock << "\n";
    some_clock = &that_time;
    cout << "No, the time is " << some_clock << "\n";
}
```

1. Why can't the stream operator functions be virtual? And why can't they belong to other classes besides **istream** and **ostream**?
2. In the **operator<<()** function for **clock**, what other way could we pass in the **clock** object, and still get the full benefits of the virtual **display()** function?

1. *To be virtual, a function must be a class member. However, the stream operator functions are already members of the* **istream** *and* **ostream** *classes, where they are overloaded, not virtual. Also, to work properly, the stream operator functions must take a stream object as their first argument. This precludes them from being members of any other classes besides* **istream** *and* **ostream***.*
2. *We could pass in the* **clock** *object using a reference argument:*

```
ostream &operator<<(ostream &strm, clock &c)
// Clock passed using a reference
{
    c.display(); // Could be virtual
}
```

Note that if we passed in the **clock** *object by value, the benefits of the virtual* **display()** *function would be lost. The* **clock** *version of* **display()** *would always be used in this case, even if the* **operator<<()** *function was called for derived class* **clock** *objects.*

Stream Oriented File I/O

Up to this point, we have been using the predefined streams **cin** and **cout**. It's now time to learn how to create your own stream objects and attach them to files.

The classes needed for stream-oriented file I/O are organized in a hierarchy as given in Figure 11.7. The classes you need be concerned about are **ifstream, ofstream,** and **fstream**. These classes are used to open files for input only, output only, and I/O, respectively.

For simplicity, we'll only be using the **fstream** class. However, keep in mind in the examples to come that we could use the other two classes, **ifstream** and **ofstream**, as appropriate.

Note ‖ To access the file stream classes, you must include the header file **fstream.h**. Since this file includes the **iostream.h** header as well, you need not specify both in your programs.

Opening and Closing Files

The **fstream** class has six basic functions that you can use to open and close files, as given in Table 11.8.

If you study Table 11.8, you'll see that there are two basic ways to open and close **fstream** files. One way is to first create an **fstream** object, and then open the file explicitly with **open()**, and close the file explicitly with **close()**. Alternatively, you can open the file using an **fstream** constructor, and have the file closed implicitly with the **fstream** destructor.

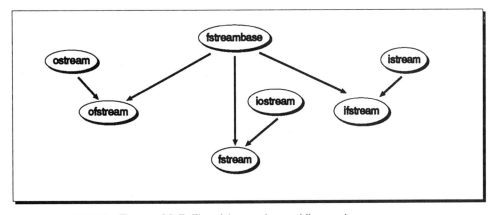

Figure 11.7. The fstreambase Hierarchy

Table 11.8. The fstream Open and Close Functions

fstream(void);	Initializes an fstream object without opening a file
fstream(const char *fn, int, om, int pm=S_IREAD|S_IWRITE);	Creates an fstream object and opens the file fn, with open mode om and protection mode pm
~fstream()	Destructor that flushes the file buffer and closes the file (if not already closed)
void open(const char *fn, int om, int pm=S_IREAD|S_IWRITE);	Opens the file fn, using specified open mode om and protection mode pm
int is_open();	Returns true if file is open
void close(void);	Closes the file if not already closed

An example of the first method is:

```
#include <fstream.h> // Be sure to include this header
main()
{
  fstream myfile; // Create unopened fstream object

  myfile.open("test.dat", ios::out); // Open file for output

  if (myfile.is_open()) {
    myfile << "This is a test\n";   // Write to file
    myfile.close();                 // Close the file
  }
}
```

This program opens the file "test.dat," writes a string out to it using the output operator, and then closes the file.

Note || Due to inheritance, all the facilities of stream-oriented I/O are available for **fstream** objects as well as **istream** and **ostream** objects.

Letting the constructor and destructor take care of the opening and closing of the file, we could rewrite our program as follows: